palms are hidden from view in the three branches of this canyon. Elephant trees can also be seen on the rocky slopes.

Elephant Trees (G-8) – Most of California's puffy looking elephant trees grow in the park. The trees are a botanical oddity, and a large stand of them grows on a rocky hillside a short distance from the mouth of Split Mountain. There are scattered specimens in Indian Canyon and Bow Willow Canyon farther south. A trail leads to the Fish Creek grove from a parking lot 1.5 miles away.

Box Canyon Historical Area (H-4) – The canyon was one of the more difficult passages on the Southern Emigrant Trail. The famous trailblazer Kit Carson, the Mormon Battalion, and the Butterfield Overland Mail all followed this route.

Calcite Canyon Scenic Area (C-9) – This is an outstanding area of unusual sandstone canyons and formations. Calcite trench mining operations still leave scars on the landscape. It is accessible only to four-wheel-drive vehicles or by foot.

Palm Spring (J-7) – A mesquite oasis with a few native palms, it is a good bird and wildlife area. It is of historical significance, and a marker tells the story of how early travellers used the waterhole.

Lookout Point (D-4) – This is an overlook near the Culp Valley primitive camp area. On a clear day, the 260-square mile Salton Sea is visible 30 miles to the east. The sea lies 235 feet below sea level and is noted for its excellent water sports and corvina and sargo fishing.

Sandstone Canyon (I-7) – Four-wheel-drive vehicles, and only narrow ones at that, can negotiate this most spectacular small canyon in the park. Flanked by sheer walls often rising to 200 feet, the canyon winds tortuously into the badlands. Here the brute, cutting power of desert thunderstorms is graphically illustrated.

SPECIAL NOTE

ALL MOTOR VEHICLES MUST REMAIN ON ESTABLISHED "JEEP" ROADS.

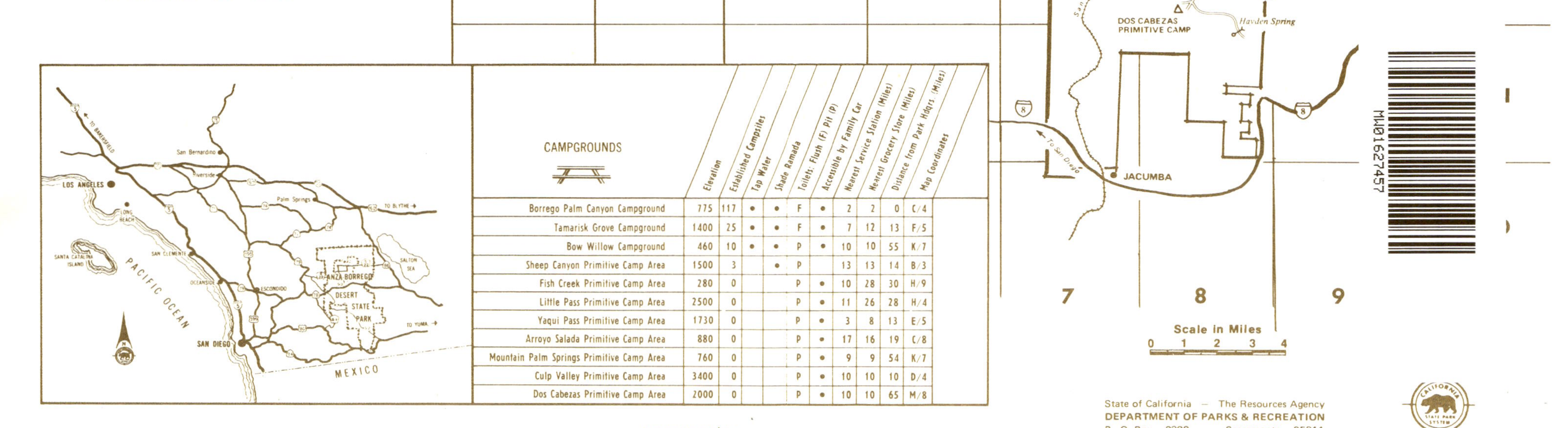

LEGEND

- ▲ CAMPGROUNDS
- △ PRIMITIVE CAMPS
- RANGER STATIONS
- ● POINTS OF INTEREST
- SPRINGS
- MAJOR ROADS AND HIGHWAYS
- DIRT "JEEP" ROADS
- RIDING AND HIKING TRAIL
- HISTORICAL TRAIL NONEXISTENT

CAMPGROUNDS	Elevation	Established Campsites	Tap Water	Shade Ramada	Toilets: Flush (F) Pit (P)	Accessible by Family Car	Nearest Service Station (Miles)	Nearest Grocery Store (Miles)	Distance from Park Hdqrs (Miles)	Map Coordinates
Borrego Palm Canyon Campground	775	117	•	•	F	•	2	2	0	C/4
Tamarisk Grove Campground	1400	25	•	•	F	•	7	12	13	F/5
Bow Willow Campground	460	10	•	•	P	•	10	10	55	K/7
Sheep Canyon Primitive Camp Area	1500	3		•	P		13	13	14	B/3
Fish Creek Primitive Camp Area	280	0			P	•	10	28	30	H/9
Little Pass Primitive Camp Area	2500	0			P	•	11	26	28	H/4
Yaqui Pass Primitive Camp Area	1730	0			P	•	3	8	13	E/5
Arroyo Salada Primitive Camp Area	880	0			P	•	17	16	19	C/8
Mountain Palm Springs Primitive Camp Area	760	0			P	•	9	9	54	K/7
Culp Valley Primitive Camp Area	3400	0			P	•	10	10	10	D/4
Dos Cabezas Primitive Camp Area	2000	0			P	•	10	10	65	M/8

43505-768 5-70 7SM △ OSP

State of California – The Resources Agency
DEPARTMENT OF PARKS & RECREATION
P. O. Box 2390 Sacramento 95811

Our Historic Desert

OUR HISTORIC DESERT

THE STORY OF THE ANZA-BORREGO DESERT

The Largest State Park in the United States of America

Bighorn Ram-BORREGO-Symbol of the Desert

Text by DIANA ELAINE LINDSAY

A COPLEY BOOK

Commissioned by JAMES S. COPLEY

Edited by RICHARD F. POURADE

PREVIOUS COPLEY BOOKS

The Explorers 1960
Time of the Bells, 1961
The Silver Dons, 1963
The Glory Years, 1964
Gold in the Sun, 1965
Ancient Hunters of the Far West, 1966
The Rising Tide, 1967
The Call to California, 1968
Historic Ranchos of San Diego, 1969
Rex Brandt's San Diego, 1969
Marines of the Margarita, 1970
The Sign of the Eagle, 1970
The Colorful Butterfield Overland Stage, 1971
Anza Conquers the Desert, 1971
From Fingers to Finger Bowls, 1972

Library of Congress Cataloging in Publication Data

Lindsay, Diana Elaine.
Our Historic Desert.

1. Anza-Borrego Desert State Park. I. Title.
F868.S15L56 917.94'98 73-11878
ISBN 0-913938-16-5

Based on a thesis for a Master's Degree on file at San Diego State University.

Dedication

To know the desert is to appreciate and love its many changing scenes.

At dawn one sees challenging vastness, promise and hope in the brilliance of the searching new sunlight.

At high noon there is an awareness of the grandeur and mightiness of the sun and its guidance of our planet.

In the night there is the majesty of the Creator in the wondrous heavens of moon and stars.

In commissioning this sixteenth book in the series we have published, we hope it will help the reader to know the desert, and consequently, love it.

James S. Copley (1916-1973)

Statue of Juan Bautista de Anza in Hermosillo

Contents

I The Story of the Ages 1

II Existence on the Desert 13

III Land of Ancient People 27

IV The White Man Arrives 41

V The Trail of Conquest 53

VI The Road to California 59

VII A March to the Desert 73

VIII To Preserve or to Abandon? 85

IX The Desert: A Way of Life 99

X The Mirages and the Myths 115

Acknowledgements 128

Bibliography 130

Index 140

BORREGO VALLEY: *Long before desert living became popular, artists followed adventurers into the land of silence and began to discover the strange and beautiful colors which flared briefly with the seasons and even at different times of the day when bleak landscapes became lighted in brilliant hues.*

One of the early desert artists was Howard Little whose painting, Borrego Valley, appears above. Little was a nationally known San Diego artist whose rich-tone paintings of the desert, ocean and redwoods have been exhibited in galleries in Washington, D.C., Denver, Colorado, and San Diego. Born in 1882, he studied art at the Ohio State University and later with Henry Reed in Denver. In San Diego he worked with such artists as Maurice Braun, Charles Fries, Alfred Mitchell and Elliot Torrey. Howard Little died in 1965.

Introduction to the Desert

The Great American Desert once was considered a fearful land, one to be crossed with as little loss of life and time as possible. But the desert has grown on the consciousness of the American people.

In California lie the hottest, lowest and loneliest deserts. The problem today is not in opening the deserts to those who succumb to their appeal, but to preserve them as nature developed them over the eons of time. This book deals with one desert, and perhaps the least known of our isolated sanctuaries.

Archaeologists believe that men may have lived in the now-arid Anza-Borrego Desert as long as 21,500 years ago, and today in the lower desert along the flanks of dry mountains and in sight of modern highways can still be seen outlines of magnificent fresh water lakes. Here huge prehistoric birds once flew unchallenged through the quiet air, and giant camels plodded across the hills in search of forage.

Although for ages it enjoyed both wet periods and dry, in the course of time it became increasingly arid until finally it ceased to be temperate, the lakes began slowly to evaporate and living things had either to adjust or disappear. In the centuries which followed, some species of plants and animals made the necessary adjustments, but many surely became extinct. Once-fresh lakes became saline and most of the early human inhabitants gradually moved to more equitable climates along the sea coast or into the mountains.

It was only two hundred years ago that recorded history began to note the events and places where Man challenged the seemingly inhospitable *terra incognito* and found not only a passage across its broad expanse but in recent times made it a place for leisure and recreation.

Our Historic Desert is a complete history of the Anza-Borrego Desert, from its geologic genesis and its early inhabitants to the modern paved roads and pleasant resorts. It presents a concise and cogent history of the things which have made this desert unique, and throughout maintains the desert mystique—that undefinable quality that can represent either a sunset or the now-stilled echoes of axes wielded more than a century ago by strong and determined Americans who literally carved a passage through Box Canyon.

But, gone today are the sounds of stagecoaches and war cries. Passed is the sight of a solitary prospector leading his burro toward the dream of untold wealth. No longer do phantom ships appear in the sandy wastes to conjure up a vision of ancient mariners forever land-locked in an inland sea. But, in this book the past is recreated and moves again across the once-uncharted expanse of time and space.

The Anza-Borrego Desert and its wealth remain for future generations, offering man the unique experience of looking into his past, and in its silence perhaps to contemplate his future.

Richard F. Pourade

RECREATING THE PAST: *This is an artist's concept of what life in Anza-Borrego Desert State Park may have been like as much as three million years ago. Depicted are only a few of the Pleistocene creatures whose remains have been found there. They are shown in a lush environment which was necessary for their survival.*

Flying above the scene are two giant, condor-like birds called Teratornis incredibilis. Fossilized remains indicate they may have had a wingspan as great as seventeen feet. By the side of the fresh water lake are a long-tailed porcupine and an early camel, while at the left is shown one of the most fierce looking of the creatures that inhabited the area, a saber-tooth cat. At the right is the massive bulk of a mastodon.

This painting and pen-and-ink sketches in Chapter II were created for Copley Books by La Jolla artist, Oliver W. Huckel, Jr.

I

The Story of the Ages

Anza-Borrego Desert State Park is named after Juan Bautista de Anza, the Spanish explorer who opened the trail to California and led the first women and children across a forbidding part of the American Desert, and *borrego,* the Spanish word for the bighorn sheep which still inhabit the area's mountain wildernesses.

The park contains a wide variety of scenic features with a striking combination of mountain and desert landscapes. Rich in fossils of giant birds, camels and saber-toothed cats of past ages, it also abounds with flowering plants and animal life as well as many signs of early flourishing populations of Indians.

In 1928, state park authorities, seeking to preserve a desert expanse, chose the Anza-Borrego area because of its outstanding natural features and valuable heritage. Nowhere else was there such a large and beautiful desert region so close to urban centers for future generations to enjoy .

Although it is the largest state park in the United States, few persons outside Southern California have ever heard of it. Some national monuments which were established in the desert at a later date—Death Valley and Joshua Tree—are better known. Taking the shape of a key, the park, encompassing almost 500,000 acres, represents about one-fifth of the total land area of San Diego County and is adjacent to Imperial and Riverside counties. Crossed by three major road systems, it is only a few hours' drive from the metropolitan centers of San Diego and Los Angeles.

The unusual combination of desert and mountain landscape offers the visitor striking contrasts. Within a range of 6,000 feet of elevation are three life zones. There are areas rich with oak, juniper, pine and ocotillo, as well as denuded mud hills, fossil shell reefs, shifting sand dunes and barren, labyrinthine gorges. Unusual geological formations, weirdly shaped sandstone concretions, mud caverns and remains of ancient lakes create scenic vistas in a setting of brilliantly clear skies with colorful sunrises and sunsets. Seemingly endless areas of tan contrast sharply with highly mineralized regions that appear red, pink, purple and blue.

The diversity of plant and animal life offers opportunities for unique scientific study. Rare, endangered and native species include the stubby-trunked elephant tree, the delicate Parish lip fern, the slow moving desert tortoise and the tiny desert pup fish. In the spring, seemingly lifeless areas blossom with more than six hundred species of flowers, plants and shrubs. Palm tree oases are common in canyons having intermittent streams or springs. More than two hundred and fifty identified vertebrate animals—animals having backbones—frequent the desert. The bighorn sheep which still roam the desert mountains are one of the last known herds.

Most landforms in the desert are sculptured by a combination of weathering, mass movements, landslides and mud flows, running water and wind. As explained by geologists, running water is the most effective agent of erosion because there is insufficient vegetation to protect slopes. Ravines, intervening ridges, and arroyos which are so typical of desert landscapes, are the aftermath of desert cloudbursts and the subsequent rapid runoff. The badlands of Borrego are due in part to this sort of conditioning. Wind also is an effective agent of erosion. Small sand particles carried by the wind act as abrasives which etch and sharpen the features that are seen.

Excellent locations to see typical badlands topography include Font's Point, Vista del Malpais and Inspiration Point in the northern half of the park. In the southern half locations are at Fish Creek Wash between Hapaha Flat and Olla Wash. Such observation points offer seemingly limitless views of barren clay hills and twisting gorges. Where the new Salton Seaway crosses the San Diego-Imperial County line—basically the route of the older Truckhaven Trail—there is a view of the underlying structure of that part of the badlands where cutting the roadbed has exposed many layers of sediment covered by a thin cap of recent alluvium.

The dry washes, often lined with smoke trees and desert willows, such as Ella Wash in the Borrego Badlands, are really very beautiful. Palo Verde Wash, in the same area, received its name from the palo verde trees. Occasionally a palm tree oasis is found, as in the case of Seventeen Palms, off the Arroyo Salado. Notable washes in the southern half of the park include Fish Creek, Deguynos Canyon, Canyon Sin Nombre—the canyon without a name—and June Wash. Two washes that turn and loop through some of the park's most interesting mud hills and sandstone forms, are Arroyo Tapiado and Arroyo Seco del Diablo. A good example of a vertically walled wash with nearly horizontal strata is located in Sandstone Canyon, an area off Fish Creek Wash.

Mud-walled caverns have been carved out of the mud hills by the action of running water. Most of the caverns are due to mud flows and landslides first bridging over a gully and then partially collapsing as running water continued eroding beneath the landslide.

Sandstone concretions found in the washes are some of the most interesting and curious features in the park. Certain natural cementing agents have caused them to be harder than the sandstone around them, and when the softer material eroded, the concretions remained in many forms, including cannonballs, bar bells and even flat plates. The nucleus of the concretions probably formed millions of years ago in ancient river beds. The Borrego Badlands also have many excellent samples, especially just east of the park in an area known as the Pumpkin Patch.

Another common desert landform is the alluvial fan, which consists of loose boulders, gravel and sand which have been washed down the mountain slopes by streams and deposited on the desert floor. As the streams leave the mountains and enter the desert floor they undergo a sudden decrease in speed which leaves the fan-shaped deposits. When these fans overlap they form a continuous apron which slopes away from the mountain and it is called a *bajada.* Some of the deposited materials in these fans and *bajadas* are loose remnants of former mountains.

Dry lakes and mud flats have resulted from mud and water runoff from surrounding mountains accumulating in undrained basins. After the moisture evaporates, a smooth surface of dried clay remains. The rushing waters of desert flash floods often collect in these natural basins. Examples located near the park are Clark's Dry Lake, Borrego Sink and Benson Dry Lake. Natural rock basins or tanks, called *tinajas,* also are scattered throughout the park and provide a temporary source of water for both desert animals and travelers. They have been carved into rock by either running or falling sediment-bearing water, or by wind blowing away the rock fragments loosened by weathering.

Rock-defended surfaces, consisting of small, tightly packed and closely spaced pebbles are sometimes found in the desert. They occur where wind has blown the finer particles away, thus leaving the larger rocks to settle and pack down together. Desert pavement or mosaic, as the pebbled surface is sometimes called, is common in various areas directly exposed to the wind and has the appearance of having been flattened with a steam roller. Polished by the abrasive action and blackened by an accumulation of insoluble residues of iron oxide and manganese oxide, the smooth surface has a varnished appearance. Anything that breaks this protective layer, such as vehicle tires, exposes the underlying sand. The newly exposed sand will then be blown away and the surface lowered to a level where new rock fragments are exposed and the desert

REMNANT OF A LAKE: *Etched forever on the rocks just outside the northeast corner of the park along Highway 86 is the shoreline of an ancient sea.*

pavement again stabilizes.

Sand dunes are a characteristic result of the depositional work of wind. They have a variety of shapes and patterns and are especially interesting for their light effects and color changes. In a day's time colors may vary from purple and pink to blue and yellow. A very striking dune is that on the eastern slope of Borrego Mountain and is visible from the highway near Benson Dry Lake.

At times in the geologic past, the desert has been covered by seas, and marine fossils more than 200-million years old have been found in some areas outside the park. However, the earliest identifiable fossil remains within the park boundaries date to the Pliocene Epoch—between three and twelve million years ago—when sea water extended from the Gulf of California northward over the lowlands. Oysters and corals are among the fossils which have been found. One of the first men to speculate on the origin of such fossils was Father Pedro Font, diarist for the Anza expedition to California in 1775. While crossing the Colorado Desert, Font wrote:

> On account of the unfruitfulness of these lands, so level, and of the aspect of the sand dunes, and especially of the abundance of shells of mussels and sea snails which I saw today in piles in some places. . . . I have come to surmise that in olden times the sea spread over all this land, and that in some of the great recessions which histories tell us about, it left these salty and sandy wastes uncovered. . . . One finds on the way many piles of oyster shells, mixed with the earth and half buried, and other shells and maritime signs.

Many land fossils in the area date from the beginning of the Pleistocene Epoch, about three million years ago. Fossils which can be seen exposed at the surface in the highly eroded badlands, especially in the Vallecito-Fish Creek area, indicate there was grassland and moderate precipitation in this region in times passed. Wooded areas grew near streams and birds roosted and nested in the trees. Turkey and quail inhabited some of the brush areas, and fossils of aquatic birds indicate that there was an abundance of water. The presence of animals similar to those found today in Central and South America suggests a mild climate existed.

The Vallecito-Fish Creek fossil site was first found in 1954 by Harley J. Garbani, a San Jacinto rancher, who took his discoveries to Dr. Theodore Downs at the Los Angeles County Museum. The discovery of the fossils created such interest that a full-scale investigation of the area was undertaken with permission of the California Division of Beaches and Parks. From 1958 to 1970, the National Science Foundation awarded several grants to the Los Angeles Museum to continue the investigation. In 1967, a helicopter was used to aid scientists in removing three tons of fossil material from the most inaccessible areas. Airlifting facilitated a more thorough and widespread search of the Vallecito Creek area.

Fossils of more than one hundred different species of mammals, birds, reptiles, amphibians and invertebrates were recorded at more than four hundred and fifty individual sites. Dr. Downs has said the Anza-Borrego area provides "one of the most remarkably complete sequences of animal life to be found anywhere in the world."

In the Vallecito and Carrizo badlands, folded layers of sedimentation have created a "file cabinet of time," exposing fossils over a 100-square mile area. Upper Fish Creek Wash of the Palm Spring formation is about three million years old while Vallecito Creek dates from about two million years ago. Other sites in the Borrego Badlands and Arroyo Salado are not as rich in fossils as the Vallecito-Carrizo badlands.

The most representative fossils in the park date from about two to three million years ago. The majority are mammals, followed in number by birds and reptiles. Among the remains are ground sloths, horses, mastodons, camels, wolves and musk oxen. Although these particular fossils are several million years old, it is known that in other areas of the Southwest, including Arizona and Texas, some varieties of these animals lived as little as 10,000 years ago in company with early man. Skeleton remains have been found in these areas with man-made projectile points near them.

REMINDERS OF A SEA: *Many marine fossils, such as these in the rock strata along the lower reaches of Red Rock Canyon, are evidence of a former sea.*

LADDER WASH: *In a tributary of Red Rock Canyon, the varying speed of erosion cut the sandstone layers on the canyon walls, giving it serrated sides.*

TWISTING FISH CREEK: *This aerial view, looking south, shows an arid panorama as the dry creek bed meanders through Split Mountain and distant mudhills.*

Other mammals found in the park have been porcupines, antelopes, bears, deer, saber-toothed cats, shrew, rodents, rabbits, peccaries, badgers, racoons, weasels, skunks, bats and pocket gophers. The porcupine apparently is an ancestor of its modern counterpart and had so adapted to living in trees that it had a prehensile tail. One of the camels was llama-like, closely related to the modern llama of South America, and another camel measured eighteen feet tall, a height greater than those found in the Rancho La Brea tar pits.

One of the best represented fossil species was a pocket gopher of the genus *Geomys*, found today only in the midwestern and southeastern states. Downs said the "genus has never before been recorded from the fossil or Recent (Holocene) record in California." He named one new species after Garbani (*Geomys garbanii*), the discoverer of the Vallecito fossil site.

Twenty-eight identified bird fossils included grebes, geese, ducks, quail, turkey, rail, coot, woodpecker, killdeer, owls, shore birds, perching birds and birds of prey.

By far the most spectacular of the bird fossils dating from two to three million years ago was *teratornis incredibilis*, a gigantic, condor-like vulture with a wingspan of about seventeen feet, forty percent wider than the largest fossilized birds found in the La Brea tar pits. At one time there were flying reptiles believed to have had wings measuring more than thirty feet, but this was the largest land bird ever found. Although the color of the bird is unknown, it is possible to identify its relationship to the condor by the remains which were found—a radius fragment in 1963 at Vallecito Creek and a portion of the upper beak in 1967 at Fish Creek Wash. The huge birds had no teeth, but tore their food, which probably consisted of carrion, with their strong beaks. Like modern condors, they were not physically able to seize and carry off live prey.

Among the reptile fossils found were turtles, lizards, iguanas and several species of snakes. Both small and giant turtles once roamed through the present badlands, together with reptiles common to the desert region today, such as the fence lizard, night lizard, desert iguana, desert night snake, rattlesnake, garter snake and the California king snake. Scientific study has been greatly aided because the fossil sites are located within protected state park lands, which decreases the possibilities of vandalism.

More than 225 million years ago, there were shifts in the earth's crust which caused some mountain building, followed by a period of erosion. When the mountain building stabilized, volcanoes erupted and laid down sheets of lava over much of the area, the results of which can be seen at Dos Cabezas, Jacumba Valley and Vallecito.

However, most of the existing landscape features of California were either created or changed to their present form between two and three million years ago during the era from which the majority of fossils date. During that time, active faults already were breaking the area into individual blocks and caused both an uplifting of mountain ranges and the depression of numerous basins. Such basins were filled as material from higher areas eroded and washed down the canyons and hillsides. Alluvium filled the adjacent Colorado Desert Basin and at times the mighty Colorado River overflowed into that basin, creating lakes which later evaporated. Wet cycles in the fluctuating climate also contributed to the moisture, and flowing streams created other fresh water lakes.

Then the last Ice Age began to diminish and the glaciers began their retreat from much of the American continent. During more recent times there also have been periods of regular rainfall—called pluvial periods—which influenced life in the lower deserts. One such is thought to have ended 10,000 years ago and was followed in historical times by a drought of 3,000 years. Another wet period of 1,500 years—from 2000 B.C. until 500 B.C.—was probably sufficient to produce permanent streams and lakes in the California Desert.

The last ancient lake, Lake Cahuilla, existed until four hundred or five hundred years ago and was probably created by an overflow of the Colorado River. It covered an area of about 2,000 square miles of the Salton Basin, including the area where the modern Salton Sea formed, and its surface was forty-four feet above sea level. Another contributing factor to the aridity, one which continues today, was the "rain shadow" effect caused by the uplifted mountains to the west which prevented rain from the windward side from reaching the protected area. Together these factors caused the region to become arid and new species of plants and animals similar to those now commonly found in the park began to evolve.

Several faults crossing the Anza-Borrego Desert are partially responsible for the topography. Movement of the blocks between these more-or-less parallel fracture zones explains the present topography of mountains and adjacent basins. Borrego Valley actually is one of these basins. The basins provided natural routes for early travel and exploration. Juan Bautista de Anza's historic trail generally followed the path created by the San Jacinto fault, a major branch of the San Andreas fault system. From southeast to northwest, the path follows from Ocotillo Wells around the north side of Borrego Mountain, across the northeast portion of Borrego Valley, along the western edge of Coyote Mountain and through Coyote Canyon.

The action of San Felipe fault created another natural trail through Grapevine Canyon east to San Felipe Creek and the old Kane Springs Road. A line made by following Grapevine Mountain, Pinyon Mountain, Hapaha Flat and Vallecito Mountain shows the direction of the Earthquake Valley fault zone and intervening valleys. Today it is part of a popular route used by persons operating four-wheel drive vehicles.

To the south, the path of the Elsinore fault crosses Mason and Vallecito valleys, Mountain Palm Springs and the Coyote Mountains from northwest to southeast, basically the route of County Highway S-2. A spur of the Elsinore fault goes to Agua Caliente where it has caused the hot springs to surface.

The intersection of these systems, with smaller faults running parallel or at right angles to the major ones, has caused irregularities in the general shape of some mountains, such as Vallecito and Fish Creek. Erosion along one such fault has created the long, straight portion of the gorge at Split Mountain, a favorite viewpoint for visitors. Other intersections have created deep valleys, including Carrizo Creek and San Felipe Valley. The fault systems are indirectly responsible for erosion of spectacular escarpments located on the west side of Borrego Valley and from Agua Caliente Hot Springs through Carrizo Gorge.

The parallel mountains which run in a northwest-southeast direction were caused by faults. They are individually uplifted, fault block mountains or ridges. The principal ridges are the Santa Rosa Mountains which rise above the northeast section of the park, while the San Ysidro Mountains close the valley on the northwest side. Bucksnort Mountain in the northwest corner of the park is the highest, with an elevation of 6,195 feet at Combs Peak. Exceptions to the northwest-southeast trend of mountains are located in the southern half of the park and include the Vallecito, Fish Creek and Coyote mountains which trend more nearly in an east-west direction.

Between the uplifted fault block mountains are sunken or deeply eroded blocks such as the valleys of Borrego, Collins, Clark, Culp, San Felipe, Lower Borrego, Earthquake, Vallecito, Mason, Carrizo, Jacumba and Blair. Most of these valleys are bounded by adjacent mountains which have steep-walled and well-eroded fault scarps.

The lowest point in the park, eighty-three feet above sea level, is found at Lower Borrego Valley near the eastern boundary. Elevation gradually descends to below sea level in Imperial Valley and the Colorado Desert area to the east.

Apparently various faults have been active throughout much of the past and into recent times. In thirty-six years, from 1934 to 1969, there were more than 7,300 earthquakes in Southern California and neighboring regions which had a Richter magnitude of 4.0 or greater. During the same period there were four such major seismic disturbances along the San Jacinto fault which registered more than 6.0 on the Richter scale. The most recent, on April 9, 1968, registered a 6.4 and was caused by dis-

NATURE'S ARCH: *What awesome force caused rocks to fold and bend upward at Split Mountain, forming a sandstone swirl that startles the imagination!*

VIEW FROM FONT'S POINT: *In the distance to the south are the Borrego Mountains, and screened by foreground hills is Anza's passage of 1774.*

placement along a segment of the Coyote Creek fault.

A large portion of the Salton Trough, of which the Anza-Borrego Desert is a part, is a wedge-shaped basin or sunken fault block which extends from the San Gorgonio Pass in the north, to the Gulf of California in the south. It is surrounded by mountains on all but the southern tip. Most of the depression lies below sea level and is covered with a thick layer of older alluvium and marine deposits which were greatly deformed by movements of the earth's crust and deeply eroded. The northern section is Coachella Valley and the southern is the Imperial Valley. Between the two is the Salton Sea, the surface of which is about 240 feet below sea level. The area is separated from the Gulf of California by the Colorado River delta. The central portion of the basin is relatively flat, but in a number of places bedrock masses protrude through the sedimentary fill, as in the case of Superstition, Carrizo and Borrego mountains.

It is difficult for today's visitor to Anza-Borrego Desert State Park to envision the forces which have created such a landscape of strange beauty, to imagine the hundreds of millions of years it took for the desert to evolve in its present form. Standing at Font's Point viewing the badlands stretching out below, it is difficult to picture lush, green lands teeming with game and dotted with lakes, or of ancient man hunting along the shores.

FAMILY PORTRAIT: *Rare Bighorn sheep—here ewes and their young—majestic symbols of the desert, stand motionless against a typical background.*

II

Existence on the Desert

Although it is impossible to accurately establish the exact age of the desert, it was almost certainly more than 20,000 years ago that temperature extremes, dry winds and lack of sufficient moisture caused increased aridity and made it necessary for plants and animals to either adapt to the new climate or disappear. Through the centuries that followed, distribution of the various species presently found in the park began to slowly evolve.

Anza-Borrego Desert lies in the rain shadow of the high Peninsular Ranges on the west which block winds carrying ocean moisture. Air coming from the west over the slopes is warm and absorbs moisture as it descends to the desert basins. Also the area is located in the mid-latitudes, the region where most of the world's deserts are found.

The park has two climates: that on high mountain slopes is classified as hot steppes and that of the valleys and lower slopes as hot desert. Temperatures vary with the elevation, as does the amount of yearly precipitation. Another factor affecting the climate is the adjacent region of Colorado Desert to the east, which is characterized by extreme heat and dryness and is one of the hottest areas in the United States.

At El Centro, where the elevation is thirty-seven feet below sea level, temperatures have ranged from a high of 122 degrees to a low of 16 degrees. Borrego Springs, which lies 625 feet above sea level, averages about 3 degrees cooler than El Centro. The record high for Borrego Springs is 121 degrees in September and the low 15 degrees in January. Daytime temperatures in the summer are consistently in excess of 100 degrees and in winter average about 70 degrees. July, August and September are the hottest months while December, January and February are the coolest.

There are two distinct rainy seasons. From November to January winter rains come from cyclonic storms originating northwest of Alaska, and have enough energy and force to cross the high Peninsular Range. These rains germinate the spring wildflowers which annually attract thousands of park visitors. Snow on the desert, although rare, has occurred from time to time. Dust and sand storms are common during May and June, months which rarely have rain. In July and August, intermittent and brief summer showers are caused by southern winds carrying moisture from the Gulf of California to the interior deserts. Runoff is usually fast during these showers and desert vegetation rarely profits from them. Annual rainfall in the desert has ranged from 5.62 inches in the city of Palm Springs in Riverside County to 2.57 inches at Brawley in Imperial County. The record for Borrego Springs is 3.99 inches.

Plant and animal life has adapted to great fluctuations in temperature, strong sunlight, high surface temperatures in summer, little rain, low humidity, extreme wind conditions, water erosion, sporadic stream flow and soils containing high mineral-salt content.

The topography particularly dictates botanical variation. Dudley A. Preston, associate professor of botany at California's San Diego State University has compiled a list of 612 different kinds of plants in the Anza-Borrego Desert. True desert species are found in the central and barren eastern sections of the park, close to the Colorado Desert basin. Plants associated with chaparral and verdant wooded areas are found in the higher elevations in the western sections which lead toward the Sunrise Highway. The area most botanically investigated is Borrego Palm Canyon, while plants in the Santa Rosa Mountains are relatively unknown.

Precipitation in the desert regulates not only the number of plant species but also the whole chain of life. Plants in the drought resistant category have adapted methods for collecting and storing water as well as preventing the loss of water, and thus survive throughout long periods of drought. Desert succulents, like cacti, have shallow roots which quickly absorb water after a period of rainfall, storing great amounts of water for long periods. Among the most common cacti are the cholla, barrel, beaver-tail and hedgehog. The rare elephant tree also has the ability to store water in its pulpy trunk, making it considerably drought resistant. The Mohave yucca resists drought through its long root system which grows at a faster rate than either wind or water erosion can expose them to the surface.

Some desert perennials reduce their leaf surfaces and have developed a resiny or leathery coating that prevents excessive evaporation of moisture. During periods of drought the palo verde tree sheds its leaves and the stem takes over the function of producing chlorophyll. The ocotillo, one of the thorniest desert perennials, produces leaves only after rainfall and loses them as soon as the ground is dry. Like the palo verde, photosynthesis continues in the green bark of the seemingly dead plant. After spring rains, a scarlet flag of blossoms tips each stem, making the blooming ocotillo a favorite of photographers. The ocotillo is also known as candlewood because the wood is so resinous that splinters can be used for torches. It also has been used in desert regions for fencing, the stems frequently taking root and forming a living fence armed with "daggers."

The desert agave, or century plant, which blooms only once in its lifetime, has sunken pores or stomata which help slow down evaporation of moisture and allow the plant to endure periods of drought. It was once a favorite food of desert Indians who baked the stalk in pits until tender.

The creosote bush is one of the most widespread and conspicuous shrubs in the park and the Colorado Desert. A wax-like covering on its leaves slows down water loss and reflects heat, which helps to keep the leaves cool. Like most desert plants, it is spaced so that it will not compete for a scanty water supply. Some plant physiologists believe that the creosote assures itself of spacing by emitting root toxins which kill plant seedlings that grow too close. The brittle bush is another plant that produces leaf toxins that wash to the surface surrounding the plant after a period of rainfall, thus creating adequate spacing. The resin of the brittle bush was burned by the early padres for incense. The production of thorns on desert plants has been said to be both a defense against browsing animals and a moisture conserving mechanism.

Several desert perennials are found along washes and canyons where intermittent streams are located. These plants must have a permanent source of water and two of them, the mesquite and fan palm, are the best indicators of water to desert travelers. Honey mesquite and screw bean mesquite send their roots very deep in order to assure themselves a permanent source of water. Immature mesquite does not grow much above the ground until it finds an adequate supply of water. Mesquite beans were once favored as a main staple by Indians who pounded them into a flour-like meal.

The fan palm is the largest of the true desert trees in the park, attaining a height of as much as eighty feet. It is the only native palm in California. Fan palms are also found on the open desert wherever a spring or seepage has created an oasis. Borrego Palm Canyon is probably the most beautiful of the palm-studded canyons and was the site first recommended for the establishment of a state park. Other areas in which palm trees can be seen are Mortero Canyon, Mountain Palm Springs and various canyons leading off Coyote Canyon.

Common water-loving perennials include the ironwood, desert willow, cottonwood, smoke tree and tamarisk. The tamarisk is also called salt cedar because it exudes a salt that forms encrustations on its branchlets. A native of western

A BOTANICAL RARITY: *A rocky hill near Split Mountain supports an elephant tree, recognized by its stubby, wrinkled trunk and ponderous-looking limbs.*

DRY SILHOUETTE: *A dead tree stands only a short distance from thriving trees at Palm Spring, perhaps the site of the first palms described in California.*

Asia and northeast Africa, it was introduced into the desert by early settlers as both a shade tree and a windbreak. A fine stand is found at Tamarisk Grove campground.

Some desert drought resisters become active only when moisture is present. The seeds of the ironwood, smoke tree and palo verde will not germinate until their outer coatings have been scarred by torrents of water rushing down the arroyos. The water must also come from above in order to leach out protective acids. In this way seeds are assured a sufficient supply of water to begin a new plant. In the case of a smoke tree, the distance carried is usually one hundred and fifty feet from the parent tree. If the seed is carried more than three hundred feet, it has usually been too scarred to germinate.

Mesquite seeds have an unusual way of disposing their outer protective covering. An animal must eat the mesquite pod so that its digestive juices will erode the grassy seedcoat, allowing water to penetrate the seeds as they pass through the animal's body. In addition, the animal's droppings provide a natural fertilizer for their growth.

Some plants and trees respond to drought by overproducing seeds, assuring a greater possibility of offspring, and also by growing only after winter rains. Germination occurs when the plant is assured enough water to flower and produce seeds, but the protective coating that surrounds each seed must first be washed off. If there is not enough moisture to soak off this outer coating it will lie dormant until a wet season occurs, perhaps for years. In wet seasons there may be a profusion of color in areas where plant life had previously seemed non-existent in other years. Among the more common spectacular annuals are the sand verbena, evening primrose, desert sunflower and wild heliotrope.

Trees not usually associated with the desert are often found in higher elevations of the park. They are similar to those located in the higher mountains of San Diego County and include piñon, coulter pine, juniper, ash, white alder, sycamore and various oaks. In the same higher areas are other species, usually found along the coast, which reach their eastern limit in the park but do not extend as far as the Colorado Desert basin. Among these are the California copperleaf and bladderpod. Other plants reach their western limit in the park and do not extend into the mountains of San Diego County.

Certain species and varieties of trees and plants deserve special mention because they are both endemic or confined to the park. Two such plants in Borrego Valley are a variety of the annual peppergrass and a species of the spring blooming forget-me-not. A cactus found from Mason Valley to Vallecito and Canebrake canyons is a hybrid between a teddy bear cactus and a silver cholla. Other endemic plants include an aster in the Split Mountain, Fish Creek and Carrizo Mountains, and sage found only in dry rocky areas 1,200 to 4,500 feet above sea level in the park's western portion. The redbud, though a common plant in the Sierra Nevada Mountains, is found only in one location south of the sierras along a section of Sunrise Highway.

The annual blooming daisy or brown turban is another plant rare to the Colorado Desert but found in the park in the Split Mountain and Fish Creek areas. The elephant tree, called *terote* by the Mexicans, is perhaps the best known of the rare trees. It is a colorful curiosity with a short swollen trunk, red twigs and sap, green foliage and blue fruit. It is found in the Fish Creek and Carrizo Creek areas. Arizona is the only other location in the United States where it grows. Though now a park attraction, it took many years to establish the fact that the trees actually existed.

During the early 1900s an old man told Edward H. Davis of Mesa Grande that he had seen trees shaped like elephant trunks which bled red. In the winter of 1911 Davis and his son found a group of them in the present Elephant Trees area of the park, north of Split Mountain. Davis' discovery and subsequent naming of the trees went unnoticed. Again, in the 1920s, a "grizzled old man" told tales about seeing trees that looked like a herd of elephants. In January, 1937, a Palm Springs naturalist, Don Admiral, and a representative of the United States Department of Agriculture, E. M. Harvey, searched for the bleeding tree. Their search ended when they found a single specimen, the discovery of which excited staffs of museums and universities who had not known of the tree's existence in the United States. Later that same year in November, the first organized search for elephant trees took place when representatives of the San Diego Museum of Natural History, the superintendent of state parks in Southern California and the director of Scripps Institution of Oceanography looked for the elusive trees. They found them north of Split Mountain.

San Diego's rarest fern, one of seven desert species in the park, is the Parish lip fern. Helen Witham, assistant curator of botany at the San Diego Museum of Natural History, discovered the fern in Sentenac Canyon. It seems appropriate that Witham earn a place in the park's history because she is a direct descendant of the widow on the Anza expedition of 1775, who in Father Font's words at camp San Sebastián "sang some verses which were not at all nice."

The very nature of plant life determines the kind and relative abundance of animals since vegetation is at the base of the food chain. The range and numbers of plants are well established, but the animal life is in need of extensive research. The fact that plants remain rooted in an area and do not need to be trapped has made it easier to find specimens. Larger animals of the park are best known because they are more easily seen. Insects, spiders, snails, and crustaceans are least known, but this should not be taken to mean they are few in number. Based on studies of related areas, authorities believe that the invertebrate species outnumber those of vertebrates by double or more.

Of the vertebrate studies, which include park birds, mammals, reptiles and amphibians, the general rule is the larger the animal and its distribution, the better known it is. Dalton E. Merkel, park naturalist, first compiled a list of park animals in 1966. He drew his material largely through observations and from the works of authorities who had done special collecting. The most recent lists indicate that there are one hundred and thirty-seven individual species of birds, seventy species of mammals, fifty-seven of reptiles and seventeen of amphibians.

Like plants, desert animals have similarly adapted to the extremes in temperature and lack of water. Some desert animals adjust to the immoderate conditions by avoiding them. Ground squirrels, spadefoot toads (a toad-like amphibian), larval butterflies, moths and snails sleep during the hottest or driest parts of the year. The desert poorwill, desert tortoise and chuckwalla hibernate in winter when temperatures are colder and there is the least amount of food. To conserve water, almost all desert animals avoid the noonday sun and the searing surface temperatures, which can be as high as one hundred and eighty degrees, by seeking shade in rock crevices, underground burrows or in the shadow of desert vegetation. Apparently no animal can survive the desert at its worst extremes and nearly all are either active at twilight or at night. Some, including the rattlesnake, respond to certain temperature ranges, so that they may be crepuscular in winter and nocturnal in summer.

Birds generally escape high temperatures more easily than other animals and are most active during the day. This possibly explains why more bird species are known in the park than other vertebrate animals. By flying, birds avoid the hot surface temperatures and perch in high places. While in flight, air moving across their bodies helps cool them and their feathers act as insulation.

Desert animals obtain water from every possible source—water holes, dew, juicy plants, and eating the bodies of animals they have killed. Some animals are not dependent on ordinary sources of water. The kangaroo rat is able to internally manufacture moisture from dry food. In addition to its nocturnal habits, which conserves body water, it also produces urine in a highly concentrated form so little moisture is lost. It also loses little water in its droppings, which are hard and dry. In addition, it eats part of its droppings to obtain necessary vitamins, and consequently reabsorbs any moisture remaining in them. Because of such methods for conserving water, the kangaroo rat is able to live anywhere in the desert. They have a wide distribution and provide a food staple for the entire meat-eating desert community.

Plants of the Desert

Jimson Weed

Peppergrass

Screw Bean

Piñon Pine

Verbena

Creosote Bush

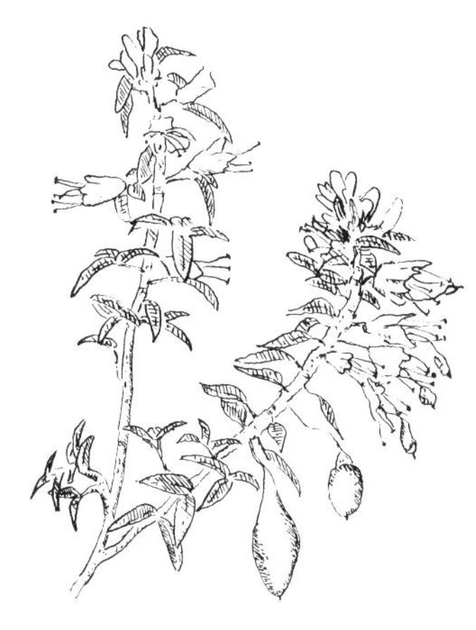

Bladder Pod

Palo Verde

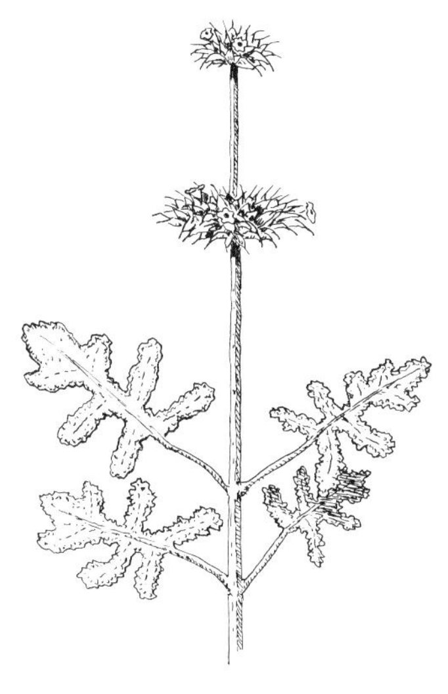

Chia

Ironwood

Birds of the Desert

Verdin

Costa's Hummingbird

Mourning Dove

Black-throated Sparrow

Western Mockingbird

Loggerhead Shrike

Gambel's Quail

Roadrunner

Phainopepla

Turkey Vulture

Poorwill

Creatures of the Desert

Bobcat

Blacktail Jackrabbit

Kit Fox

Coyote

Ringtail Cat

Desert Horned Lizard

Desert Kangaroo Rat

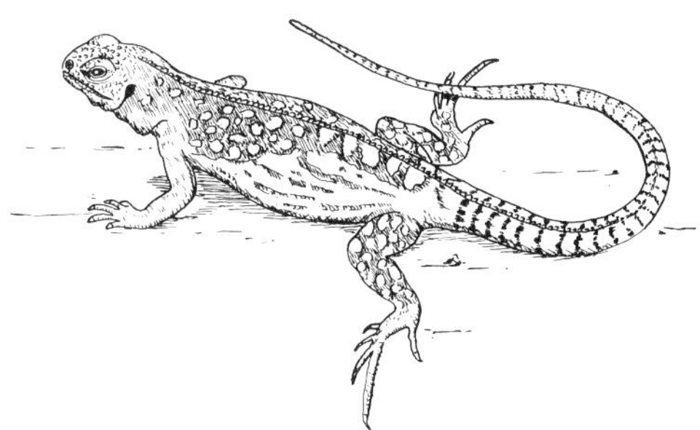

Desert Iguana

Chuckwalla

Antelope Ground Squirrel

Desert Tortoise

Side-Blotched Lizard

The desert tortoise, one of the few reptiles believed by some not to be native to Anza-Borrego Desert, has the ability to store water for long periods of time in a pair of sacs located between its flesh and shell. That makes it much less dependent on a permanent source of water.

Like a number of plants, some desert animals produce offspring only after a wet season. Rain signals the mating period to spadefoot toads which deposit eggs in temporary pools of water. A few days later tadpoles appear and within a month an adult spadefoot emerges. Tadpole shrimp and fairy shrimp hatch from eggs deposited perhaps years earlier when a puddle had formed in the same spot. The life cycle is so short that birth, maturity, mating and laying of new eggs occur before the puddle evaporates. Moisture also stimulates the development and growth of bees. Drought is a signal to the cactus wren and thrasher to lay fewer eggs or forego mating and nesting altogether for the season.

Another natural adaptation of desert animals is protective coloration which both helps to conserve body moisture and to conceal them from predatory enemies. The coloration of the horned lizard allows it to blend into the surrounding landscape, the sidewinder rattlesnake has adapted its locomotion to better travel in sand, and the long ears of the jackrabbit help regulate body temperature as well as warn of an enemy's approach.

Unlike the plants, animals have a wider area of distribution, and no species is known to be confined to the park. However, a few reach the periphery of their distribution within its borders. One barrier to the distribution of certain species is the natural boundary between the desert and mountains at the western edge of Borrego Valley and extending south into the Pinyon and Vallecito ranges. The Volcan and Laguna mountain ranges influence the distributional limitation of both coastal and desert species, particularly reptiles and amphibians, and the Tierra Blanca Mountains also serve as a barrier.

Birds are not restricted to specific areas and many are migratory, pausing on their journey north to feast on ripening seeds or drink at desert water holes. One of the easiest native birds to identify is the red-eyed, crested, and black-feathered phainopepla. The white wing patch of the phainopepla flashes as the bird flaps its wings in flight. It usually is found near mesquite where it nests. Another common species of bird found around mesquite is Costa's hummingbird.

The roadrunner, often seen scurrying before oncoming cars, is perhaps the most popular and best-known bird. The cactus wren, which builds its nest in cactus bushes or palo verde trees, is also conspicuous. Other common birds include the California thrasher, raven, Gambel quail, verdin, hawk, turkey vulture, black-throated sparrow, golden eagle, mourning dove, poorwill and loggerhead shrike.

Rodents are the most important mammals in the desert. According to Richard C. Banks, past curator of birds and mammals at the San Diego Museum of Natural History, rodents are the major herbivores, feeding directly on plants. Because they are food for carnivorous animals and reptiles, Banks says their abundance determines to a large extent the number of larger animal species. The inclusion in his report of voles, a small mouse-like animal, is significant because it is a species which lives in areas of permanent water and lush grass, not usually associated with a desert climate. Finding voles at Sentenac Canyon, Vallecito and the northeast corner of Earthquake Valley proves that "a desert is not in all places as dry as most people think." In Bank's study the cactus mouse was found to be the most abundant rodent with its nearest rival in numbers being the kangaroo rat. However, a park visitor is more likely to see the antelope ground squirrel and the jackrabbit than these animals.

Most sought after and asked about, but most infrequently seen, is the desert bighorn sheep. This symbol of desert wilderness is honored by the park in its name, *borrego,* the Spanish word for yearling lamb or sheep. Classified both rare and endangered, the bighorn has been a fully protected species in California since 1873. They are unable to live in civilized areas and Ernest Brown, a park naturalist, has said "the rugged, wild, undisturbed wilderness of Anza-Borrego is ideal for the protection and preservation of this rare animal." They are usually found in the more remote rocky areas near natural watering spots. The 1972 annual sheep count conducted by the park naturalist and volunteers listed 192 sheep in Palm Canyon, Sheep Canyon and Coyote Creek areas. In 1971, in similar areas, the count was 121. The 1970 survey, centered in the Santa Rosa Mountains, noted 219 bighorns.

Even though the sheep are fully protected by law, poachers have killed trophy rams. One man, a taxidermist, was fined, jailed, and placed on five-years' probation in 1971 for killing more than one hundred and fifty sheep. He was well informed of the locations for finding the sheep, having been a board member of the Society for the Conservation of Big Horn Sheep and once the organizer for the annual tally in the park. During his probationary period, he again was charged with violating laws designed to protect the animals, and in May, 1972, was accused of conspiring to arrange trips to hunt the desert bighorn.

Other protected but endangered species include the ringtail cat and the kit fox. Related to the racoon, the ringtail is a nocturnal animal which has a banded tail with seven alternating white and black bands and a black tip. Its face looks like a fox and its feet are cat-like with sharp claws. The ringtail was once called the "miner's cat" because, being a good mouser, miners encouraged it to make its home in their cabins. The kit fox also is a nocturnal animal, about the size of a house cat, with a thick coat and bushy tail. Although lacking a keen sense of smell, it has an acute sense of hearing. Its ears are very large and move independently, easily picking up sounds in any direction. It preys on small animals, especially the kangaroo rat.

The coyote, unlike the bighorn sheep, ringtail cat and kit fox, is commonly seen and heard in the park. It travels a wide area in search of food, and although it prefers small rodents, rabbits and ground squirrels, it will also eat vegetation if hungry enough. Other mammals native to Anza-Borrego are the bobcat, mountain lion and mule deer.

By far the most conspicuous and frequently seen desert reptile is the lizard, the heaviest and most impressive being the chuckwalla, which feeds on plants. When pursued they rapidly crawl between rocks and inflate their bodies so they cannot be removed. The Cahuilla Indians, who ate chuckwalla, removed them from the rocks by puncturing their inflated skin with a pointed stick. The only other herbivorous lizard in the park is the desert iguana which surpasses even the eighteen-inch total length of the chuckwalla. All of the other lizards eat insects. The smallest is the scaled lizard, and the one most commonly seen is the side-blotched lizard.

Four species of rattlesnake are found, all of which are venomous. Their diet consists of lizards, small rodents, ground squirrels and mice. However, the rattlesnake is not free of enemies, as hawks, roadrunners, coyotes and man control its numbers. It is probably the most singularly feared creature in the desert.

The desert tortoise, like all reptiles, is protected by law within the park. John Sloan, formerly curator of herpetology for the San Diego Natural History Museum, believes it is not native to the area but was purposely introduced into the region within the last fifty to one hundred years.

Prior to 1916, the desert pupfish was found in natural pools in Fish Creek. That year a flash flood laid a carpet of sand and gravel in the wash, completely covering both the pools and the creek. In June, 1970, pupfish were reintroduced into a man-made pond at the mouth of Borrego Palm Canyon. Naturalist Ernest Brown has explained that the purpose of the pond was to provide a stronghold for these fish should they become extinct elsewhere.

Plants and animals are probably the chief factors which contribute to the park's value as an outdoor laboratory for the study of ecology. Richard Banks, in a government report on rodents, found Anza-Borrego an excellent place to do research and commented, "I know of no other area where so many exciting and important problems can be studied so effectively." In the park, where the essential character of life is left to itself and where its cycle is allowed to function freely, scientist and layman alike can study the forces of nature.

SLEEPING CIRCLES: *Early desert-dwelling Indians formed circles of rock on the ground and, perhaps adding brush, used them for shelter at night.*

RED ROCK CANYON: *Geologists believe the color was caused by overflow lava baking the sandstone, but an Indian legend attributes it to the coyote.*

Land of Ancient People

Recent evidence from an Indian burial site near the Anza-Borrego Desert State Park indicates that people may have been in the area for at least 21,500 years, predating the evolution of the desert climate. As the ice age receded and an arid climate evolved, life forms changed and adapted in order to survive. Man had to create new hunting and gathering techniques, tools, home industries, and life styles.

Four distinct layers of human culture in the Anza-Borrego area have been identified. Archaeologists describe them as the San Dieguito, Pinto Basin, prehistoric Yuman and Shoshonean, and the modern Indian tribes who were encountered by White civilization two hundred years ago. Studies of early cultures are fragmentary and only the most recent period has been adequately documented.

The earliest human remains found near the park were discovered in 1971 in a boulder cairn in the Yuha Desert by W. Morlin Childers, an amateur archaeologist. The site was subsequently excavated by the Archaeology Department of Imperial Valley College, and radiocarbon dating of caliche deposits on the bone fragments indicated an age of about 21,500 years. Because dating was not done on the bone itself, some experts question this early age, and aspects of the find are still under study. However, further investigation may help to substantiate the presence of man in North America prior to 10,000 years ago. It is believed that the Yuha Man belonged to the San Dieguito culture.

The main body of evidence of San Dieguito and Lake Mojave culture dates back to 9000 or 10,000 B.C., after glaciers in the Great Basin retreated, leaving scattered lakes in the area of the Mojave and Colorado deserts. San Dieguito sites have been found along the Kane Springs Road west of Ocotillo Wells and near the Truckhaven Trail in Imperial County. Evidence at these sites has led archaeologists to draw tentative conclusions about San Dieguito people.

San Dieguito Indians hunted and fished for a livelihood with spears or darts which they hurled from a hand-held device called an *atlatl.* Bows and arrows were not used. They lived on high ground above lakes and streams where they could better spot both game and enemies.

Forty years of extensive research on the San Dieguito occupation, over much of the West, was carried out by Malcolm J. Rogers while on the staff of the San Diego Museum of Man, or on his own with financial assistance. He described round cleared areas, which still remain embedded in the desert pavement today, as "sleeping circles." Usually surrounded by rocks, they may have served as rock supported brush shelters. Strange rock alignments of various forms found near these circles have not been interpreted but may have been used for ceremonial purposes. Traces of artifacts, such as mortars and pestles have not been found, an absence which suggests a general disinterest in plant and seed gathering, which was common to later desert tribes.

James Moriarty III, an archaeologist at the University of San Diego, believes that the San Dieguito Indians—or the Early Playa-Flake Complex as he calls it—had a very generalized subsistence pattern, living "on foods that were easily secured and processed without highly specialized tools." Stone for tools was obtained from an eighty-acre quarry site in the Truckhaven area. This location, one of the largest and oldest rock quarries in the United States, also was used by later Indians.

Moriarty and Malcolm Rogers suggest that San Dieguito people were oriented toward lake shores where waterfowl, freshwater mussels and plants abounded. Lakes were probably surrounded by large expanses of arid or semi-arid land. Juniper and piñon forests grew at lower elevations than those of today. Though large animals were not numerous, many smaller animals were similar to species presently found in the area.

Little evidence of San Dieguito occupancy after 7000 B.C. has been found in the park area and Moriarty thinks that this complex "ceased because of the necessity to adjust its tools and subsistence techniques to the increasing aridity," and the group apparently migrated to the west where it settled along the coast in an essentially marine environment to which it was accustomed.

Using information gathered at only one site, the next clearly defined occupation dates some 4,000 years after that of the San Dieguito people. Known as the Pinto Basin culture, this group apparently was the first in the area to follow a typical pattern of life adapted by desert Indians in North America. One concept of the desert tradition singles out the basket and the flat milling stone as twin hallmarks of a life pattern in which seed gathering took precedence over hunting. Other characteristics are described as small social units of twenty-five or thirty persons, seasonal wandering within a limited territory in search of plants or animals, and few material possessions. The desert tradition began in the Great Basin after 7000 B.C., spread to California about 2500 or 3000 B.C., and continued with slight variation into the time of recorded history.

Four sites of the Pinto Basin culture, which Malcolm Rogers called Amargosan, have been reported. One of these in a rock shelter at Indian Hill located at the southern end of the Anza-Borrego Desert State Park, was first visited in 1958 by a team of University of Southern California archaeologists under the direction of William J. Wallace. The team concluded that Pinto Basin aborigines used the Indian Hill rock shelter as a temporary residence, and there was evidence of continued, seasonal occupation. Milling stones, mortars and pestles, and some Olivella shell beads and bone awls were found. Judging from these implements, Indians gathered wild seeds and vegetable foods in the area. Other sites were either few in number or had been erased by erosion.

Archaeologists believe that the overall population of the Pinto Basin culture was greater than that of the previous San Dieguito period, due largely to fluctuating climatic conditions which at this period brought increased rainfall and lower temperatures. However, as in the former San Dieguito culture, projectile points were used to tip darts rather than arrows, and there was no pottery. After about 3,000 years the Pinto Basin culture seems to have declined.

About 1,000 years passed between the Pinto Basin occupancy and the prehistoric Yuman and Shoshonean cultures. Documentation of human habitation throughout all California deserts is rare during this period and no sites have been found in the Anza-Borrego Desert. However, Wallace conjectures that there could have been a continuation of Amargosan or Pinto-like culture, or perhaps the presence of an intermediate group which preceded modern Indian cultures.

About A.D. 900 or 1000, ancestors of the modern Yuman and Shoshonean Indians entered the California deserts from the east. These people best fit the description of following a desert tradition in which seed collecting was paramount. They commonly used milling stones, hand stones, and mortars and pestles while at various camps, apparently storing many of their tools when they moved on to another site. Small seasonal camps were made along streams, waterholes, and lake shores, with larger semi-permanent villages located where there was a water supply in relative abundance, at such locations as Scissor's Crossing, Vallecito, Mason Valley, and Coyote Canyon.

Population fluctuated considerably from year to year. When wild crops were bountiful, several bands may have camped together, while in poor years, some areas may have been vacant. Two innovations appeared among these Indians: small projectile points used to tip arrows rather than darts, and pottery. The method used in making pottery probably was introduced to the region

MARINE FOSSILS: *Nearly actual size, they were photographed with official permission in the closed and potentially dangerous Carrizo Impact Area.*

SIGNS OF THE PAST: *Two Indian ollas—clay utensils—and an early settler's iron cooking pot were utilitarian but a far cry from present cookware.*

through the influence from lower Colorado River Indians.

Even with this information there is presently not enough data available to describe native customs or to reconstruct the physical characteristics of these Indians. Erosion, cremation of the dead, and destruction of all personal artifacts of the deceased, have hindered such research. Even though precise information is limited, some scholars have speculated that Yuman Indians preceded the Shoshoneans into the Colorado Desert during the late Amargosan period. This would account for the influence of Yuman pottery in the area.

The Yumans were perhaps attracted by Lake Cahuilla, a new lake and oasis created in the Salton Sink. Though no definite date has been established for the formation of the lake, archaeologists believe it existed as early as A.D. 60, when the Colorado River overflowed its west bank near present-day Yuma. Mesquite and willow trees grew around the lake and in late Amargosan times, Yuman villages dotted the lakeside. Evidence indicates that at one time an unexpected increase in water level flooded the villages. Later, the water receded, and about A.D. 1400, the natives abandoned the lake due to its increasing salinity. Indians who lived on the eastern shore of Lake Cahuilla returned to the Colorado River, and those who occupied the western side moved into the mountains of San Diego County. The old shoreline and the remains of four identifiable village sites can still be seen just east of the park boundary in the San Felipe Hills.

These village sites, and others south of State Highway 78, have been investigated by archaeologists from U.S.C. Surveys of the Indian Hill district, Mountain Palm Springs, and the entire Bow Willow Canyon were conducted. The Indian Hill area, more than other sites, abounded in archaeological remains. Wallace's team concluded that the mode of life was similar to that of Yuman-speaking Indians who have occupied the same district in recorded times.

Another team of archaeologists from the University of California at Los Angeles, under the direction of Clement W. Meighan, explored north of Highway 78, taking samples from six main districts. These included Grapevine Canyon, northern Culp Valley, Collins Valley and Indian Canyon, Coyote Creek, Rockhouse Canyon and Clark Dry Lake. They discovered one hundred and seventy-three sites dating back to about A.D. 1000. Extensive vandalism by uninformed and careless relic collectors created difficulty in obtaining artifacts and Meighan angrily noted:

> It represents the greatest amount of archaeological looting known to the writer anywhere in California. Even sites in the most remote and inaccessible parts of the park have suffered from the collecting and digging activities of vandals. . . . Like most sites of the desert area, the Borrego archaeological villages consist mostly of surface remains, and in some areas these have been picked over so intensively that nothing but a few small potsherds can now be found. In the few large sites which justify excavation, active digging was going on during the time of our survey.

Despite such vandalism, Meighan's team found traces of Indian settlements throughout the park. Some areas appear to have been widely used while others were almost uninhabited. The most heavily populated site was San Felipe Creek, especially in its Grapevine Canyon tributary. The largest site in the northern half of the park was found at Santa Catarina Spring in Coyote Canyon.

In 1969 another group of archaeologists from U.C.L.A., headed by Alex Apostolides, checked Meighan's survey and also investigated sites in Henderson Canyon, Borrego Palm Canyon, Hellhole Canyon, Hawk Canyon and Clark Dry Lake. Surveys corroborated the findings of the former team and also found that Meighan's warning about destruction of surface sites had been valid. Users of recreational vehicles were, and still are, the primary offenders. Apostolides found alluvial fans of canyons such as Henderson Canyon "literally covered and churned up with jeep tracks, including areas where, in witless joy, they drove around and round in a large circle." Predictably, the best preserved locations were those that could be controlled by the park rangers.

Apostolides recommended the building of

interpretive centers so park visitors could be made aware of the archaeological richness of the area, and especially suggested such a display in Borrego Palm Canyon. Subsequently greater effort was made to locate and preserve such sites by the park's first full-time archaeologist, William Seidel. An effort also was being made by the park's Natural History Association to build an information center.

The U.C.L.A. teams surveyed areas which primarily were occupied by Shoshonean Indians, who at an early date had pushed the Yumans south and about the year 1700 had established themselves in well-defined territories. These two cultures are distinguished from each other by differences in language and variations in social patterns.

The terms Yuman and Shoshonean refer to distinct linguistic families within different language stocks of the Southern California tribes, and these families in turn are divided into native groupings. Separate dialects of the Yuman Diegueño and the Shoshonean Cahuilla, recorded after 1769, included the Southern or Desert Diegueño, located in the section south of the San Felipe drainage; Mountain Cahuilla in the northern and northwestern portions above the San Felipe drainage; and Desert Cahuilla on the southwestern edge of the Santa Rosa Mountains and at Travertine Point.

Many anthropologists believe another dialect, the Kamia, also existed in the area between the Colorado River and San Diego. A. L. Kroeber, author of the *Handbook of the Indians of California,* has listed them as a variant of the Kumeyai, the name the Southern Diegueño used for themselves. Anthropologists from the San Diego Museum of Man and others who have specialized in this area, believe the Kamia were actually part of the Southern Diegueños who moved into Imperial Valley, possibly in the early 1800s, where they became greatly influenced by the Colorado River Yumans, even to the extent of adopting farming techniques.

E. W. Gifford, a proponent of the existence of the Kamia, offered the opinion that they relocated in the New River area to avoid Spanish missionaries who had established *rancherias* west of the park. Lowell Bean treated them as a distinct group, but Gifford was not certain that they should be considered "separate people." Anthropologist Philip Drucker believed the Kamia were Desert Diegueños who drifted back and forth between a gathering and an agricultural existence.

The material subsistence and environment of Yuman and Shoshonean groups were basically the same. Frequent contact took place between the Diegueños and Cahuillas, especially in the Borrego Valley area where the groups converged. Father Francisco Garcés, missionary and diarist who accompanied the first Anza expedition to California in 1774, noted the mixing and acculturation of Indians in this area, but modern anthropologists have not determined the extent of the integration.

Recent Indians, regardless of their linguistic family or native grouping, followed the desert tradition. They lived in local village groups in dwellings made of posts, earth and thatching and made seasonal rounds within their territory to gather wild vegetables, hunt game, and visit and trade with other Indians. Villages were usually located no more than sixteen miles from food gathering areas, with eighty percent of the food resources found within five miles of the village.

As many as two hundred different varieties of plant foods were used. Many plants also were utilized for medicinal purposes, creosote being the most common. The main staples included mesquite beans, the agave or century plant, native palm and cactus fruit from desert areas, and acorns, sage and conifer seeds from the mountains.

The yearly food gathering cycle began in January and February when the Indians harvested agave. In addition to furnishing food in the form of leaves, blossoms and stalks, the plant also provided fiber which was utilized in the making of sandals, skirts, bowstrings, cord, cradles, nets, mats and snares. Even the thorns were used in producing baskets, and the burned stalks provided a dye which was used for coloring tatoo marks. During those months little else was available for gathering, so the tribes relied on supplies which had been stored from the previous season and supplemented their diet with some hunting. This also was the period of greatest ceremonial activity.

In the Spring, Indians were able to gather ripening wild food near the villages—staples such as ocotillo, certain buds, grasses and greens. The Mohave yucca also was a plant of many uses. The fruit pods were eaten, the roots were used to make soap and the strong fiber was utilized in making string, rope, nets, bowstrings, sandals and paint brushes.

However, the most intense gathering period was during the summer months when plants increased their yield. The fruit of the fan palm was important because of its dependability. Palm trees were periodically burned both to destroy harmful pests and to improve the quantity of the fruit produced. The palm tree also was important as building material for the Indians' dwellings.

Mesquite beans were the most important of all the summer produce. The blossoms, green pods and dried yellow pods were all eaten. The green pods were pounded in mortars, producing a pulpy juice, while the pounded dried pods furnished a flour meal which was easily stored. Mesquite wood was also used for making mortars and bows and arrows.

In the fall, Indians gathered grass seeds, chia, berries and pinyon pine nuts. A brew made from the seeds of the chia plant, roasted, ground and mixed with water, was said to have been of such high nutritional value that one teaspoonful was enough to sustain a person during a forced march of twenty-four hours. Large groups of people would leave the village for a week or more to harvest the pinyon nuts which often were located more than ten miles from the camp.

The gathering of acorns became the prime concern for the entire tribe during the months of October and November. Villages would be almost deserted for as long as three weeks during harvest, and the women who had the responsibility of gathering the acorns took processing equipment to the oak groves each year. Acorns were either ground and leached, being made into a kind of bread or mush, or stored in baskets for later use. The men hunted game while the women gathered and prepared the acorns. Tons of acorns were taken back to the village at the conclusion of the gathering. By late November, when harvesting activities had slowed down, ritual activity again took precedence. It also was a time for making goods, trading, visiting, recreation and the education of the young.

Indians instinctively left behind a stand of what they were harvesting so the plants would produce more food in the future. Individual ownership of some food resources, such as oak and mesquite groves, also helped protect the environment. Although food gathering was normally an activity of the female members of the tribe, men were almost certainly the exclusive gatherers of agave because of the amount of labor involved in collecting it.

Common animal staples included rabbit, hare, rodents, quail, tortoise, lizards and snakes. Important large game animals were antelope, deer and bighorn sheep. Hunting implements included snares, traps, nets, and bows and arrows. The bow was usually made of mesquite, as was the rabbit stick, a throwing club used to kill small game. Salt was obtained from the Salton Sink.

Mortars and pestles as well as milling stones and hand stones, called metates and manos, were used to pound and grind various foods. Mortar holes, some quite deep, ground into the surface of boulders, can still be found in the park.

Basketry was a highly developed industry. Produced in a variety of shapes, sizes and designs, baskets were used for carrying, storage, and as serving dishes. Most were made with the coiling process, but a few were twined or woven rather than sewn. A basket cap also was worn by both men and women to protect their heads and keep hair out of the way when grinding meal. Kenneth Hedges, curator of the San Diego Museum of Man, has noted that the Diegueño baskets "exhibit qualities of form and texture which are esthetically pleasing and highly prized by Indian and non-Indian alike."

Pottery was made by the coiled paddle-anvil method. The wall of a vessel was built up with

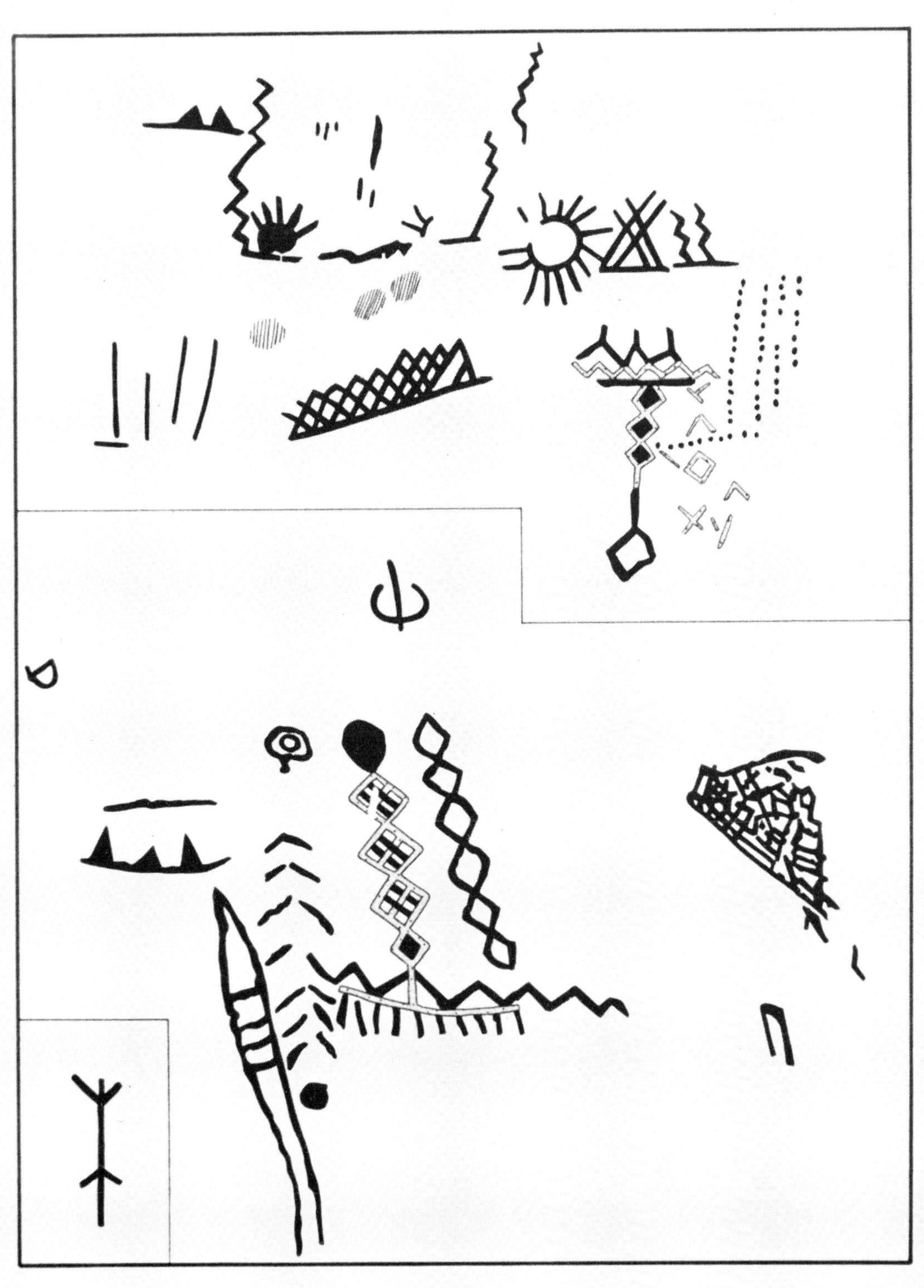

INDIAN PAINTING: *This Diegueño pictograph located in Smugglers Canyon, is unusual for its well-executed designs using a diamond chain motif.*

coils of clay which then was shaped with a paddle while a small anvil was held inside. The clay, which became red when fired, was also used to make tobacco pipes and figurines. Both Rogers and Hedges rank Diegueño pottery as among the best in the Southwest and Hedges says, "It is only in matters of painted designs that Southwestern pottery excels that of the Diegueño, and then only in technique, not in inspiration."

Pictographs were commonly painted by the shamans who were the tribal doctors and religious leaders. There are excellent examples of such rock art at Indian Hill. The only Diegueño representation of a man on horseback is located at Dos Cabezas. Rock paintings in the Blair Valley region show the influence of the Luiseños. There also are many paintings in Coyote Canyon.

Indians wore little clothing prior to contact with Spanish missionaries. Diarists accompanying the Anza expedition noted the nakedness of the men, although women usually wore a two-piece apron made of willow bark or agave fibre with the longer apron in the back. Robes made of rabbit fur and cord twining were used for warmth. Agave fibre sandals were worn for travel but were not used in campsites. Using cactus spines as needles, women tatooed designs on their chins as part of a puberty ceremony. The Indians painted their faces and bodies for ceremonial purposes. They wore beads, pendants and hair ornaments made of shells, stone or pottery.

Generally the tribes were peaceful and traded with each other over established Indian trails, some of which are now followed by major roads in the park. Intertribal fighting between Cahuillas and Digueños usually grew out of territorial or food preserve encroachment.

Diegueños and Cahuillas had substantially the same material possessions, but differed from each other in social pattern. Digueños were organized into patrilocal bands in which married couples resided in the geographical territory of the husband's family, permitting the hunter to remain in familiar territory. Tribal consciousness was slight and the local group acted as the most important unit. Political and social organization was based on lineage with one line of descent usually dominating. Lineage was associated with a restricted locality, one which probably served as its usual summer home. Most village sites have disappeared, but some can still be traced in San Felipe (*Mitltekwanak*), La Posta, La Laguna, Manzanita, Vallecito (*Hawi*), Carrizo (*Ahta* or *Hapawa*), Jacumba (*Hakum*), Cuyapaipe, Agua Caliente, Hapaha Flat, Scissor's Crossing, Grapevine Canyon, Yaqui Well, Mountain Springs, Pinyon Mountain, Dos Cabezas and Mason Valley. Usually any canyon with a water supply was a seasonal village site.

Diegueños were exogamous, no marriage being allowed within the lineage. No formal marriage ceremony was conducted and a legal union took place when the woman went to live with her new husband. She retained her lineage and tribal membership, but her children took the father's lineage. Each tribe had an hereditary chief who officiated at religious ceremonies centered around puberty rites, mortuary customs and mythology. In the mid-Eighteenth Century, Diegueños became strongly influenced by northern groups in ceremonial matters, but the story of creation had a Yuman origin.

Puberty rites were conducted for both sexes. The one for boys was elaborate and greatly influenced by the Gabrielino *toloache* ceremony, which was introduced by Luiseño neighbors on the north. Only those boys who were to receive instruction in shamanistic magic and dancing took part. After using *toloache* (jimson weed), an hallucinogenic drug which induced dreams, initiates fasted for six days prior to learning dances and ceremonial rites. Songs used in the ceremony were sung in the Gabrielino tongue. Fifty years ago, anthropologist Constance DuBois wrote that the Southern Diegueños had received the cult only within the preceding two or three generations. Diegueño women never drank *toloache,* but the Gabrielino and Luiseño women did.

For the girls' puberty rites a pit large enough to hold the reclining initiate was dug in the ground. After stones were placed inside the pit a fire was built. When the stones became hot the fire was removed, the pit lined with herbs

DOS CABEZAS ROCK ART: *This painting, found at a small rock shelter, is the only known representation in Diegueño art of a man riding on horseback.*

PATH OF AN ANCIENT PEOPLE: *A park ranger inspects an old Indian trail worn into the rock-strewn earth near Truckhaven Trail east of Arroyo Salado.*

or brush and the girl placed on top. She was then covered with more herbs and "roasted" in the pit for as long as she was physically able to tolerate it, usually about a week. Periodically the pit would be reheated. The girl was allowed to leave the pit for only short periods of time and was instructed to remain as still as possible while in it. At night, ceremonies were conducted, the men and women singing songs in the Diegueño tongue and dancing around the pit. The initiate's face also was tatooed—usually on the chin—and she was required to follow certain dietary restrictions for a limited time.

Like other Yumans, the Diegueños cremated their dead, placing the ashes in a jar before burying it. The dead person's house also was burned but personal effects and clothing were saved for a memorial observance conducted a year later, when all clothing, articles and images of the deceased were consumed in flames. The purpose of the ceremony was to keep the dead content and to end the survivors' period of mourning. Indians did not begin burying their dead until after contact with Spanish missionaries.

Cahuillas also were organized into patrilocal lineages but there was a further division into two exogamous clans called moieties: the wildcat (*túkut* or *túktum*) and coyote (*ísil* or *ístam*). The primary functions of moieties were cooperation in matters of ritual and the regulation of marriage. A member of the wildcat group could marry only a member from the coyotes. A marriage usually was arranged by the two fathers, and the girl's family customarily received a gift.

Clans were small and few in number and derived their names from specific places or certain localities. The chieftainship was hereditary, as with the Diegueños. The Cahuillas placed greater importance on their shamans than did the Diegueños, thus having more control over malpractices, as the killing of a malevolent shaman among the Coyote Canyon Indians testifies.

The story is that the *wiwaiistam* people had an evil shaman whom they called Gopher. Having bewitched and killed many people, Gopher's actions incurred the wrath of his own daughter who asked the tribe to kill him. After discussing it, they entrusted the assignment to *Morui,* a Bear shaman. As Gopher sat eating ripe summer watermelon, Bear came up behind him and hit him a blow on the head with a digging stick. The blow did not kill the evil Gopher, so the people piled rocks on him until he died.

Religious emphasis centered on puberty rites, the mortuary ceremony and the creation myth. The *toloache* ceremony was practiced by Mountain Cahuilla, but to a lesser degree by the Desert Cahuilla. The creation myth had elements similar to that of the Diegueños.

William Duncan Strong, who published a paper on the aboriginal society of Southern California in 1929, distinguished two main groupings of the Mountain Cahuilla. The more northerly was oriented toward Santa Rosa and the present Cahuilla Reservation. Two villages were located in Rockhouse Canyon and were called Old Santa Rosa or *kilwovakut* or *kewel.* The village of *sewiu* was located at New Santa Rosa. In the northern end of Horse Canyon was the village of *nacuta,* and to the east on Terwilliger Flats was *pauki.* The large village at the Cahuilla Reservation was called *paui,* and other villages were situated to the north and east.

The Southern Mountain Cahuilla were oriented toward Coyote Canyon and called themselves *wiwaiistam,* or coyote people. Because they were members of the coyote moiety, suitors took brides from the Diegueños, who, having no moieties of their own, were designated the wildcat moiety for the purpose of intermarriage. Before 1875 five villages of wildcat moiety (*wancham sib*) were located at *ataki* near Rockhouse Canyon. After that, when villagers moved east to the Coachella Valley, men had to travel outside the park area to find a Cahuilla girl of the wildcat moiety.

Five different lineages trace themselves to the *wiwaiistam* people of Coyote Canyon. The main village in the canyon was *wiliya,* where the clan chief lived. The four other villages can be thought of as "colonies" of *wiliya,* with another to the north being only an extension of the main village. The other three villages were named *tepana, sauivil,* and *sauic* (in Collins Valley), all of which eventually were moved to Rockhouse Canyon. These villages were in contact with

Cupeño, Luiseño and Diegueño neighbors and resembled them in many ways.

The southernmost Mountain Cahuilla village was *patcawal* at San Ignacio, situated within the present Los Coyotes Indian Reservation northwest of the park. South of San Ignacio and still within the domain of today's reservation was San Ysidro, the site of the more recent village of *wilakal,* which contained a mixture of Cahuilla, Cupeño and Diegueño families. Present-day residents of San Ysidro call themselves Los Coyotes, indicating the presence of some Mountain Cahuilla who formerly lived in Coyote Canyon. However, it is believed that there are only a few modern descendants of the original Los Coyotes tribe.

In the early 1880s Indian lands and gathering places in San Ysidro, Coyote Canyon and San Felipe were usurped by homesteaders such as Chatham Helm, William B. Fain and Paul Sentenac. Helm came into San Ysidro Canyon and took up a homestead three miles above the Indian village site, cut off the greater part of the water supply and took over some of the cultivated fields. The Indians grew poorer and poorer. When one of the villagers once attempted to get water from the stream, he was shot for trespassing.

When William Fain appeared in the Los Coyotes Valley, the Indians living there supported themselves by keeping stock and cultivating beans, pumpkins, wheat, barley and corn. Their houses were built of hewn pine timber and had thatched roofs. The village numbered twenty-six men, twenty-one women and thirty-six children. Fain offered the Indians $200 for their lands. When they refused to sell, Fain told them he had filed on the land and would stay in any event, and then proceeded to cut down trees and build a corral.

Paul Sentenac likewise usurped Indian lands at Scissor's Crossing, taking away the water from the Indian village. He told the captain that the land belonged to him and that if anyone so much as hunted a rabbit on the place he would put him in prison.

In 1886, the United States Indian Commission investigated some of the alleged deprivations of the Indians. One of the commission members was Helen Hunt Jackson, well-known author of the novel *Ramona* and the *Century of Dishonor* which concerned government dealings with the Indians.

In 1891, the Cahuilla Indians were confined to Los Coyotes Reservation and Diegueño reservations also were established. In the same year, while installing a public watering trough at Vallecito, County Supervisor James A. Jasper met an old Diegueño Indian who was clad in tattered rags and appeared at the camp half starved. Jasper recorded:

> He lived all alone in a wickiup at the cane brakes a few miles away and was a Mission Indian. . . . He was born at Vallecito, his father and grandfathers were born there; they were dead. His wife was dead, his children were dead, all his people were dead, and he alone of all the Vallecito Indians was left.

The Anza-Borrego Desert was home territory for the Indians, who not only found subsistence in the arid environment but also had important personal, religious, mythological and ceremonial ties to the land. To later Spaniards, Mexicans and pioneer Americans, the desert was only a barrier to cross in attempts to reach settlements on the Pacific Coast, a place to pass through, but not to settle. The desert seemed a poor choice for a home when better lands were available for development. The Spaniards, the first to encounter park Indians, viewed themselves as bearers of an advanced culture, as did later waves of White civilization. The White man had little appreciation for the life and customs of the Indians and persistently sought to subdue them, forcing upon them an alien economic system and new political and religious values. To historian Jack D. Forbes, the initial years of Spanish contact between 1769 and 1821 were devastating for California Indians:

> By the later years all of the coastal natives were living in the missions or on nearby ranchos and virtually all of the ancient villages were depopulated.

As with coastal tribes, there was a drastic decline of park Indians, stemming primarily from disease, changes in food, and social and genetic factors. Lowell Bean reported that the Cahuilla Indian population prior to Spanish contact could have been more than 5,000 or 6,000, but by 1850 had dropped to 2,500 and in 1910 to about 800. Diegueño population, as estimated by A. L. Kroeber, was about 3,000 in 1770, around 800 in 1925, and 322 in 1930.

By the beginning of the Twentieth Century, the last of the park Indians had been moved onto reservations and were forced to live far from their ancestral homes. Anthropologist Peter Farb concluded that the complex web of Indian "social, religious, and political life had been irreparably torn apart."

COYOTE CREEK: *The only stream in the park which flows year long, is shown here as it passes through Lower Willows near the mouth of Coyote Canyon.*

IV

The White Man Arrives

To the Spaniards, the Anza-Borrego area was a land passage that afforded water and pasturage between the deserts to the east and the mountainous areas north and west. Father Pedro Font saw it as an area nearly devoid of plants and animals and occupied only by aborigines. But it was vital for communication and as a route to supply isolated California settlements on the coast. Juan Bautista de Anza and his expeditions deserve credit for opening a road through the area, for describing its Indians, and for bequeathing a name and a mystique to the largest state park in the United States.

The possibility of a land route to California lay open ever since 1702 when Father Eusebio Francisco Kino confirmed the almost forgotten reports of some earlier explorers that California was in fact a peninsula, and not an island. As early as 1737, Anza's father had proposed taking a more northerly route across the deserts to the western coast of the American continent. However, the untimely death of the elder Anza during an engagement with the Apaches ended his plans, and it was left to his son to fulfill them. In 1769, Inspector General José de Gálvez sent Captain Gaspar de Portolá and Father Junípero Serra to New California to establish missions and presidios, because of a reported threat of Russian encroachment south from Alaska. In Sonora, Anza III heard rumors from local Indians of the Spanish activity in California. If word could travel so easily among the Indians, Anza believed that a road must exist between the California settlements and the Colorado River.

In 1771, the Spanish priest Francisco Hermenegildo Garcés, missionary at San Javier del Bac near present-day Tucson in Arizona, proceeded west down the Gila River to the Colorado River and followed it south into the barren delta country of Sonora and Baja California. Turning northwest, Garcés wandered to within sight of Signal Mountain, just below the present international border near Calexico. Looking across the Anza-Borrego Desert he saw a break in the Peninsular Range which suggested a pass or a river course through the mountains which might lead to the coast and the California settlements.

This opening in the mountains marks Coyote Canyon. But Garcés did not see the entrance to the Carrizo Corridor which led across the western part of the Anza-Borrego Desert to the spring at Vallecito, where a series of valleys lift easily up through the mountains to Warner's Spring. When finally discovered a half-century later, the pass would play a major role in the destiny of California.

The small and limited number of supply ships and the long journey north from the port of San Blas on Mexico's mainland, against adverse winds and tides, made the sea route to Baja California hazardous and uncertain. The trip across the Gulf of California and then north through the interior of the peninsula also involved more hardships than the results merited. Without a practical land route to supply the Upper California settlements, their existence seemed doubtful.

The information brought back by Garcés made Anza even more confident that a practical route did exist, and he offered to personally finance an expedition to find one. His first proposal was rejected but the critical need for improved communication with the California settlements gave Anza another chance to propose an overland expedition.

Anza ultimately led two expeditions. The first proved the feasibility of his idea and the second took colonists and soldiers from Sonora and Sinaloa to San Francisco where they established a settlement.

Members of the first expedition included Anza, Garcés, Father Juan Díaz of Caborca Mission, Juan Bautista Valdes who was a soldier familiar with the California mission roads, twenty volunteer presidial soldiers, five muleteers and two servants, and more than two hundred animals. Apaches raided the cattle and mules and caused a delay in Anza's departure from Tubac until after Mass on Sunday, January 9, 1774. In order to try to replenish his stock, Anza was forced to abandon his original plan of proceeding to the Gila River and following it down to the Colorado. Instead he retraced the old mission route through Sonora, from where he would eventually swing northward toward the Colorado crossing at Yuma.

The delay, however, proved to be rewarding. At Altar in Sonora they encountered a runaway Indian from the Pacific Coast, named Sebastián Tarabal. Originally from Baja California, he had gone north with Portolá and settled at the San Gabriel Mission near today's Los Angeles. Tired of mission life, he fled with his wife and a companion in the winter of 1773, descended the mountains in the vicinity of Coyote Canyon, and crossed Borrego Valley to the Colorado Desert. Only Tarabal survived the rigors of the journey. His arrival at the presidio at Altar proved once again there was a route across the desert, difficult as it might be, and Anza drafted Tarabal as a guide for the expedition.

Leaving the Altar Valley, Anza's expedition crossed the land of the Pápagos into Yuma Indian country, following Kino's original trail to the Colorado River and its junction with the Gila. Here the expedition met Salvador Palma, chief of the Yuma Indians. The vital link to the road to California was the Yuma area and its Colorado River crossing. Without control of the Indians at this strategic point, a road would be impossible. Knowing this, Anza viewed friendship with Chief Palma as indispensable. Chief Palma was treated with every courtesy and was presented a medal in the likeness of the Spanish king.

The route west from the Colorado River was blocked by great sand dunes and the expedition was led by the Yumas on a southerly course toward a small lake created by an overflow of the river, located deep in the wasteland of northern Baja California, and which they named Santa Olaya.

Friday, February the thirteenth, was an unlucky start for the expedition. On that day Palma bid Anza farewell and the expedition set off westward from Santa Olaya. For the next ten days they wandered about in still more sand dunes where both Tarabal and Garcés were unable to recognize the trail. In a dangerous situation, with no water or pasture available, Anza ordered the expedition back to Santa Olaya to recuperate.

On March 2, after sending part of his expedition back to the protection of Palma at the Yuma crossing, Anza again left Santa Olaya, this time circumventing the sand dunes by traveling even farther south, eventually swinging west and then north toward California. Passing Laguna Salada and Signal Mountain, and entering what is now Imperial County, Anza reached the first good water at Yuha Well or Santa Rosa de las Lajas (Santa Rosa of the Flat Rocks), as he called it, on March 8. The well is north of Signal Mountain, four miles from the present international boundary and seven miles south of what today is Plaster City. Anza described the wells, dug several feet into the sand, as having the "finest water." It was at Yuha Well that Tarabal recognized his outgoing trail, and Garcés also remembered the area as the place where he had turned back to the Colorado River in 1771. At that point success seemed reasonably assured for the expedition.

The next day's march brought the party to a dry camp, called Arroyo del Coyote, located a few miles north of Plaster City. Continuing north the following day, they came to a level plain roughly paralleling the present San Diego - Imperial County line, and had to walk their horses through the dunes between Fish Creek Mountains on the west and Superstition Moun-

WIND-SWEPT DUNES: *Low hills or banks such as these located northwest of Borrego Sink are the result of wind continually depositing fine sand.*

SHARP CONTRAST: *Lakes and evergreens in Laguna Mountains overlook the desert area through which Anza passed to reach the Spanish coastal settlements.*

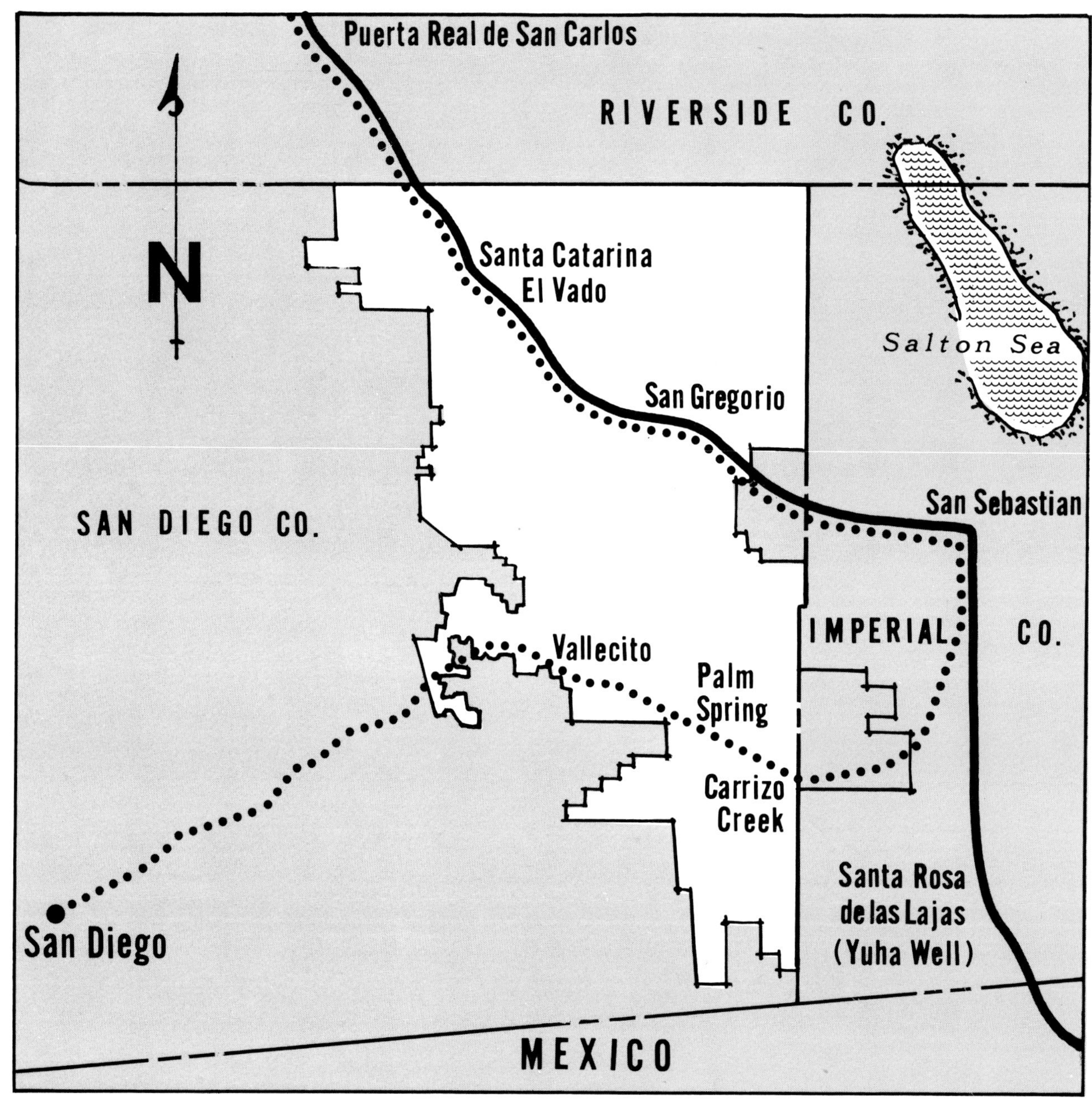

EARLY TRAILS: *In 1772, Lieutenant Pedro Fages started east from San Diego in pursuit of deserters from the presidio. The dotted line shows his progress as he crossed the Cuyamaca Mountains, down Oriflamme Canyon on an Indian trail and then out into the desert by way of the Carrizo Corridor. Fages went deep into Imperial County before heading northward to San Sebastian and then across Borrego Valley. Between the San Ysidro and Santa Rosa mountains he found Coyote Canyon which led him into Riverside County and he eventually reached San Luis Obispo. Two years later, the first expedition of Juan Bautista de Anza crossed the desert on its way to Monterey. Anza traveled from Tubac, near the present day Tucson, but had twice turned south into Mexico. His expedition entered Imperial County and made its first camp near Yuha Wells before proceding north to San Sebastian where it joined the Fages Trail.*

tains on the east. After traveling a grueling twenty miles that day they made camp at the junction of Carrizo and San Felipe creeks near what is now called Harper's Well. There was a good supply of water as Tarabal had promised, and in his honor they named the camp San Sebastián. Some of the Indians in the area recognized Garcés and Tarabal.

At San Sebastián, Anza learned that other Spanish soldiers already had passed that way. In 1772 Captain Pedro Fages had reached the Anza-Borrego area from the Cuyamaca Mountains by way of Oriflamme Canyon, Mason Valley and Carrizo Corridor while in pursuit of deserters from the presidio at San Diego. After arriving at San Sebastián, his party turned northwest, crossed Borrego Valley and entered Coyote Canyon. Anza and Garcés later saw Fages' tracks in Coyote Canyon, and Garcés correctly concluded from the evidence that two roads were already opened: one to San Gabriel in the Los Angeles area and the other to San Diego.

Thus, Pedro Fages and not Juan Bautista de Anza made the first official entry into the Anza-Borrego Desert and found not one, but two land routes through it. Consequently, the only segment of the desert explored by Anza was a thirty-mile area between Signal Mountain and San Sebastián. Garcés had previously explored as far as Signal Mountain and Fages had explored the Carrizo Corridor and the northern half of the "Anza trail." Perhaps because Fages' discoveries were made by chance rather than in a planned expedition, and because there were no significant records of his feat, he has not received the credit due him.

While at San Sebastián, Anza took note of about four hundred Indians living there. He described them as less robust and darker complexioned than the Colorado River Indians. Though they had more bows and arrows, they were less warlike. They had no horses, and in fact were afraid of them. Like the Yumas, the men went naked but the women wore skirts of mescal fibre.

On the morning of March 11, Anza left San Sebastián and his party headed west toward the mountains. By evening they were on the other side of a marsh where they were forced to camp, though it proved to be a poor site with no water and having saline pasturage, resulting in the death of two saddle animals. More reassuring was news from Indians living in a nearby village. They told Anza that the sea was only three days to the west and a Spanish settlement six days away. Anza believed this to be San Diego.

The next day the expedition followed San Felipe Creek northwest around Borrego Mountain and entered Borrego Valley from the southeast. Now within the boundaries of the present Anza-Borrego Desert State Park, the expedition found at San Gregorio the best water and pasturage they had had since leaving Pimería-Alta. Nearby they saw more than sixty Indians hunting and sent Tarabal to invite them over. However, the braying of the expedition's pack animals caused the Indians to flee, but not before Tarabal had had sufficient time to learn that they spoke the language of San Diego.

Garcés painted a vivid picture of these Diegueños, whom he called Cajuenches:

> These Cajuenches do not paint themselves as much as the Yumas. With their macanas (wooden ax or club) they are accustomed to kill many rabbits and some deer, with whose skins the women cover themselves behind, but in front they wear aprons of the fiber of *arria,* made of the inner bark of trees. These multitudes of fibers some wear like a net and others loose, but all cover themselves well, and even little girls three years old and even infants are never seen naked. In these regions the women use the nets to carry wood, herbs and ollas in which they carry water, and also to carry their little children. The men build corrals with the nets, stakes and flat rocks, and, driving the game from long distances to a corral, they kill it in abundance. Since these mountain Indians eat much mescal and, in some parts, the roots of the tule, their teeth are very badly decayed and damaged. Some carry a lance with a good point, which appears to be a weapon of war, and even the women carry poles that are shorter and thicker. They eat a great quantity of wild onions, which abound in these parts. Although these Cajuenches are not such people as the Yumas they are friendly and more timid.

After a day's rest, Anza traveled northwestward through Borrego Valley to the entrance of Coyote Canyon and followed the flowing creek to Lower Willows, which they called Santa Catarina. Anza was quite pleased with this camp and the spring, finding "much grass and other green plants, as well as wild vines and trees, which announced to us an improvement in the country from here forward." Here Anza and Garcés found traces of hoof marks from the horses and mules of the Fages party. They also noticed a new tribe of Indians, although some "Cajuenches" were mixed among them. This tribe, the Mountain Cahuillas, occupied all the mountain country north of Santa Catarina. Anza noted in his diary:

> These new Indians are less warlike people than those farther back, much smaller, and more unhappy in every way. Most of them employ their hands solely with a stick shaped like a sickle, which serves them to kill jack rabbits by throwing at them when they are on the run, because the weapon flies so. These miserable people were given presents, and they stayed with us until a mule brayed, when they precipitately fled, terrorized.

Father Díaz noted that their dress was the same as the river people, except for sandals of maguey and nets of the same material which they wore about their heads. There were more Indians living in the mountains than in the valleys, but they appeared less robust.

On March 15, a difficult march up Coyote Canyon brought the Spaniards to the summit of the mountains and Puerto Real de San Carlos (Royal Pass of San Carlos), named for the Spanish king. Garcés made note of the Indians there and their unusual speech "in tones like some little crows which abound in this region." When they spoke they moved their feet high behind them and waved their arms as if complaining. Because of these strange gestures they were called "Dancers."

Continuing its journey, the expedition reached Mission San Gabriel at sunset on March 22. Anza and an escort proceeded to Monterey by the established mission trail, but as Mission San Gabriel had a limited food supply and could not sustain the remaining men for long, Father Garcés and the other soldiers returned to the Colorado River. They traveled without incident until reaching Coyote Canyon where Indians killed one of the fattest horses of the loose herd out of "a hankering for meat." Garcés carved a note of warning for Anza on one of the willow trees in the canyon. From San Sebastián, Garcés attempted a shortcut across Imperial Valley, stopped at Kane Springs and reached Santa Olaya on April 24.

When Anza returned a few weeks later the Indians in Coyote Canyon wounded some of his horses, but Anza caught the chief culprit and gave him a whipping. Using Garcés' shortcut, he traveled the ninety miles from San Sebastián to Santa Olaya in twenty-five hours. He concluded, however, that the longer trail would be better for colonists.

Pleased with the results of the first expedition, Viceroy Bucareli authorized the newly-promoted Lieutenant Colonel Anza to lead another, this time with more than two hundred colonists and soldiers to reinforce the presidio at Monterey and establish a colony at the port of San Francisco. In addition to Anza, the expedition included Father Pedro Font, missionary at San José de los Pimas, who was chosen as chaplain and diarist, primarily because he knew how to determine latitudes; Father Garcés and Father Thomás Eixarch who would travel as far as the Colorado River; Anza's second in command, Lieutenant José Joaquín Moraga, who would command the future presidio of San Francisco; and Sergeant Juan Pablo Grijalva. In all, one hundred and seventy-seven persons left Horcasitas on September 29, 1775. Sixty-three others joined them at Tubac in present-day Arizona, making a total of two hundred and forty persons, of which the majority were women and children. There were more than eight hundred head of mules, horses and cattle.

As with the first expedition, this one also suffered a shortage of pack animals and mounts due to a last mtnute Apache raid. From Tubac the expedition traveled north to the Gila River which they followed down to the Yuma crossing, where Anza again was warmly received by Chief Palma. After leaving Garcés and Eixarch under Palma's protection, the party crossed the river and proceeded south to Santa Olaya where they

SANTA CATARINA SPRINGS: *Coyote Creek meets the famous springs near the spot where, in 1774, Father Garcés carved a warning about Indian trouble.*

prepared to cross the sand dunes.

To avoid exhausting the supply of water in the desert wells, the expedition was divided into three sections, each traveling a day apart with the livestock placed at the rear. On December 9, the first division, led by Anza, left Santa Olaya. They traveled across the dunes to Santa Rosa de las Lajas, Arroyo del Coyote, and on to San Sebastián. Unusually cold winds and storms multiplied the hardships but on December 13, Anza's section arrived at San Sebastián where they waited for the others to join them.

The next day it snowed and became so cold that six cattle and a mule died during the night. The second division, led by Sergeant Grijalva, arrived on the fifteenth, having been delayed by the snow storm which had caught them when they were midway between Santa Rosa and San Sebastián. When they finally reached camp several persons suffered from frostbite, one so badly that "in order to save his life it was necessary to bundle him up for two hours between four fires," according to Anza.

The third division, led by Lieutenant Moraga, fared even worse. When Anza sent two soldiers with twenty saddle animals to search for them, they were found only a few hours from camp. The storm had caught them in an exposed position between Santa Olaya and Santa Rosa where several members of the party nearly perished from the cold and ten mounts had died or were left by the wayside. Moraga himself became temporarily deaf.

These hardy pioneers apparently encountered one of the worst cold spells known to the Imperial Valley and the Anza-Borrego Desert. Even Eixarch's diary mentions the cold and snow at Yuma and the Indians there said they had not experienced such extreme weather before.

However, there were two reasons for optimism at San Sebastián. Of the fifteen invalids that had been counted nine days before, less than five were still incapacitated. Anza attributed their recovery, in spite of the cold and poor weather, to the many watermelons given to them by the Indians and eaten at Santa Olaya. Also, on the previous expedition many of the stock had become ill and some had died from eating the salty pasturage which grew around San Sebastián, but on this trip the animals were spared because rain and sleet had neutralized it.

When all members of the expedition were reunited, they celebrated with a *fandango*. Father Font disapprovingly described that night of the seventeenth as being "somewhat discordant, and a very bold widow . . . sang some verses which were not at all nice."

After spending four days at San Sebastián, and with the sun again shining, the expedition moved on, camping at the entrance of Borrego Valley at Los Puertocitos, just west of the old lake bed or marsh encountered on the first expedition. Despite the care given the animals, cattle continued to die almost every day, and Anza noted that all the mountains were covered with snow except for the Fish Creek Mountains.

After leaving camp, they traveled west over sand dunes, stopping in San Felipe Wash at San Gregorio. Font described the site as having good grass and water, though scanty in amount, and wrote that the surrounding hills were "so dry that not a little tree or even brush is seen on them, and only in the flats is there a little hediondilla." One day in the future a site northeast of their camp and overlooking the majestic Borrego Badlands would be named Font's Point.

At Los Puertocitos, Anza ordered several wells dug down to a depth of six feet, and though water was found in all of them it was insufficient to prevent some of the animals from stampeding back to San Sebastián during the night. The cold was so intense that most of the colonists stayed awake feeding the fires, and the next morning Font could not celebrate Mass. The expedition packed up and continued its march to El Vado, the mouth of Coyote Canyon, while Sergeant Grijalva, accompanied by three soldiers and a vaquero, went out to look for the lost animals. The expedition waited two days for the sergeant to return with the strays. When he arrived, he reported that the cattle had made it all the way back to San Sebastián where about fifty of them died in the mires. This news was a severe blow for Anza who had taken the greatest care for the well-being of the livestock throughout the expedition.

SNOW IN THE DESERT: *Anza's people encountered snowstorms which caused them to fear what lay ahead as they journeyed northward toward San Francisco.*

WHITE-CROWNED PALMS: *Two hundred years later, rare snow such as this seen in Borrego Palm Canyon is an attraction, appreciated for its bleak beauty.*

HENDERSON CANYON: *Located northwest of Borrego Springs, it is not far from the mouth of the large Coyote Canyon which runs into Riverside County.*

SUNRISE AT FONT'S POINT: *A similar dawn may have been seen in 1775 by Father Pedro Font, the diarist who accompanied Anza's second expedition.*

Despite rain the next day, the expedition moved up Coyote Canyon to Santa Catarina Spring. Unlike the impression Anza had of the canyon on the first expedition, Father Font formed a dismal opinion of it:

> The canyon is formed by various high and very rocky hills, or better, by great mountains of rocks, boulders, and smaller stones which look as if they had been brought and piled up there, like the sweepings of the world. Consequently it is arid, fruitless, and without trees or any green thing. Of grass in this place there is none, and on the way there are only a few small willows on the banks of the arroyo. The road in places is somewhat broken and grown with shrubs or brush and a little hediondilla, for since this is a shrub of evil augury, it is not lacking in these salty and worthless lands.

Reaching Upper Willows at Fig Tree Spring, camp was made early because a woman had begun having labor pains, and that night the third child of the expedition was born. This happened just outside the limits of the park boundary in what is now Riverside County. Near the camp was the Indian village called Los Danzantes (Dancers), seen on the first expedition. They celebrated Christmas Eve with another *fandango* and again Font complained:

> They were very noisy, singing and dancing from the effects of the liquor, not caring that we were in so bad a mountain in the rain, and so delayed with the saddle animals and the tired and dead cattle.

On January 4, 1776, the expedition reached San Gabriel from where they would later proceed to Monterey and San Francisco. Anza immediately began a reconnaissance of these northern sites, and four months later returned to Tubac. His second expedition had proven the practicality of taking large groups of people and herds of animals across the desert.

In the five years which followed the opening of the trail, more than three hundred colonists used it to reach Calfornia. A census taken in 1790 indicated that thirty-five to fifty percent of the colonists in California came by way of the Anza trail. Also, there were no large herds of cattle or horses in California until the route had been opened from Sonora.

To assure that the Colorado crossing, the key to the Anza trail, would remain open, two missions, Concepción and San Pedro y San Pablo, were established near Yuma. But in July, 1781, Yuma Indians destroyed the missions and killed Garcés, Díaz, and Captain Fernando Rivera y Moncada and his soldiers. Salvador Palma, who for a while was torn between his former loyalties to the Spanish and those of his people, joined in the attacks which effectively closed the Anza trail. Although Pedro Fages led a punitive expedition against the Yumas, nothing of consequence was accomplished, and without control of the river crossing, the trail fell into disuse.

Quite appropriately, it may have been Pedro Fages himself who used the Anza trail for the last time in the Spanish era. In the spring of 1782 Fages delivered dispatches from San Gabriel to Yuma. On his return, he stopped at San Sebastián to rest, and hearing rumors of trouble in San Diego, decided to go there instead of returning to San Gabriel, again using his road through Oriflamme Canyon and over the Cuyamacas. At Palm Spring he found "a small spring of good water, near which there were three or four very tall palm trees." Thus Fages wrote the first description of a palm tree oasis in California. At Vallecito, which he named San Felipe, Fages found "plenty of pasture and two pools of water" and recommended the site for a future presidio.

Further efforts by Fages and Governor Diego de Borica to reopen the Anza road were never realized. In June, 1783, the Fages route from San Diego to San Sebastián was mapped by Alférez José Velásquez. He called the whole Carrizo Corridor the Arroyo de San Sebastián and placed the Indian village of Cuñamác at the summit of the trail. Velásquez later recorded that Fages last used the road in 1785. When Lieutenant Governor José Arrillaga attempted the passage from San Diego to San Sebastián and Yuma in 1796, he found the Yumas still hostile and the road impractical. The Anza trail and the Fages road were abandoned and in time forgotten. They would wait to be rediscovered by the Mexicans some thirty years later.

BLOOMING CACTUS: *Delicate flowers atop the thorn-covered beavertail pads contrast with subdued colors usually associated with the desert.*

The Trail of Conquest

Mexico won its independence from Spain in 1821 and the mission system in California began to collapse. Mission lands were parceled out to old soldiers and settlers who became the dons of a fabled California. Interest was renewed in communication and transportation between Mexico and the Pacific Coast. However, forty years had effectively clouded the memory of the Spanish land route, so once again, trailblazers in the spirit of Anza, Garcés, and Fages rose to the occasion and rediscovered a passage over the desert.

In 1822, Mexican Emperor Agustín Iturbide had sent Agustín Fernandez de Vicente to California to inspect the growing Russian interests along the Pacific Coast, particularly at Bodega Bay north of San Francisco. Fernandez was alarmed by his findings and recommended the immediate reopening of a route between Mexico City and the California settlements in order to strengthen Mexico's position. While Fernandez was making his investigation, California Governor Pablo Vicente de Solá sent a similar inquiry to Captain José Romero, commandant of the presidio at Tucson in present-day Arizona. In September, 1822, Lieutenant Colonel Antonio Narbona, civil governor and military commander of Sonora, ordered Captain Romero to organize an expedition to investigate a possible mail route connecting Tucson with Monterey.

As with Anza before him, Romero knew such a route existed because Indians frequently crossed the desert. On April, 1823, a Dominican priest, Father Felix Caballero, and two companions from the northern Baja California missions of San Miguel and Santa Catalina, arrived in Tucson. In twelve days they had crossed the Colorado delta which had thwarted earlier expeditions. The great excitement caused by their arrival was further proof that the Anza route had been forgotten.

The Romero expedition of ten men left Tucson on June 8, guided by Father Caballero. In July, they reached the Colorado River, where Yuma Indians, pretending to help them cross, stole their horses and baggage and left them practically naked and without shoes to make the sixty-five-mile trip to Mission Santa Catalina. Although Romero did not give details of this journey between the Colorado River and the mission, the same trip was made five years later by an American trapper, James Ohio Pattie, whose rather fanciful autobiography described this segment of the desert as "a more fitting abode for fiends, than any living things that belong to our world."

After obtaining clothing and supplies from Father Caballero's mission, the Romero party proceeded to San Diego. In California, Governor Luis Antonio Arguello, Solá's successor, ordered an escort of forty men and a cannon under command of Lieutenant José María Estudillo to accompany Romero back to the Colorado River. This time they would try the Cocomaricopa trail, an Indian route from San Gabriel Mission which went through the mountains by way of San Gorgonio Pass to the Mojave Desert, the Colorado River, then to the Gila River and on to Tucson. This more northerly route presumably would avoid any hostile Yuma Indians on the lower Colorado.

Starting from San Gabriel Mission on December 15, 1823, the Romero expedition traveled eastward into the desert through San Gorgonio Pass, but the guide became lost and the animals began to suffer from thirst. After six weeks of wandering, the expedition admitted defeat and returned to San Gabriel Mission. Lieutenant Estudillo later wrote that "it is well known that there are no other roads more suitable than the ancient ones explored by . . . Juan Bautista de Anza . . . and Pedro Fages."

However, Estudillo's letter was premature, for within a year the link which completed what would become the famous Southern Emigrant Trail would be discovered by Lieutenant Santiago Argüello.

Argüello, an officer from the San Diego presidio, discovered the San Felipe Valley while chasing Indian horse thieves. Although he was unsuccessful in apprehending the thieves, he suggested that in the future, instead of following the old Anza route from the Colorado all the way across the Borrego Desert and up Coyote Canyon, it would be better to go by way of the Fages trail westwardly directly across the desert and through the Carrizo Corridor and Vallecito. Then, in Mason Valley, instead of taking Fages' road up Oriflamme Canyon into the Cuyamaca Mountains, one could continue northward through Mason and Earthquake valleys into San Felipe Valley, a long sloping valley lifting gently from the desert to Warner's Hot Spring, from where the trail would proceed north through high flat valleys to Temecula, eventually picking up the Anza route to San Gabriel Mission.

Meanwhile the Yumas, fearing that their enemies to the north, the Cocomaricopas, would greatly benefit by a regular road through their territory, announced they now would welcome the Mexicans' use of the Yuma crossing. Romero, still waiting at San Gabriel to make a second attempt at the Cocomaricopa trail, also had second thoughts and encouraged the use of Santiago Argüello's route. But the new governor, José María de Echeandía, insisted that Captain Romero continue his exploration of the Cocomaricopa trail, and sent a labor force under the command of Romualdo Pacheco, a lieutenant of engineers, to clear the way.

In November, 1825, they reached the Colorado River. When Pacheco returned to San Diego, he recommended the Fages-Argüello route as the better road. It soon became the official Mexican mail road from Sonora to California, and Lieutenant Pacheco established a fort near the Colorado River to control the Yuma Indians. Although only a horse trail, the main Sonora Road, as it was called by the Mexicans, went through Carrizo and San Felipe valleys and continued to Los Angeles. The San Diego branch, or the Fages trail, left the Sonora Road at Mason Valley and crossed the Cuyamacas to San Diego.

In January, news of Captain Romero's feat reached Mexico City and he received credit for reopening the land route. He was awarded a promotion for his efforts, just as Anza before him had received recognition fifty years earlier for his 1774 expedition.

While the Mexicans were opening trails to California, Americans were doing the same. In 1826, trapper Jedediah Strong Smith became the first known American to reach California overland. Crossing the Colorado River above Yuma, Smith proceeded across the Mojave Desert and reached San Gabriel Mission in November. A year later another trapper, James Ohio Pattie with his son Sylvester further opened the Gila River route to California. Arriving at the Colorado River, they followed Father Caballero's route southwest to Mission Santa Catalina in Baja California and then proceeded northwest to San Diego. Mountainmen William Wolfskill, Ewing Young, Kit Carson and David E. Jackson blazed other trails to California during the Mexican period, opening routes later to be used by early American pioneers.

Although Mexico made the Sonora Road an official mail route, it was poorly marked and was not well known. Most likely the first American to reach California's Pacific Coast by land, after presumably crossing the Anza-Borrego Desert was Richard Campbell, a trader. In 1827 his party arrived at San Diego from Santa Fe, New Mexico, and he later reported that he had found water and grass along the entire route and that a good wagon road could be opened to San Diego as well as to the Mexican puebla of Los Angeles. Several years later, however, in December of 1831, the trapping party of David E. Jackson found no one in Tucson or Altar who knew the exact route to California. A member of the party was Jonathan Trumbull Warner who would remain in California, marry a Mexican girl and build the ranch house that became a famous stopping place for immigrants and stages. The route of his party also led across the Anza-Borrego desert. He wrote:

> The trail from Tucson to the Gila River at the Pima villages was too little used and obscure to be easily followed, and from those villages down the Gila River to the Colorado River and from thence to within less than a hundred miles of San Diego there was no trail, not even an Indian path.

Another possibility for a "first" American in the Anza-Borrego area was Thomas Long "Pegleg" Smith, a fur trapper, horse thief, and adventurer. His biographer, Alfred Glen Humphreys, believes Smith first entered California in the early part of 1829. Having collected a good supply of pelts in the Virgin River area of Utah, Smith and another trapper, possibly Maurice LeDuc, traveled to Los Angeles to sell them. Their route is not recorded, but it is believed they followed the old Anza trail from the Colorado River to Los Angeles.

Either on this trip or one he made in the 1830s, Pegleg Smith claimed to have found gold in the area north of Borrego Springs. However, in later explorations he could never relocate the site and as time passed, the legend of the Pegleg Gold Mine grew. Many historians doubt both the existence of Pegleg's gold and his claim of arriving in California as early as 1829. Nevertheless, a monument honoring Peleg and his gold stands today in the park.

In 1832, an English scientist named Thomas Coulter arrived at Monterey by ship and between March and July traveled over the Sonora Road to the Colorado River and back. While in San Felipe Valley, he collected screw-beans and noted various plants in the area. He also recorded "the rapid decrease and approaching annihilation of the Indians."

Perhaps one of the most rapid couriers to travel the Sonora Road was Rafael Amador. In 1834 he was sent overland from Mexico City to Monterey by President Antonio López de Santa Anna with dispatches rescinding orders, which had been sent by ship to California Governor José Figueroa, to relinquish the governor's office. Amador made the trip in forty days, despite the theft of his clothing and horse by the Yuma Indians. Governor Figueroa was impressed with his feat and awarded Amador $3,000.

There are few other records concerning the use of the Sonora Road between Amador's journey in 1834 and the outbreak of war between the United States and Mexico in May of 1846, a period which marked increased American use of the road. Christopher "Kit" Carson, who originally came to California with Ewing Young in 1830 and later served as a guide for John Charles Frémont, took part in the first phase of the California conquest. In September, 1846, Carson left California carrying dispatches to President James Polk from Commodore Robert F. Stockton and Frémont. South of Socorro, New Mexico, he met Brigadier General Stephen Watts Kearny and his Army of the West. Kearney had left Fort Leavenworth, Kansas, on June 30, leading his Dragoons on the trail to California.

From the dispatches which Carson carried, Kearny learned that Commodore Stockton apparently had extended American control over all of Mexican California, and made the fateful decision to send half of his army back to Santa Fe. He persuaded Carson to send the messages on to Washington with a scout and to accompany him to California.

Confident of the situation, Kearny, Carson and 110 men of the First Dragoons marched along the Sonora Road. On November 23, they intercepted and temporarily detained Filipe Castillo, who was found to be carrying letters urgently asking help for California from the Sonoran state. From this encounter Kearny learned that American victory in California was not as decisive as Carson's dispatches had led him to believe, and the remnant of his original army was faced with unexpected hazards.

In his diary, Lieutenant W. H. Emory describes Kearny's journey as one of extreme hardship, with many animals left on the road to die of thirst and hunger while coyotes followed them, fighting over the carcasses of dead animals. Reaching Carrizo Creek on November 28, 1846, Emory noted the creek had little flowing water, and what it did contain quickly disappeared into the sand. The source of the stream he described as "a magnificent spring, twenty or thirty feet in diameter, highly impregnated with sulphur, and medicinal in its properties." He found the water of the creek to be warm, the temperature varying from sixty-eight to seventy-five degrees. He also described the mountains bordering Carrizo Pass:

> The portal to the mountains . . . was formed by immense buttes of yellow clay and sand, with large flakes of mica and seams of gypsum. Nothing could be more forlorn and desolate in appearance. The gypsum had given some consistency to the sand buttes, which were washed into fantastic figures. One ridge formed apparently a complete circle, giving it the appearance of a crater.

The next day they followed the sandy creek bed to Vallecito. Captain Abraham Johnston believed "Bayou Cita" would be a poor camp if in Arkansas, but added:

> Here it is fine; the green grass reaches two or three miles along the narrow valley where the water comes to the surface, and then all is dry and barren again, except the greenness given by the stink-bush and its kindred plants, inhabitants only of dry places. A few willows on the water furnish fuel, and the mountains hang over, high and bleak, destitute of trees, and almost vegetation . . . agave abounds, and the Indians have baked it in every direction.

They rested for a day, killing a horse for food. Captain Johnston noted how the rigors of the trip had affected the soldiers, and commented that "they are well nigh naked and some of them barefoot—a sorry looking set." Yet the men kept their spirits up and even had time to investigate their surroundings. Johnston frequently saw pieces of pottery which led him to conclude that many Indians had traveled the road in the past. Some of the troopers who had taken part in the earlier Florida campaigns described the palms as "cabbage trees," and Emory mentioned seeing ocotillo in full bloom. Meeting an Indian couple in the area, he commented on their athletic figures, but found them "prematurely wrinkled from poverty and exposure to cold."

After leaving Vallecito, the army continued through Mason, Earthquake and San Felipe valleys. Captain Johnston found the part of the route devious and "a bad road for our little howitzers, and impassable, without work, for wagons." On the night of December 2, 1846, they arrived at Warner's Ranch house, a short distance south of the hot sulpher springs. Four days later, at San Pasqual near present-day Escondido, Kearny's army fought a pitched battle with the lancers of Andreas Pico, losing eighteen men, including Captain Johnston. A column of 180 American sailors and marines from San Diego relieved the dragoons and escorted them safely to the coast.

Though the American trader, Richard Campbell, two decades earlier had suggested that an easy wagon trail could be established across the desert, it was not until the military expedition of the Mormon Battalion that the Sonora Road became advertised as an all-weather route and began carrying heavy traffic. Commanded by Lieutenant Colonel Philip St. George Cooke, the Mormon Battalion's march from Iowa to California was one of the longest and hardest ever made by untrained men.

Traveling in the wake of Kearny's Army of the West, the objective, besides entering the war with Mexico, was to find a practical wagon route to California across mountains and deserts. Leaving Council Bluffs in Iowa in July, 1846, the Mormon Battalion was guided by mountainmen, among them Antoine Leroux, Jean Bautiste Charbonneau, and the feminine-named Pauline Weaver. Following essentially the same route as Kearny, the battalion passed through Santa Fe and down the Rio Grande, reaching Socorro, New Mexico, in October. En route to Tucson and the Colorado River, the battalion met a small party of Mexicans on November 23 and recorded:

> They gave a good report of a route to San Bernardino; and one of them was engaged as a guide, and to assist in opening communications with the Apaches, whom they report to have plenty

of mules.

After a difficult march they reached Carrizo Creek on January 16, 1847, with five wagons, the others having been abandoned on the way. The water supply had run out the day before, and many of the men were in a sorry state, as Cooke mentioned in his diary:

> A great many of my men are wholly without shoes, and use every expedient, such as rawhide moccasins and sandals, and even wrapping their feet in pieces of woolen and cotton cloth.

On the seventeenth, after reaching Palm Spring, Cooke noted twenty to thirty palms, but because there was no grass, the battalion continued on to "Bajiocito, a wet swampy valley, with willow bushes, bad rank grass and no fuel." They camped until the following morning and the men renewed their spirits by singing and playing the fiddle.

The most crucial part of the journey came on January 19, when the men and wagons reached a rocky chasm, called Box Canyon, and found the passage too narrow for the wagons. Pauline Weaver, who had ridden back to inform Cooke, was ordered to "find a crossing, or I should send a company who would soon do it." But after Cooke himself had ridden up to the canyon, he "found it much worse than I had been led to expect." The only other way out of Mason Valley was the old Fages route through Oriflamme Canyon to the Cuyamaca Mountains, much too difficult for wagons to negotiate. Having lost their picks, shovels, and spades while crossing the Colorado River, the men had no choice but to follow Cooke's example and begin hacking away at the walls of the canyon with axes.

The first wagon had to be taken apart and carried through in pieces. After hours of hewing at the walls, the men were able to lift the second wagon through. With yet more work, the last two wagons rolled through with their loads undisturbed. On January 20, 1847, the battalion reached San Felipe Valley, and nine days later reported to General Kearny in San Diego. The following day Cooke issued a statement commending his men:

> History may be searched in vain for an equal march of infantry. Half of it has been through a wilderness where nothing but savages and wild beasts are found, or deserts where for want of water, there is no living creature. There with almost hopeless labor we have dug deep wells, which the future traveler will enjoy. . . . With crowbar and pick and axe in hand, we have worked our way over mountains, which seemed to defy aught save the wild goat, and hewed a passage through a chasm of living rock more narrow than our wagons. . . . Thus, marching half naked and half fed, and living upon wild animals, we have discovered and made a road of great value to our country.

Unknown to them, the war in California had ended before they reached Carrizo Creek. They had crossed the park in the aftermath of the war, but many Californios were using the road to flee to the interior of Mexico.

The Sonora Road to Mexico faded in importance and was replaced in history by a new routing that led from New Mexico and Arizona and became known to Americans as the Southern Emigrant Trail. Popularly, it was known as the Gila Trail. It passed through the Carrizo Corridor to Warner's Ranch, where one branch led westward across and down the mountains to San Diego by way of Santa Ysabel, and another continued north through the higher mountain valleys to Temecula, San Gabriel and finally Los Angeles. The Oriflamme trail to San Diego now also was forgotten.

The military conquest, the subsequent Treaty of Guadalupe-Hidalgo in February, 1848, and admission to statehood in 1850 insured American control of California.

BOX CANYON: *In 1847, the Mormon Battalion used axes to hack a wagon passage through this canyon, the road later being used by the Butterfield Stage.*

VI
The Road to California

For three decades, from 1848 to 1880, a steady stream of California-bound traffic crossed the Anza-Borrego Desert on the Southern Emigrant Road. Popular as the only all-weather overland route, the road also became the first mail and stage route between California and the East.

On January 24, 1848, less than a week before Mexico and the United States signed the Treaty of Guadalupe-Hidalgo, formally ending hostilities and ceding California to the United States, James Marshall discovered gold at Sutter's Mill. Within a few months news of the discovery had reached many parts of the world, and by the end of the year the gold fields had already yielded \$10,000,000. During 1848 the California population rose from 26,000 to 115,000, some immigrants arriving by ship and others by overland trails across the great plains or up through Mexico.

Two principal cross-country routes were used, both beginning in Missouri and each about 2,000 miles long. The northern route went through South Pass in the Rocky Mountains and then west to the Sierra Nevada in California. The southern, all-weather route followed the Santa Fe Trail through New Mexico, down the Gila River to the Colorado River, then crossed the Anza-Borrego Desert and went north by way of San Felipe Valley and Warner's Ranch.

The first to arrive at the gold fields in large numbers were Mexicans. They came up from the interior of Mexico and once again followed the old Sonora road into the Anza-Borrego Desert. Dragoon Lieutenant Cave J. Couts, a member of Brevet Major Lawrence Pike Graham's battalion, recorded this migration in his diary during the battalion's arduous and disorganized march from Monterey in Mexico to Tucson and California at the conclusion of the Mexican-American War. Soon after crossing the Colorado River in November the battalion saw the effects of the gold rush. Couts noted in his diary that it seemed like the whole state of Sonora was passing them daily on the way to the *abundancia* of the gold mines. To avoid the Americans, most Sonorans traveled the old Anza trail up Coyote Canyon, but many used the Southern Emigrant Route as Couts testified.

It is estimated that 6,000 Mexicans crossed the Colorado River in 1849 and the next year about 1,000 per month entered California, with as many as 10,000 having arrived by the end of the year. Most of them apparently came in spring and returned to Mexico in autumn. The number of Mexican emigrants reached its height in 1850 and rapidly decreased until 1854 when it virtually ceased because of the great friction that had developed between Mexicans and Americans in the gold fields.

While traveling the Southern Emigrant Trail in the fall of 1849, William H. Chamberlin met a group of Mexicans camped at Carrizo Creek and commented:

> They are resting their stock, before they undertake crossing the desert. . . . They gave us glowing accounts of the gold diggings, and had large quantities of the dust in their possession.

Chamberlin also found campsites in the Anza-Borrego area heavily used and littered. He described Carrizo Creek as "a general encamping place, but the stench arising from the number of dead animals strewed about is almost sickening." Palm Spring was no less polluted with dead horses and mules lying in the springs or about them. At Vallecito his party saw the ruins

FLOWER CARPET: *Welcome winter rains cause flowers to spring to life and create a carpet of color on the alluvial fan at the mouth of Hellhole Canyon.*

of Graham's camp, part of which had made quarters there the previous December. Some of the adobe and mud huts which they had constructed on the site were still standing.

The great number of prospectors crossing the Anza-Borrego area were mentioned by Couts who was escorting the American surveyors of the International Boundary Commission, which had been established by the Treaty of Guadalupe-Hidalgo to determine the border between the United States and Mexico. Under the command of Amiel Weeks Whipple, the commission first crossed the site of the present park in September and again in December, 1849, on its way to survey the Gila River region. Couts and Whipple were continually harrassed for supplies and directions by the emigrants. Couts gives a clear picture of the frustration and annoyance it caused:

> Friday, Sept. 21st. (Vallecito) . . . the emigrants continue flocking in. . . . Have been troubled nearly to death by the emigrants inquiring the route to Los Angeles and San Diego. If I have made one I have made a hundred way-bills for them in the last three days. Left one stuck up on a board for their guidance.
>
> Wednesday, Sept. 26th . . . The emigrants! Ah! Still they come. I never was in my life so annoyed.

Despite the bothersome immigrants, Whipple and Couts were among the first Americans to note the beauty of this desert. The moonlit landscape reminded Whipple of ancient temple ruins and on September 21 at a small oasis six miles east of Vallecito he described the comparison:

> The scenery here, by moonlight, was beautiful. The hills in the background, with angles sharp and sides perpendicular, were singular in the extreme. By the dim light it was hard to believe that they were not ruins of ancient works of art—one had been a temple to the gods, another a regularly bastioned fort.

Couts was awed with the extremes of the unusual desert weather they experienced:

> We had a very severe storm . . . about two hours, the most beautiful sight I ever saw . . . at five, the terrible sand hurricane struck us. . . . Twenty minutes after, it commenced raining and hailing. . . . The whole desert was one complete sheet of water. . . . Whilst the storm was raging, I was setting on my horse with my back to it, until the hail got too severe, when my horse jumped from the effect of an earthquake, and I saw a large opening break into the surface of the earth. Afterward we saw a great many places which had opened the same way.

The Mexican boundary team was commanded by General Pedro García-Conde. One of his officers was Felipe de J. Iturbide, the official interpreter for the Mexican commission and the son of the former Emperor of Mexico.

Benjamin Hayes, an emigrant who later became a well-known judge in Southern California, met the Mexican commission while at the Colorado River. He talked to García-Conde's escort, Colonel Carrasco, concerning the great numbers of emigrants, and renewed his friendship with Iturbide, whom he had known at St. Mary's College of Maryland. Carrasco used his position to obtain reduced fares for the Hayes party on the ferry.

One of the more famous travelers passing through the park area was Colonel James Collier who was en route to begin his newly appointed job as the first collector of the port of San Francisco. In the Imperial Valley he met Andrew B. Gray, a civilian engineer for the boundary commission, who was traveling to the Gila River to check Whipple's survey. Gray told Collier that he had come by a shorter route from San Diego. Collier persuaded Gray to lead his party to San Diego on the new route, which followed Carrizo Creek south through Carrizo Canyon, Carrizo Gorge and Jacumba Pass, then west to San Diego. Gray believed that Collier's party was the first to attempt this route with packs and equipment.

Thousands of sheep and cattle were driven to the gold fields along the emigrant trail. Tremendous herds from Texas and Mexico were ferried across the Colorado River and, after the difficult desert crossing, fattened in the Laguna and Cuyamaca mountains before being put onto the trail for San Francisco.

While the immigrants poured into California and through the park, tensions increased among the area's remaining Indians. The White man had repeatedly changed the life of the Indians in an attempt to "civilize" them. Now, the seemingly endless tide of emigrants aggravated the many problems already confronting the Indians.

In 1850, a band of desperados led by John Glanton began to terrorize both immigrants and Indians at the Yuma crossing. On the night of April 23, the Yumas attacked the ferry camp and killed a number of men. A punitive expedition was ordered by California Governor Peter H. Burnett but it was ineffective in capturing the illusive Indians. In an attempt to control the Yumas, Major Samuel P. Heintzelman in October led three infantry companies from the post at the San Diego Mission and established a camp opposite the mouth of the Gila River, called Camp Independence, which later became Fort Yuma.

San Diego County, in need of tax money, asked nearby Indians in 1850 to pay taxes on their cattle and property. While some Indians agreed to the demand, others decided to resist. Led by an Indian from Warner's Springs, Antonio Garra, they planned a widespread rebellion that would include Cahuillas, Cupeños, Yumas, Cocopas, Quechan, and Diegueños in a united front against the White man. Widespread alarm was caused by rumors that the Cahuillas would attack Los Angeles and that river tribes along with Diegueños and Luiseños would descend on virtually unprotected San Diego.

On November 10, 1851, the Indians struck. The *San Diego Herald* reported that seven men who were crossing the Colorado River with 1,500 sheep were menaced by one hundred Indians, but were chased off by Lieutenant Thomas W. Sweeney, who at that time was in charge of Camp Independence. The seven men left the crossing safely but were met by Yuma and Cocopa Indians under command of Garra in the desert between the river and the Algodones sand dunes. Four of the herders were killed and the sheep driven off.

Less than two weeks later, another group of Indians led by Antonio Garra's son attacked Warner's Hot Springs and killed four San Diegans who were taking the hot baths. Simultaneously the Los Coyotes Indian chief Chapuli, with fifty Indians, attacked and burned the buildings at Warner's Ranch and drove off the cattle. Garra's son and Chapuli then retreated to the Cahuilla village in Coyote Canyon.

Later in the same month a volunteer company under the command of Army Major E. F. Fitzgerald marched from San Diego to the hot springs where they buried the four dead White men and burned the Cupeño village. At the site of Warner's store they found only ruins and the bodies of Indians killed in the raid. Meanwhile, San Diego sheriff Agoston Haraszthy went to Santa Ysabel with a small party and arrested three Indians and a renegade White by the name of Bill Marshall. Marshall was accused of having assured Garra that if he led a rebellion against the Americans he would be aided by the Californios and Mexicans. After a trial in San Diego, Marshall and an Indian, Juan Verdugo, were sentenced to be hanged. Warner's servant boy was given twenty-five lashes and Marshall's father-in-law was reprimanded and released.

Indian hostility became so intense during this period that Lieutenant Sweeney was forced to abandon the camp at Yuma in December. A speedy retreat over the emigrant road brought Sweeny and his men back to San Diego and they reported that the mountains were covered with Indian signal fires from Carrizo Creek to Santa Ysabel.

For Garra's rebellion to have been successful it was imperative that he receive the assistance of all neighboring Indian tribes. However, Juan Antonio, chief of the main body of Cahuillas, though he wanted to preserve his Indian nation and society, greatly feared the power of the Whites and felt it best for the Indians to cooperate with them rather than to fight them, as Garra had chosen to do. Consequently, he sent a message to Garra, arranged to meet him in a village in the desert, captured him and turned him over to military authorities. Garra's son, after receiving a message from his captured father, surrendered to northern authorities.

In late December while Garra was being held captive, Major Heintzelman divided the United States Army forces, then headquartered at Santa Ysabel, into two columns and sent them to the Los Coyotes village to capture the remaining ring-leaders of the rebellion. One column under Major J. B. Magruder went through Warner's Ranch to Anza Valley and down Coyote Canyon while Heintzelman followed the trail down San Felipe Valley, crossed up through Borrego Valley and entered Coyote Canyon from the south. Heintzelman's unit was attacked by Indians led by Chief Chapuli. After Chapuli and another chief were killed, the Indians fled. Troops burned the village and hunted down the other rebellious chiefs. Two days later a military trial was held. On Christmas Day, while about eighty Indians looked on, four chiefs were executed as they knelt before their graves near what now is known as Middle Willows. Two days later Garra's son was executed at Chino in San Bernardino County. Garra himself was tried by a military court-martial in San Diego and executed.

The execution of Garra ended the last Indian uprising in Southern California. In retrospect, neither Garra's revolt nor Juan Antonio's compromising position with the Whites was successful. Village sites in Coyote Canyon were abandoned after the massacre, and for the next forty years the Indians used the area as a gathering ground but not as a home. After 1891 the Indians were confined to Los Coyotes Reservation. In 1916, a flash flood washed away what remained of both the village sites and the graves of the Los Coyotes Indians.

With the apparent end of the Indian threat, immigrants again passed undisturbed, and the boundary commission was able to continue surveying. The commission returned to San Diego from Texas as the Garra insurrection ended. In January, 1852, Whipple and the surveyors were the first to arrive, followed a day later by Dr. Thomas H. Webb, commission secretary. John Russell Bartlett, the new commissioner who had arrived by ship, met them in San Diego. This time the Americans were not joined by their Mexican counterparts because of the death of General García-Conde.

In June, 1852, the survey party traveled east through Anza-Borrego for the last time. Bartlett's journal entries for Vallecito described the military depot and the Diegueño Indians then living in the valley:

> A depot of provisions is kept at this place, with a file of soldiers, for the supply of Fort Yuma, and of government trains passing and repassing. A few horses are also kept here, to facilitate the communication between Fort Yuma and San Diego.

The Indians at Vallecito were dressed in holiday clothes with nearly all wearing white or fancy calico shirts, their only garment, because, as Bartlett wrote, "pantaloons were regarded by them as useless articles of dress." These were former mission Indians who lived in huts scattered around the valley. Although still dependent on acorns for food, they also cultivated beans and pumpkins and occasionally killed and ate mule. The Diegueños were attentive to the needs of the boundary commission, bringing them wood and water and assisting in camp. In return, the Indians were repaid with a few old clothes and fragments of food that remained from the tables:

> Our culinary department was always the great point of attraction to these poor creatures, who would often form a double circle around the camp fires, much to the annoyance of the cook.

After leaving Vallecito and taking the way east across the desert, Bartlett wrote:

> All traces of grass disappear. . . . But the cacti and agave seem to delight in such arid and desert regions, as though the intense heat and dry atmosphere were the vivifying influences that nourish them.

En route to Carrizo Creek, they passed the bleached bones and dried carcasses of oxen, mules and sheep, mute signs of the hardships experienced by earlier parties. Bartlett found Carrizo Creek to be one of the remarkable streams which sometimes appear in deserts, rising in the center of barrenness and flowing for about a mile before being absorbed.

After leaving the present boundary of the park, the commission encountered Lieutenant Sweeny who was in pursuit of two deserters from Fort Yuma. The fugitives later shot Bartlett's escort, Colonel L. S. Craig, in a skirmish and fled toward Vallecito. Indians in the Anza-Borrego area, after learning of the deserters and the reward for their capture, tricked the men into let-

PUMPKIN PATCH: *This garden of delicately shaped but heavy sandstone concretions is located outside the park south of the Salton Seaway near Tule Wash.*

ONCE THERE WERE FIVE: *The life and death battle in the desert is difficult enough without vandalism—this is one of two trees left in Five-Palms.*

ting them look at their guns and captured them for the authorities.

Later in the year, Lieutenant Sweeny noted the passage of a returning filibuster party through the park. Filibustering was a phenomenon of the 1850s, attracting young, restless Americans who were perhaps frustrated in their professions or their attempts to become rich. Many Californians who left the gold fields empty-handed started searching for other areas in which to make their fortunes. Imbued with a feeling of Manifest Destiny and the belief that the borders of the United States should be extended to their natural frontiers, some misguided Americans, along with other adventurers, began crossing the border in hopes of colonizing Mexican lands rich in mineral wealth. In 1852, Gaston Raoul de Raousset-Boulbon attempted to seize the ore-rich mines of Sonora. He met heavy Mexican resistance, and the survivors of his expedition retreated to California by way of the emigrant road.

Perhaps the best-known filibusterer to cross the Anza-Borrego Desert was Henry A. Crabb. He was a northern California politician who once served in the State Legislature and had married into a well-known Sonoran family which claimed to be descended directly from Juan Bautista de Anza. Crabb supposedly made arrangements to establish a mining and agricultural colony in Sonora with political strongman, Ygnacia Pesqueira, in return for helping to take control of the governorship.

In 1857, Crabb led more than one hundred men south from Los Angeles through Anza-Borrego to Sonoita in Sonora. The rest of his force was to sail to Guaymas. The sea-borne expedition never materialized and Pesqueira, who became governor of Sonora without help from Crabb, warned him to stay out of Mexico. Nevertheless, Crabb persisted, crossed the border, and was defeated at Caborca after a six-day siege. Crabb and his men surrendered and were executed on April 7, 1857. According to contemporary accounts in the *San Diego Herald,* Crabb was first shot more than one hundred times and then beheaded. Afterwards his head was preserved in mescal and the bodies of his company were left to rot or be eaten by birds and hogs. Only a sixteen-year-old boy named Charles Edward Evans was spared to tell the gruesome tale.

Filibustering was common along the border in the 1850s, but while some men dreamed of riches in foreign lands, others were concerned in building a nation. The rapid influx of people to California created an ever-increasing need for better communication and transportation. In 1853, after James Gadsden negotiated the purchase from Mexico of almost 30,000 square miles of southwestern lands down to the Rio Grande, Secretary of War Jefferson Davis ordered surveys of five proposed routes for a Pacific railroad. In November and December of 1853, the Southern Pacific Railway group, headed by Lieutenant Robert S. Williamson, surveyed the Southern Emigrant Trail and the surrounding area in Anza-Borrego. Williamson, assisted by Lieutenant J. G. Parke and geologist William Phipps Blake, surveyed the emigrant road and Sentenac Canyon. Parke investigated Jacumba Pass and areas west of Warner's Ranch and Blake explored San Gorgonio Pass and the northeastern corner of the park.

William Blake is perhaps the best known of the group. He traced the old shoreline of Lake Cahuilla, sometimes called Blake's Sea, proving the existence of the lake in times past. Traveling south from San Gorgonio Pass, the survey party passed Travertine Point and entered the Borrego Badlands as the sun set on the evening of November 18. As Blake looked west he noted "the intensity and richness of the colors of the distant hills" which were "very striking and beautiful" with blue, purple and red being the prevailing tints and their "clearness and depth were remarkable." That evening they crossed the badlands traversing various washes and barrancas by wagon with great difficulty. Blake surmised that the ravines were formed by flash floods from the mountains or from unusual winter rains.

Early on the morning of the 19th the party once again set out to find the emigrant road. Thousands of concretions of all sizes and shapes were found, as Blake related:

> One of the more sandy beds furnished great spherical nodules as large as tenpin balls or bomb

> shells. Some of the balls were connected together by a smaller sphere, which made them resemble dumbbells. . . . Such was the variety of forms displayed on the surface that it was not difficult to find specimens resembling various fruits and vegetables, fancy pastry and confectionery.

They were forced to travel at night in hopes of soon reaching water and continued crossing deep ravines and plodding through sand dunes. In spite of the rugged terrain, Blake was impressed by the purity and clearness of the atmosphere. After two nights and a day without water or grass, the mules began to give out. Blake commented that unless water was found the wagons would have to be abandoned. At about 4:00 on the morning of November 20, everyone noted a change of atmosphere. Blake wrote:

> There was an occasional dampness, or sudden coolness, together with the odor of vegetable decomposition. . . . The mules of the train were the first to recognize these indications of the proximity of water, and they became animated and pressed forward with eagerness. . . . We soon reached the brink of a chasm or ravine in the clay . . . (where) there was a small shallow stream of water at the bottom.

Thus the party came upon San Felipe Creek near Harper's Well, which they called Salt Creek. There they rested for the day before continuing to Carrizo Creek. Blake took advantage of the time to explore the area and near camp found pieces of "silicified" wood and calcite crystals.

The next day the expedition left in the morning and reached Carrizo Creek by afternoon. They found the creek dry and were forced to do a considerable amount of digging in order to find water. On the march of the following day between Carrizo Creek and Vallecito, Blake, like Bartlett before him, noted carcasses of dead animals on the road and mentioned that the air was filled with the smell of decaying animals. However, he found Vallecito a pleasant camp where they pitched tents near the military depot which had been abandoned by the Army earlier in June. From Vallecito the expedition went eighteen miles to the northwest to the Indian village of San Felipe, where they noted small fields of corn along the borders of the creek. Blake wrote that "the squaws were gathering mesquite beans, and some were seen carrying jars of water on their heads in true oriental style."

On a return trip through the park in December, Blake stopped at the adobe depot at Vallecito and obtained a supply of barley. At Carrizo, he wrote concerning the palm trees at Palm Spring:

> There are three or four palm trees, each about thirty feet high. . . . They are much injured by fire and the persevering attacks of emigrants, who have cut down many of the finest of the group, as if determined that the only trees that grace the sandy avenue to the desert, and afford a cool shade for the springs, should be destroyed.

After a thorough investigation of the area, the railroad engineers found the emigrant road and the route farther south through Jacumba Pass impractical and recommended San Gorgonio as a better route. Because the railroad was to terminate in Los Angeles and would not be built for some time, other means were found to provide better communication and transportation between San Diego and the East. In 1854, Joseph Swycaffer and Sam Warnock—both of whom were San Diegans retired from the Army—established a semi-weekly service to carry military mail between San Diego and Yuma, occasionally using Vallecito as a relay station, and at times going by way of Jacumba. This was the first regular mail service between these points since the one established by the Mexican government seventy years earlier, and for many years it was the only road to San Diego.

In 1856, Congress passed legislation creating mail and passenger service between San Francisco and the Mississippi River. Authority for the selection of both the route and the contractor was given to the Postmaster General, Aaron V. Brown, but Congress specified that an interim service should begin at once. John Butterfield of New York and James Birch of California submitted bids. The original four-year contract was awarded to Birch in June, 1857, with service to begin the following month. His line was to run from San Antonio, Texas, to San Diego, Cali-

CARRIZO STAGE SITE: *Willow trees supported by water from the Carrizo Creek drainage, stand near a former outpost of the Butterfield Stage Line.*

SMOKE TREE CLUSTER: *The action of running water and gravel are necessary to grind away the tough cover on the seed of this tree before it can grow.*

fornia, a distance of 1,470 miles. It would follow the Southern Emigrant route across the desert to Carrizo Creek and Vallecito which were selected as way stations by the advance agent, Isaiah Churchill Woods. After Vallecito, however, the line would leave the now-established emigrant road and once again turn up the old Fages road that led through Oriflamme Canyon.

The first stage coach, driven by James E. Mason, left San Antonio in July and arrived in San Diego in August. Charles F. Runing, a correspondent for the *San Francisco Chronicle*, described his stay at Vallecito while a passenger on the San Antonio and San Diego Mail Line:

> We . . . slept in a house on a hard dirt floor. Here we met passengers coming from the other end of the route, five in number; they complained very much, and had a very hard time of it; one was a newly married lady, and I thought it must have been a rather dangerous honeymoon; however, she was fat and hearty and had got along better than any of the men. The place is called Vallecitos, and from the name one would expect to see a few houses, but we found only one solitary habitation.

The line became popularly known as the "Jackass Mail" because the section of the route that led up Oriflamme Canyon into the Cuyamacas and then down to San Diego was not suitable for regular stagecoaches. At Vallecito the mail bags and passengers were transferred from the coach to mules. This would be the shortest and most direct route to the coast. There was no easy wagon route to San Diego. It was not difficult to reach the ridge of the mountains, by way of San Felipe Valley, for example, but the descent of the west side meant traveling sixty miles down steep, rock-strewn hills and valleys, as later railroad surveys would prove.

The portion leading through Oriflamme Canyon was already being utilized by James Lassitor who hauled wild oats from the Cuyamaca Valley to supply his store and hay station at Vallecito. His route was then popularly known as the "hay road."

Though the "Jackass Mail" continued until almost the outbreak of the Civil War, it declined in importance after Butterfield was awarded the Great Overland Mail Contract to carry mail and passengers from Tipton, Missouri, to San Francisco, a distance of nearly 2,800 miles. Early jubilation in San Diego over the prospect of the new service was short-lived. Instead of going to San Diego, before proceeding up the coast to San Francisco, the Butterfield stage would follow the Southern Emigrant Road up San Felipe Valley to Warner's Ranch, and then through the high interior valleys by way of Temecula to Los Angeles, and eventually to San Francisco.

During 1858 Warren F. Hall was employed by Butterfield to establish the route and locate stations between Tucson and Los Angeles. Carrizo Creek and Vallecito were to be retained as stage stops and a station between the two was established at Palm Spring. Box Canyon also was widened to permit easy passage of the coaches.

The station at Carrizo Creek was a large adobe building, forty-eight feet square, with four rooms. It was the first stop where travelers could see green vegetation after crossing the barren Imperial Valley. Nine miles northwest of Carrizo station was the Palm Spring stop. Today a plaque identifies the site and palm trees planted by park personnel have replaced the original ones which were destroyed by passersby. A solitary stump, all that remains from the original grove, has been stored by park officials.

The Vallecito station was built around the old adobe military depot and in 1858 Lassitor was put in charge of the station. He and his wife were the first White settlers to permanently locate there. Good grazing and an adequate supply of water made it possible for rundown livestock to recuperate. Early in 1859 the company built a blacksmith shop and coach repair facility near the station and constructed quarters to accommodate the convoy of soldiers detailed to protect the route.

On September 16, 1858, stagecoaches left San Francisco and St. Louis, thus inaugurating the semi-weekly Butterfield service. Waterman L. Ormsby, a correspondent for the *New York Herald*, recorded the journey of the westbound coach. Arriving at Vallecito on October 6,

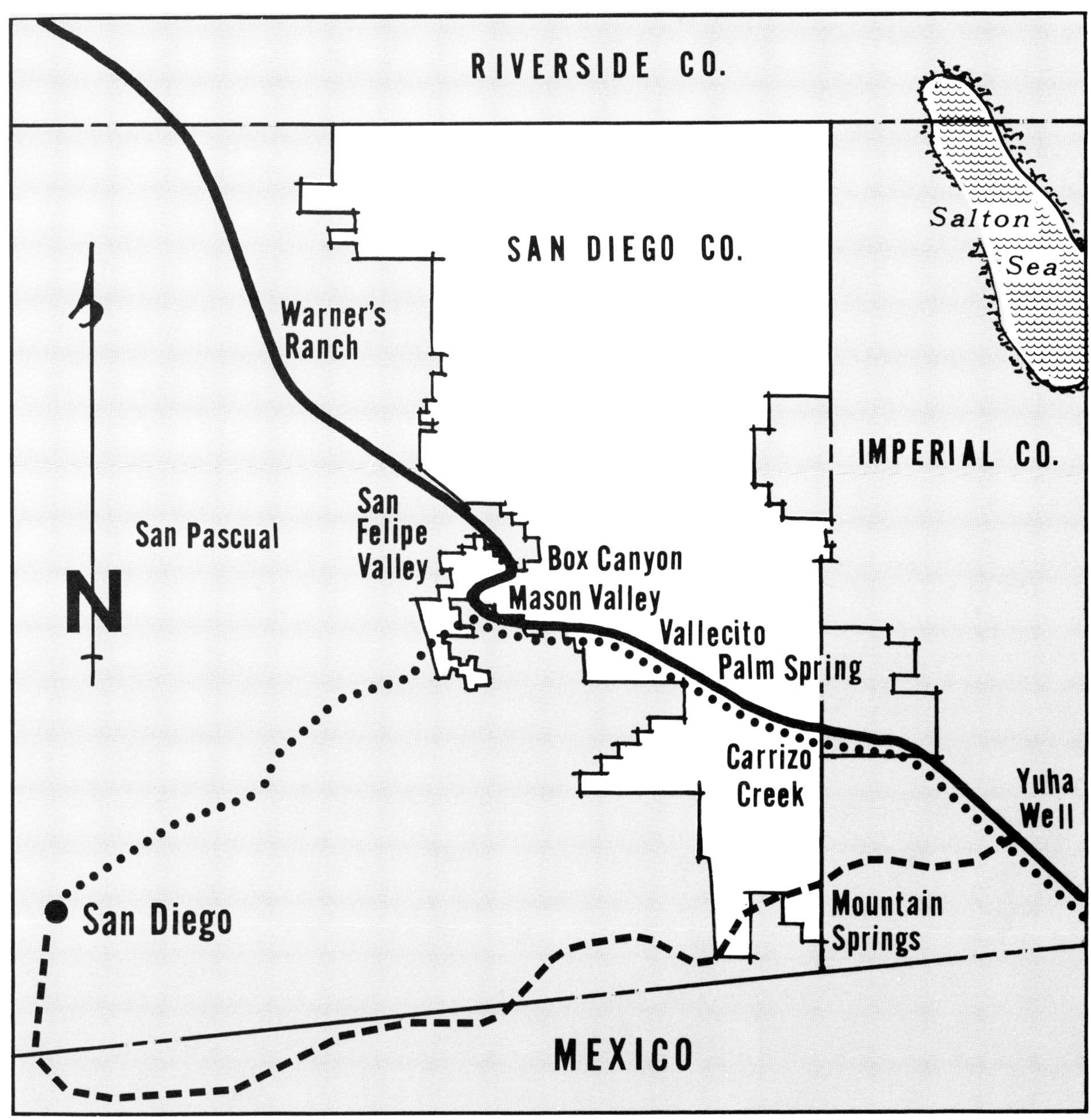

PIONEER TRAILS: *The solid line represents one of the most famous pioneer roads in the country, the Southern Immigrant Trail which also was known as the Gila Trail. During the Gold Rush it carried prospectors and adventurers through the park on their way to the gold fields. In their wake came the first transcontinental mail service, the dotted line showing part of the route of the short-lived San Diego & San Antonio Mail Line which left the immigrant trail and turned up Oriflamme Canyon, striking out toward San Diego on the old Fages road. Because passengers had to ride mules part of the way from Vallecito, it was dubbed the "Jackass Mail." Later, the Butterfield Overland Stage would also follow the immigrant route as it regularly traveled between Missouri and San Francisco. The broken line on the map represents the development of an alternate road to San Diego by way of Mountain Springs. Traffic on this route included people who boarded ships in San Diego and continued their journey north by sea.*

Ormsby found it to be "a beautiful green spot—a perfect oasis in the desert." He noted the number of springs in the area but made no mention of any Indians living nearby. He wrote that the "sand sparkles in the sun with large quantities of mica, which the uninitiated often mistake for gold dust, as it much resembles the precious metal in color." From Vallecito, Ormsby continued west and north to San Felipe and finally to San Francisco.

Another passenger who was aware of the desert's beauty was J. M. Farwell, special correspondent for the San Francisco newspaper, *Alta California*. Farwell was probably the first to record the absence of palm trees at Palm Spring station:

> This place takes its name from a species of palm trees which formerly grew here, and which within a few years were standing, as I saw the trunks as they lay upon the ground, and the stumps from which they were cut. The hills are within a short distance, and have the appearance of being suddenly broken off, leaving a square but furrowed front. It was bright moonlight while we remained here, and the beauty and singularity of the scene will not soon fade from my memory.

Until 1861, travel on the Butterfield route kept a steady pace. However, the company suspended operations at the beginning of the Civil War in favor of a more northerly route. Civilian traffic and trade on the emigrant road suffered in consequence of the war, but military use of the route increased. Yuma again became significant as a gateway to Southern California and the emigrant road was one of the main passages. From 1861 to 1866 travelers would include Southern sympathizers on their way east to join Confederate forces, California Volunteers who manned and supplied Fort Yuma, the California Column on its way to Arizona and New Mexico and finally, returning war veterans as well as Southerners fleeing their ravaged homeland.

Some of the first war traffic through the park included California secessionists. Failing in attempts to take California out of the Union, they organized parties that would march east to join the Confederacy. Among these were General Albert Sidney Johnston, Colonel Thomas T. Fauntleroy, Major Henry H. Sibley, and other officers—both Army and Navy—who resigned their commissions in the United States forces before the outbreak of hostilities.

In June, 1861, Johnston and thirty others crossed the emigrant trail en route to join the Southern forces. In November the Don Showalter party of seventeen well-armed men attempted to reach the South but was captured by the First California Volunteers at the John Minter ranch at Mesa Grande. They were transferred to Fort Yuma and kept under guard until May, 1862. All signed oaths of allegiance to the United States but, after being paroled, again headed toward the Confederacy where Showalter became a lieutenant colonel in the Confederate States Army and fought in several major battles.

In October, 1861, Lieutenant Colonel Joseph R. West was ordered to take three companies of volunteers from Camp Wright, established near Warner's Ranch, to Yuma to relieve the regular troops. The companies marched as individual units, five hours apart, to make the desert crossing easier. Although water was limited they found good pasturage, and in addition, provisions of stored food for the animals had been left at Vallecito by the mail line. West complained of prowlers along the road and also noted that the only mail station at Carrizo had been abandoned. After being relieved by the California Volunteers, the regular troops began their march to San Diego on the emigrant road.

Troops and supplies for Fort Yuma caused steady traffic on the emigrant trail during the war years. San Felipe, Vallecito, and Carrizo Creek were used as supply stations with barrels of water and supplies of hay stored for animals. One civilian contractor, Phineas Banning, hauled military supplies by wagon from Camp Drum at Wilmington and Camp Wright to Fort Yuma. In 1861, imported camels were pressed into service in parts of the arid west for transportation and communication. These "ships of the desert" were never successful but were on one occasion used to carry dispatches from Fort Yuma to Camp Wright.

Until 1861 the California Volunteers were in

a defensive position at Fort Yuma. However, in December, Colonel James H. Carleton received orders to cross the Colorado River in an attempt to retake Arizona and New Mexico which had fallen under control of Confederate sympathizers. Carleton's army, known as the California Column, left their barracks at Camp Drum in mid-Ajril, 1862, and arrived at Yuma in early May. The column was reinforced with a light howitzer battery commanded by Lieutenant John B. Shinn. One company was sent a day ahead with barrels which they filled at all the desert water holes. Cattle which would be slaughtered when needed were driven on the march, and each wagon carried 3,000 pounds of feed for the animals. The troops were ordered to travel by night if the days were too hot and to "practice as you march along, one hour each day, the saber exercise." The column marched to Arizona, New Mexico and part of Texas. Although they did not engage in any battles, their presence apparently helped regain control of those areas from the Confederacy, which in turn helped assure the safety of Fort Yuma and Southern California.

In 1865, both Union and Confederate veterans and some deserters began following the emigrant road to California. The last known active troops to travel west along the trail were the California Volunteers who returned from Texas in 1866.

At the beginning of the Civil War, the Vallecito station manager, James Lassitor, was murdered in Arizona. In 1861, Mrs. Lassitor sold the station to John Hart and his wife who continued to run the store and managed the station during the war. When the war ended, business along the route picked up for several years as travel increased. However, by 1867, traffic had decreased in favor of a more northerly route. After Hart died in 1867, his widow, Jane Fillen Hart, and John C. Wilson, a stage driver who later married Mrs. Hart, continued to manage the station for the convenience of occasional passersby. The completion of the transcontinental railroad in 1869 diverted even more of the remaining traffic from the emigrant road and for the next six years it had only minimal use.

In February, 1870, gold was discovered at Julian, to the west of the park, and the subsequent development of the town focused attention on the Anza-Borrego Desert as a possible locale for a new road connecting the Julian mines with the gold town of Ehrenberg, Arizona. Five years later a group under the direction of Henry I. Wyllie surveyed the Anza- Borrego area for such a road.

The survey party followed the emigrant road east towards Carrizo Creek and made their first desert camp at what the party named "Borego Springs because of many evidences of the presence of sheep." Thus the springs, and eventually the community that developed there, received its name. The Americans were not familiar with the Spanish spelling of *borrego,* meaning yearling lamb or sheep. Their error would remain on maps until 1950, when the United States Department of the Interior settled a controversy by correcting the misspelling.

While exploring the desert, Wyllie's party found themselves short of supplies and he traveled to Julian to get them. On his return to the desert, Wyllie's horse gorged itself with barley while Wyllie rested at San Felipe. Later it drank some of the alkaline water at Carrizo Creek and became ill. Wyllie dragged the suffering beast eight miles into Borrego Springs where the horse died, and then, as he related, spent a dismal night with the dead animal, fending off a pack of coyotes by shouting and throwing cow chips at them.

The next day, Wyllie walked across Borrego Valley to join the other surveyors at Clark's Dry Lake. Despite the suffering endured by Wyllie and the efforts of the entire party to find the best route for the Julian-Ehrenberg road, nothing ever came of it.

A new road over Mountain Springs and up through Campo and Jacumba was established by John G. Capron in 1865, and continued to divert traffic south of the park. In 1877 the Southern Pacific Railway Company completed its line from Los Angeles to Arizona and the fate of the old emigrant road to California became sealed. From that time the Anza-Borrego Desert would be seen in a different light and a new era in desert history would begin.

NATIVE WASHINGTONIA PALMS: *Named for the first President, more than seven hundred individual trees have been counted in Borrego Palm Canyon.*

VII
A March to the Desert

The 1880s marked the beginning of a new era for what eventually would become Anza-Borrego Desert State Park. Previously considered too hostile for development, the desert gradually became a place where optimistic land promoters, cattlemen, prospectors and homesteaders hoped to settle.

Discovery of gold in the Julian-Banner area had attracted many people and with the Southern California land boom of the 1880s, interest in real estate and irrigation began to extend east into the desert areas. Portions of the future park were advertised in promoters' pamphlets and local newspapers, and the area began to be appreciated for its economic potential as well as for its own special kind of beauty. One article called the Anza-Borrego Desert a land of promise, rich in flowers, and also gave one of the earliest descriptions of Borrego Palm Canyon:

> . . . the trees tower fully 100 feet, their trunks being three feet in diameter. None of the branches of any were lower than forty feet, and there was no way of getting at the great branches of fruit that averaged three and a half feet in length. Some are turning black, and resembled dates.

In 1849 a man named Oliver Meridith Wozencraft nearly perished in the sand dunes west of the Colorado River. Undaunted by his experience he envisioned an agricultural empire in the desert, if only water could be brought to it. Ten years later he succeeded in getting the California Legislature to pass a bill entitled "An Act to encourage the supply of fresh water on the Desert west of Yuma." Included in this bill was a grant of ten million acres of land to Wozencraft from the state of California in return for supplying a sufficient amount of fresh water for irrigation purposes. The grant of land was to include almost all of the area enclosed in today's Anza-Borrego Desert, all of Imperial County and almost all of Riverside County.

The success of Wozencraft's scheme depended on his receiving rights to all federal lands in the same desert area, and authority to proceed with irrigation. When Wozencraft's desert land bill was brought up in the United States House of Representatives in 1862, it was blocked by an Ohio representative, and despite revisions again failed to pass in 1876 and 1878. After Wozencraft's death in 1887, the proposed irrigation project began to materialize.

Dr. T. S. Stockton explored the area during early years and reported he found it rich in marble, gypsum and cement. The soil also was considered excellent. Optimistic promoters even described Borrego Valley as a place where tropical orchards would grow.

Despite such advertising and praise, the first public land was filed on by cattlemen, not prospectors or farmers. In September, 1883, Paul Sentenac filed claim to one hundred and sixty acres east of Scissor's Crossing near what is known today as Sentenac Canyon and Cienega. Little is known about this early homesteader other than that he built a house and corral near the canyon and raised cattle and goats. He also had a cattle camp and cabin at Yaqui Well, near the future Tamarisk Grove campground. Sentenac later sold his property to George Sawday who leased the land for grazing to another cattleman, Ralph Jasper.

On November 1, 1884, James E. Mason filed on and received one hundred and sixty acres at Vallecito, which included the old stage station building. His was the first patent on the station site since its abandonment in 1877. Mason was well acquainted with the area, having been the stagecoach driver who took the first westbound overland mails between San Antonio and San Diego on the initial 1857 run of James E. Birch's line. Three years later Mason sold his property to Charles F. Holland of Los Angeles. Today the former Mason homestead is part of Vallecito County Park, adjacent to Anza-Borrego State Park.

In 1891 Mason received patent for another one hundred and sixty acres of land in what is known now as Mason Valley, which he occupied until 1912. While hunting deer in the valley in 1900, Colonel R. C. Wueste and Charles S. Moore of San Diego noted that Mason had a lot of black cattle. Twelve years later a cowboy named Lester Reed, on a cattle drive through the area, saw Mason, but records do not indicate how long Mason remained on his homestead after 1912.

John McCain, another early cattleman in the park, came to San Diego County with his parents in 1867. After his marriage in 1872, he and his wife lived with his niece, Mrs. John Hart, at the Vallecito stage station. McCain was a former stagecoach driver who had worked for the Butterfield line and once hauled supplies and hay to desert stations from Warner's Ranch. He is credited with building an old road from Sentenac Cienega through Plum Canyon to Yaqui Well. Later McCain settled in Julian and sometime after that ran cattle in the Borrego Valley and other desert areas.

At Borrego Springs, Anza's San Gregorio camp, McCain built a small cabin about eight by ten feet and some water troughs to use the area as a base for his cattle operation in Borrego Valley. He received title to the springs through the Homestead Act. McCain's original springs, surrounded by a series of sandhills and mesquite trees, later dried up, but about a half-mile to the north a new Borrego Springs surfaced.

J. L. Kelly, who went to Borrego Valley in 1894 to pasture two hundred and thirty head of horses in Palm Canyon and Coyote Creek during a dry year, visited McCain and his cattle camp. Kelly described McCain as "one of the genuine, old fashioned cowboys of the West." He was uneducated, rough, used extensive profanity, but was good hearted. Once when Kelly started to throw out some bacon grease, McCain stopped him, poured it on his saddle, got on his horse and rubbed it in with his overalls and explained that "you couldn't get too much grease into leather down on this --- ---- desert." According to Kelly, McCain came down from Julian only to check on his cattle once every two weeks and would stay at the camp for two or three days at a time.

Joel Reed claimed squatter's rights in Coyote Canyon, which included water rights to Santa Catarina Spring. He had a great deal of trouble with people who attempted to get his claim. On several occasions William B. Fain threatened him with violence, but on November 3, 1891, Reed received legal patent to the lands, settling the dispute with Fain. However, soon after getting title to the land, Reed moved out of the canyon.

In 1897, John and Ella Collins and their family of three children moved into Coyote Canyon and squatted on the land, disputing Reed's right to the land and water. The family lived there for five years, growing fruits and vegetables. Unfortunately for Reed, Collins was present when the area was surveyed by the government and the name of Collins instead of Reed was used to designate the valley off Coyote Canyon. In 1902 Collins was ordered to move by cattlemen who killed a cow and one of the burros, set fire to the fence and attempted to burn the house down while the family was asleep. According to Collins, Reed did not own the land because he had made a mistake in filing the section number. Collins also believed that a section marker had been moved a quarter of a mile by the cattlemen. When he reported this to county authorities, one of the cattlemen, possibly Reed, was arrested. A trial followed in which the judge bound the defendant to keep the peace for six months, a decision which Collins thought was a gross miscarriage of justice.

Upon returning to Coyote Canyon, Collins found his home burned to the ground. Three separate fires had been started. At this point the family packed their few remaining possessions and left, moving to a vacant log cabin at the Ella Mine located between Julian and Banner. The land dispute ended in 1922 when Reed sold his acreage and moved back to Mississippi.

Although cattle had been driven through the park since the days of Anza, 1882 saw the appearance of cattle camps. In that year Walter Vail drove cattle from his Empire Ranch in Arizona to pasturage at Warner's Ranch. Vail decided to cross the desert directly instead of using the railroad and paying what he considered a prohibitive charge. While Vail was watering 2,000 head at Carrizo Creek, a sheriff's posse came into camp looking for two brothers who were accused of stealing horses in Arizona and who had joined the cattle drive at Yuma. The brothers were in camp and were disarmed and arrested, but one, Frank Fox, was later killed while attempting to escape. His body was buried a few hundred feet west of the old stage station. His brother, Will Fox, was taken to Yuma territorial prison where he served four years.

The safe arrival of Vail's cattle at Warner's Ranch helped popularize the notion among ranchers in Arizona that the old emigrant road could be used as a regular cattle trail to Southern California. According to a contemporary, this so alarmed railroad officials that they immediately lowered their freight charges.

Perhaps the best-known cattlemen of the park were the brothers, Fred and Frank Clark, for whom Clark's Dry Lake is named. In 1891, Fred purchased land above Nance Canyon, a tributary of Coyote Canyon, from a Cahuilla Indian named Pisqual. The area is sometimes called La Puerta but was known to Anza as San Carlos Pass. The Clarks began investigating the desert for a possible cattle range. Locating water not too far below the surface of Clark's Dry Lake, they dug a well and established a cattle camp. In the winter and spring their cattle fattened on desert wildflowers and were then driven up Coyote Canyon to spend the summer and fall months in the higher elevations. Occasionally on these drives the Clarks stayed at the Joel Reed cabin in Collins Valley. With homesteaders coming into the Borrego area, Frank Clark purchased land in the valley to assure continued pasturage and Borrego Valley became his main cattle camp.

Some years winter droughts on the coastal plain attracted other cattlemen to the Anza-Borrego Desert, as Lester Reed explained:

> Going to the desert with cattle in those days could be a good gamble if the rains there came early, but when the rains failed to come the gamble on the desert could turn out to be a poor one. I know of no place where cattle will fatten faster than on the desert when the flowers come. . . . I never have sold fatter cattle than some I sold out of Borrego one year.

The winter of 1897-1898 was an unusually dry season and William and Shasta Tripp, who lived in the Anza Valley area, drove their cattle to the desert in an effort to save them from starvation. They arranged with James Mason to range two hundred and sixty head of cattle on his land. The Tripps then found a site near Borrego Springs to winter another one hundred head of their livestock. The following spring, when they rounded up their herds for the drive back to Anza Valley, they found the cattle had done very well in Borrego Valley, while at Mason Valley one hundred had died and the rest were very thin.

After 1900, the Tripps and other cattlemen began taking their cattle through Anza-Borrego to new pasture lands in Imperial Valley. On one such drive, Lester Reed saw several abandoned vehicles on the road between Box Canyon and Vallecito, which presumably had been left by homesteaders on their way to the newly reclaimed Imperial Valley.

At this time, man was reclaiming the desert with water from the Colorado River which at some points flowed almost four hundred feet above the lower parts of Imperial Valley. Irrigation again was making the land habitable, as it had been for the early Indian tribes who lived on the banks of freshwater lakes created by the flooding river. Lake Cahuilla had been one of these lakes, and marshy remnants may have existed as late as the time of the Anza expedition more than a hundred years before. But the lakes had dried up and been forgotten and the majority of Indians had long since moved away to coastal areas or to the mountains. Few settlers even knew that such lakes had existed, nor did they know the tremendous power of the then-peaceful river.

In 1904, the low state of the river and the resulting lack of water for the irrigation system caused widespread alarm among valley farmers. In September a breach sixty feet wide was made in the river bank at a point four miles below the International Border. A 3,300-foot channel was dug connecting the river with the lower end of the original Imperial Canal. In three weeks the work was completed, but abnormal winter floods soon began coursing through the cut. During the preceding twenty-seven years there had been only one such flood each season. Now, in frightening succession there were three. Near El Centro, waters destroyed levees and flooded the town of Imperial. Calexico was partly destroyed and Mexicali, just beneath Calexico in Mexico, was partially carried away by the raging water.

By the beginning of summer the whole of the river was pouring out into the delta through the breach which was then more than a half mile wide and was racing down the slope to the Salton Sea. The water level in the sea rose at a rate of more than seven inches a day over an area of four hundred square miles. It was not until February, 1907, that the raging river was checked after months of labor. The ancient inland sea had been recreated and measured forty-five miles long, twelve to seventeen miles wide and in some places reached a depth of eighty-three feet.

Many ranchers drove their cattle to Imperial Valley for wintering, but others continued to use the Anza-Borrego area. Arthur Stone and the Angel brothers, Vance, Buck and Jack, wintered cattle at Palm Creek, the site which in time became the main campground in the park. Other cattlemen who used the Anza-Borrego area were Ralph Benton and Archie Chillwell in the Vallecito Valley; Bert Moore and George McCain in Mason Valley; Bob McCain at Canebrake Canyon, Carrizo Creek and Fish Creek; and Julius D. and Amby H. Harper at Pinyon Mountain. However, the area was not restricted to the grazing of cattle as there were also goats and sheep. In the early 1900s, Theodore Ebens, who had a cabin at the mouth of Coyote Canyon, even raised hogs.

At the turn of the century there was considerable interest in oil wells in the desert. Prospectors dug wells where subsurface oil was indicated in areas that had sedimentary deposits rich in gypsum, conglomerates, travertine, mineral springs, gas flows, bleached sand and clay shales. Among the early oil developers were the Carrizo Creek Oil Company, Palm Spring Oil Company, Vallecito Oil Company, Cactus Oil Comany below Palm Spring, Mesquite Oil Company at Fish Creek, and Yuha Oil Company. When geologist Stephen Bowers visited the site of the Palm Spring Company in July, 1900, he found they had a well down to one hundred and seventy feet and planned to continue drilling to a depth of 1,000 feet. However, speculation in desert oil came to a halt with unsuccessful drilling.

Interest in gold mining and searching for Pegleg Smith's lost gold mine, on the other hand, continued. Jim Green, a well known resident of the Julian-Banner area, prospected for gold in Borrego Desert in the 1880s. His permanent camp at Borrego Springs became a focal point for active prospecting. Some of the cattlemen also searched for gold in the park area. Barrel Springs was a favored location for Ozro and Chester Tripp and others who worked a mine called Three Buttes. After it was abandoned, stories spread about a "ghost" who haunted it. Howard Bailey and Bert Simmons spent many hours in the Fish Creek Mountains at their Hyacinth Mine in the early 1900s.

In 1906 a miner named Nicolas Swartz built and occupied a rock house in what is known today as Rockhouse Valley and Canyon. He claimed to have taken $18,000 in gold nuggets from his mine before leaving for Chicago where he died. His mine was never found again. Other early prospectors included Charles McCloud, Charles M. Knowles, William J. James (cousin of Jesse James), Charles Ferguson, Charlie Carstesen, Henry E. W. Wilson, Charlie McVickers, Dad Hardy and many others. Granite Mountain was another site actively mined for

PROSPECTORS' POST OFFICE: *Old timers say miners deposited their mail in glass jars or kegs hidden beneath thick palm skirts at Seventeen Palms Oasis.*

gold in the mid-1920s. However, in later years prospectors would search for other minerals, including calcite, tungsten and uranium.

After 1910, farmers began coming into the Anza-Borrego area and gradually pushed the cattlemen to the park edge. Lester Reed has recalled that the last cattle drive he was on was in 1932, the year the state park was created. After that cattle were moved by truck between Imperial Valley and higher elevations west of the park during the hot summer months. After the park was established, cattlemen who had winter ranges in the park area were allowed to keep their grazing rights under an agreement with the state.

Throughout the second decade of the Twentieth Cenutry, settlers became attracted to the desert because of the results of reclamation of the Colorado Desert a few years before, and also because of favorable comments of desert travelers. Farmers knew that success was possible in the desert if they could find a reliable source of water. Imperial Valley was proof enough. Desert writers such as John C. Van Dyke, Arthur Burdick and George Wharton James described the desert in a new light—a place of solitude, mystery and adventure. Van Dyke was possibly the most poetic:

> In sublimity—the superlative degree of beauty—what land can equal the desert with its wide plains, its grim mountains, and its expanding canopy of sky! . . . Never again shall you see such light and air and color; never such opaline mirage, such rosy dawn, such fiery twilight. And wherever you go, by land or by sea, you shall not forget that which you saw not but rather felt—the desolation and the silence of the desert.

James, perhaps more than any other early writer, deserves credit for giving the park a "magical aura." He described events from Anza's crossing of the desert to the Mormon Battalion and Butterfield Stage Line. He provided detailed descriptions of the natural features of the Colorado Desert and discussed the reclamation potential of the desert. Most of the pioneers who arrived with high hopes of success probably departed somewhat disillusioned.

In 1895, County Supervisor James A. Jasper erected signboards at desert water holes, and as desert travel became safer more people began visiting the park area for pleasure. One of the first to do so was Karl Bennis who in 1910 drove a Jackson automobile by way of Grapevine Canyon, Yaqui Well and the Narrows into Borrego Valley. After 1910 Howard Bailey and Alfred Armstrong Beaty introduced people to the Anza-Borrego area through hunting trips and desert tours.

The first settlers attracted to the park area after 1910 attempted, for irrigation purposes, to use water from Palm Spring near the old stage station. Little is known of their activities and only the ruins of their buildings remained in the 1970s.

Beaty, who was probably interested in the area as a result of hunting trips he led into the valley, decided to try desert homesteading in November 1912. With his wife and daughter, he entered Borrego Valley by way of the Narrows and the recently completed Julian-Kane Springs Road, selecting a site near what is today the Borrego Valley Airport. They lived in a tent and cooked on a wood stove under a mesquite tree. There were only four other homesteaders in the valley at the time. During the next three years Beaty found he was hindered from further development because of an inadequate water supply, his well providing only enough for domestic needs. He supplemented his income by hiring out his Fresno-scraper and horses to other homesteaders for leveling their land. Road crews from both San Diego and Imperial counties also rented his horse-drawn scraper.

After having proven his claim, Beaty moved his family to the mouth of Coyote Canyon and began homesteading another one hundred and sixty acres, this time at what is now the De Anza Ranch. Using water from Coyote Creek, Beaty constructed irrigation ditches that allowed him to cultivate as much as twenty acres. He grew alfalfa but had to travel three days to Brawley by mule-drawn wagon to market it.

On one of his return trips, Beaty found an old eight-inch crucifix at Kane Springs. Representatives of the Roman Catholic Church later told Mrs. Beaty that a crucifix of that design was carried by early padres. Beaty also found a copper kettle at Santa Catarina Spring that was later designated as one similar to the copper utensils carried by the second Anza expedition.

In 1916, Harry Oliver, a desert writer, homesteaded an area near the present Peg Leg Monument in Borrego Valley, and Everett W. Campbell established the first large desert ranch in Vallecito Valley. Campbell came to the desert because of his health and was engaged both in dairying and growing apricots. By 1955 his ranch had been enlarged to 5,572 acres. He later recalled:

> Everyone thought we were crazy when we went down into the desert to homestead the ranch, but there was a wonderful spring on the land and I was sure I could utilize the water for irrigation purposes.

In July, 1918, desert traveler J. Smeaton Chase recorded a vivid picture of desert homesteading in the Anza-Borrego area. At Seventeen Palms and at Borrego Springs, Chase found abandoned and littered campsites with "cascades of cans, scraps of rawhide, horseshoes, rock specimens, and stove-in canteens." At a corral gate at Borrego Springs, he found the signatures of a party of government surveyors who had scrawled their names, from "Lieutenant Tripod, Chief Engineer" down to "Pete Ortega, Chief of Remuda." At Collins Valley, Chase saw only one abandoned cabin, but there were several settlers' homes in Mason Valley:

> . . . here, as at Borrego, three or four men have taken up homesteads, and are holding on in hope that some day matters will improve, through the striking of abundant water by deeper borings. Meanwhile it is mainly the jackrabbits that profit by the crops planted by the pioneers of Mason Valley.

At Vallecito, Chase found another cabin occupied by a settler who ran a few head of cattle—perhaps the beginnings of the Campbell ranch. Continuing east, between Fish Creek Mountains and Harper's Well near Fish Creek Wash he came upon a derrick, a house, an old shed and two men, a Norwegian and an Irishman, who had posted on the door of the shed a sign which read "San Felipe, 71 feet below sea-level, Watch it Grow, Population 1920, 1000." Chase called this a good example of western optimism.

After Chase visited the San Felipe townsite, other hopeful settlers moved into the area, erected buildings, dug wells and planted crops. But the effects of heat, flash floods, high winds and drifting sand soon caused newcomers to give up the struggle. Few surface remains are evident today in this location.

Around 1920, Harry Cross of El Centro built two little cabins at the base of Dos Cabezas in a cove northwest of the spring. He used the cabins as a camp for his apiary whenever there was a good flowering season. As late as 1940, Cross still camped there on occasions and extracted honey from his bees.

With the end of World War I and with improved roads and greater use of automobiles, Southern California experienced dramatic growth and another land boom. Growth extended even to the park area by the mid-1920s, with attention being focused on Borrego Valley. In 1922 the Borrego Valley Land Company was formed, but records do not indicate whether it was successful. In 1924 E. A. Wynn opened a small store and auto repair shop and became Borrego Springs' first postmaster, each week bringing the mail from Julian. Three years later he sold his homestead and store to E. DuVall, who continued to run the operation.

At the beginning of the land boom, few homesteaders met with success. Campbell and Beaty were favored because they had permanent sources of water, but for many others there was only failure. In 1926 the first important well was dug and a good source of water tapped in the Anza-Borrego Desert. This made large-scale irrigation possible and gave impetus to farmers, especially those who grew dates.

O. H. Ensign and his sons, Paul and Roy, selected a homestead tract of one hundred and sixty acres under the Desert Land Act and purchased additional land from the Borrego Fruitlands Association. Ensign's selections were based on his knowledge as a reclamation engineer and his choices proved to be the best in the entire area. Their well was the first good one in the valley, pumping 1,000 gallons per minute. It supplied enough water to irrigate vast fields of alfalfa and became the main source of water for other homesteaders in the valley. Later the first park custodians hauled water from the Ensign well to the Palm Canyon campground where a water supply was yet to be developed.

Such wells, which today account for the entire water supply of Borrego Valley, tap vast reservoirs of "ground water" stored in the porous layers of the earth's crust, some of it less than three hundred feet beneath the surface. Although no one can know the exact amount of such water, reliable engineers have made very rudimentary calculations and theorize that underlying the Colorado Desert itself are perhaps as much as 235-million acre feet of water, each acre foot containing 43,560 cubic feet.

Soon after the Ensigns settled on their land, A. A. Beaty introduced them to Dr. Walter T. Swingle, a leader of the date industry in Coachella Valley. In 1926, Swingle had planted Borrego Valley's first fruit-bearing date palms on the Beaty homestead at Coyote Canyon. Beaty recognized the potential for the date industry in the valley but lacked the money to undertake a large-scale project. However, the Ensigns did have the capital and in 1927 planted twenty-seven Coachella shoots in Borrego Valley. The following year 119 more were planted and the first harvest was in 1939. By 1946, the twenty-four-acre plantings were said to be the largest pest-free date garden in the world. The ranch slowly grew until it reached 1,160 acres.

Many families moved into the valley between 1926 and 1930. Fred Lanz and his Uncle Henry Lanz each homesteaded land in Tub Canyon, growing some of the valley's finest winter vegetables which occasionally were sold in San Diego. Gilbert Rock, who was still living in Borrego Springs in the 1970s, with Lanz's help claimed land on Clark's Dry Lake in 1927. Joseph A. Kelsey, in addition to being the first justice of the peace of Borrego Springs, raised garden produce. Harry Woods, who originally moved to the desert because of his health, became an early promoter of Borrego Valley. Melbourne G. Small helped develop the Ensign Ranch and attempted homesteading on his own in 1927. For these and other early residents of Borrego Valley the future looked bright. On May 6, 1928, *The San Diego Union* reported:

> This long-neglected land of long-recognized agricultural possibilities is on the eve of what is predicted will be one of the most interesting developments in San Diego's back country.
>
> More and more settlers are filing water claims, following successful development of several wells, road conditions are being improved, mail service has been provided and hydroelectric service is promised.

In 1926 the Borrego Valley School District was formed with twenty-seven students, meeting at the Harold W. Bemis homestead. However, this was not the valley's first school. In 1915 Bemis and a woman named Mrs. French had become concerned about their children's education and hired Mrs. Ruth Brice from San Diego to teach at a salary of $5.00 per pupil per month, plus board. Class began in the home of Charles Ferguson, who originally came to the valley in 1904 searching for Pegleg Smith's lost gold. Later, in 1930, a schoolhouse was built on land donated by Dana Burks.

According to homesteader Mabel G. Small, most of the settlers in the late 1920s remained in the valley only long enough to prove their homesteads. To receive title it was necessary to live on the land for six months a year for three years and show property improvements. After receiving title, most homesteaders left. Albert L. Mathes, who had a homestead south of the present site of Pegleg's Monument, described what he saw in the valley in March, 1929:

> The Ensign Ranch was the only producing farm, not much to brag about either. About twenty families comprised the community.

In spite of the small population, 1929 was a significant year for Borrego Valley. In December residents signed the articles of incorporation of the Borrego Valley Chamber of Commerce and Community Club. Its purpose was "to promote the welfare of the residents of Borrego Valley and environs socially and from a civic standpoint and for the extension and promotion of trade

THE CANYON WITHOUT A NAME: *Canyon Sin Nombre deadends, surrounded by steep sandstone and mudstone cliffs which dwarf vehicles attempting the journey.*

BASIN WASH: *Smooth, denuded hills provide a narrow passageway for modern 4-wheel drive vehicles negotiating terrain southwest of Seventeen Palms.*

OLD DOC BEATY ROAD: *The Truckhaven Trail, rough and rugged, was built by local residents in 1929 as the link between the valley and Highway 99.*

and commerce." Called the Booster's Club, it was active in sponsoring the Pegleg Smith Liar's Contest and in building a monument in his memory. A graduation ceremony for the first four students from the Borrego Springs School District was conducted.

Also in 1929 the Truckhaven Trail from Borrego Valley east to Salton Sea was constructed. Believing that this route would make it easier for Borregans to transact business in Coachella Valley, Beaty and other residents personally worked on the twenty-eight-mile road. Until then only two dirt roads led into the valley, one entering through the Narrows and the other by way of San Felipe Creek. Both of them joined the Julian-Kane Springs Road. Work on the Sentenac Canyon Road had begun as early as 1917, but it was not completed until 1932 and it was another two years before the Yaqui Pass Road to Borrego was opened. With the backing of Coachella Valley businessmen and the help of Borrego residents, Beaty and his crew used mules, horses, picks, shovels, and his Fresno-scraper to complete the Truckhaven Trail. Unfortunately the road was in continued disrepair due to periodic flash floods.

By 1930 residents formed the Borrego Springs Township and began the process of selecting a justice of the peace and constable. Records indicate that the post office served one hundred and twenty-five people and held fifty-five mail boxes. A year later the population had increased to three hundred and there were one hundred and forty-eight registered voters. Yet the township had no commercial center. There was no actual town, no crossroads and no centralized settlement. The valley still appeared relatively undeveloped and, according to *The San Diego Union,* the new constable, Milo C. Porter, and the judge, Joseph A. Kelsey, had "little to do."

However, the small community had public spirit. In the early 1930s, Borrego Valley citizens placed on Font's Point a jar which was to be filled with names and pennies everytime anyone visited the location. The pennies were to pay for a future road to this scenic area. The jar and the tradition of placing money and names into it continued until the early 1940s when someone took the money and scattered the names.

Growth of the valley remained slow during the early 1930s, lack of capital being the main reason. As the full effects of the national depression settled over Southern California, most of the early settlers gave up their desert homes, and in 1932 the school district was closed when attendance fell to less than five students. Finally, by 1936 the permanent population had decreased to twenty-five persons.

One of those remaining was Eugene P. Woillard who moved into the barbershop of the abandoned and since-vanished fourteen-room Miracle Hotel in Little Borrego, a townsite near Ocotillo Wells which had been an early victim of the depression. "Doc" Woillard achieved uncertain fame as a healer, treating people with radium water and electricity. He practiced in his hotel office and on the road in his Model-T Ford Sedan, called the "Princess Radium Health Car." In the late 1930s, Woillard was killed when he drove his car off the Yaqui Pass Road.

Marshall South and his poetess wife, Tanya, who decided to experiment in primitive living, selected a site on Ghost Mountain at the east end of Blair Valley, and in February, 1932, began constructing a hand-built adobe house which they called Yaquitepec. They lived like the early Indians, surviving off the desert and wearing little in the way of clothing. Treasuring the peace and solitude of their desert home, they remained there until the mid-Forties, writing about their "back-to-nature" experiment. The ruin of Yaquitepec could still be seen in the 1970s.

Since the 1880s, cattlemen, prospectors and homesteaders had tried to develop the Anza-Borrego Desert and Borrego Valley. Most were frustrated, but their failures were to have a long-range benefit to people of California. The lack of expansion in the desert and Borrego Valley had kept the area a veritable wilderness, preserving it for the future desert park.

SAND VERBENA: *The Santa Rosa Mountains, east of Clark Dry Lake, make an impressive backdrop for blossoms which spring to life following the rains.*

AT SWEENEY PASS: *Looking toward Canyon Sin Nombre offers a typical view of the topography of the southern part of the park as seen from Highway S-2.*

VIII

To Preserve or to Abandon?

More than four decades ago a group of farsighted people realized that accessible scenic land in California was rapidly being appropriated. They had seen threats to the Yosemite Valley and the redwoods, and had witnessed the destruction of Hetch-Hetchy Valley by the building of a dam to provide another source of water for San Francisco. They realized that California's remaining open areas, mountains, coasts and deserts were being threatened. Founders of the state park system believed the state had a duty to preserve several desert areas for future generations.

Anza-Borrego Desert was selected as being representative of the typical wild and beautiful California deserts because it was believed that certain natural and historical features made it particularly valuable as a park site. In 1932 several prominent San Diegans donated both land and money to help make the idea a reality. Soon after, they hoped to extend the proposed park to a million acres, stretching from the Mexican border north to Mount San Jacinto and from the Salton Sea west to the Laguna Mountains. There also were those who had a more utilitarian outlook. Proponents of the park extension met unexpected opposition from the San Diego County Board of Supervisors, who were concerned with the future economic development of the county. Supervisors believed the lands within the proposed park extension could be put to better use than "maintaining it as a desert waste."

The present Anza-Borrego Desert State Park is the product both of insight to the needs of the future and of the struggle to preserve open space. Nowhere else can such a large and beautiful desert park be found so close to population centers easily accessible to the public. In the 1970s, with growing urban problems and greater manipulation of the earth's surface, interest in ecology and environmental preservation has increased. As the founders of the California park system looked to the past for insight, so today's conservationists must look to the past to better understand the challenge of the present.

In 1864 President Abraham Lincoln signed an Act of Congress ceding Yosemite Valley to California, setting it aside as the first public preserve which was designated as a national park. This marked the beginning of a burgeoning movement for the preservation of unique wilderness and scenic areas in the United States, arising as a reaction to and as a consequence of almost two centuries of land exploitation. As scenic areas throughout California and the nation became increasingly threatened with destruction and development, conservation organizations began to be established. In 1892, the Sierra Club was created and in 1918 the Save-the-Redwoods League was formed, both in California. These early conservation groups had as their purpose the protection and preservation of scenic resources and hoped to secure some of these areas for the state.

By 1923, almost 6,000 acres had been conveyed to the state by conservation groups, but no organization had been established to administer and care for the land. John C. Merriam, president of the Save-the-Redwoods League, appointed a committee to study and recommend the agency they believed best qualified to receive custody of the land and to have the responsibility of managing the parks. In the fall of 1924 the committee reported that in its opinion the state was the best agency to provide administrative machinery. They further recommended that the California Legislature establish a state park commission to administer the parks and furnish funds to pay the cost of a comprehensive state-wide survey of scenic and recreational resources that would form the nucleus of a state park system.

In 1926, the Save-the-Redwoods League was enlarged to include representatives from all conservation organizations in the state and was given the title of the California State Parks Council. The council submitted to the 1927 State Legislature two recommendations and in addition called for a park bond issue of $6,000,000. The money would be used to obtain additional park lands upon receipt of matching private funds. The three bills passed almost unanimously and on May 25, 1927, Governor Clement C. Young signed them, establishing the first state park system in the nation.

Young appointed five leading conservationists as members of the initial State Park Commission which met for the first time on December 13, 1927. At that meeting the nationally recognized landscape architect, Frederick Law Olmsted Jr., was selected as director of the survey. Olmsted was already well known in the San Diego area because he and his brother, John, had drawn some of the preliminary sketches for the 1915 exposition grounds in Balboa Park, although Olmsted's idea that buildings were an unnatural intrusion upon parks led to his withdrawal from the project.

As director of the 1927 park survey, Olmsted had one year in which to submit to the governor and legislature recommendations for a state park system. A proponent of a desert park also figured in the first commission meeting. Dr. Ray Lyman Wilbur, a commission member who would later serve four years as President Herbert Hoover's Secretary of the Interior, advocated setting aside a desert region in the southern section of the state so some of the rapidly disappearing desert plants and animals could be preserved.

The day the meeting took place, Clinton G. Abbott, director of the San Diego Natural History Museum, wrote to W. B. Rider, acting chief of the California Forestry Service, urging him to immediately set aside the areas of Borrego Palm Canyon and Thousand Palms Canyon, now known as Salvador Canyon which is located to the west of Coyote Canyon, because of their easy accessibility and the possibility that vandals might destroy them.

Abbott and Guy L. Fleming, both Fellows of the Natural History Society, had made a reconnaissance of the Borrego Valley and surrounding areas only two months before, after it had been recommended to the Fellows as a possible park site by Dr. Walter T. Swingle, the date palm expert who supervised the planting of the original date palms on the Ensign Ranch in Borrego Valley. Abbott and Fleming were so enthused with what they saw that they persuaded members of the society to vote unanimous approval of the desert park concept. The San Diego Chamber of Commerce Conservation Committee and the San Diego Community Service and Citizens Committee soon announced their endorsement of Borrego Park.

In March, 1928, Fleming, representing the Natural History Society and the Chamber of Commerce, went to San Francisco, where he urged the newly formed State Park Commission to include Borrego Desert in their selections. A month later, the commission asked him to assist in the selection by working as a volunteer in the San Diego and Imperial County areas. Fleming accepted the assignment and filed a report on the possibility of a Borrego park. He suggested a park which would enclose 120,000 acres with a possible 184,000-acre extension east to the Salton Sea and north to the San Jacinto State Park project. The name Borrego Palms Desert Park was officially assigned the project. It was from the information submitted that Frederick Olmsted made his recommendations.

The real boost to the Borrego project came as a result of Olmsted's survey, submitted on December 31, 1928. He gave full approval of the idea of a desert sanctuary:

> Certain desert areas have a distinctive and subtle charm, in part dependent on spaciousness, solitude, and escape from the evidence of human control and manipulation of the earth, a charm of constantly growing value as the rest of the earth becomes more completely dominated by

BORREGO PALM CANYON: *One of the most accessible areas in the park, this canyon features a small creek which flows from the San Ysidro Mountains.*

> man's activities. This quality is a very vulnerable one. . . . Nowhere else are casual thoughtless human changes in the landscape so irreparable, and nowhere else is it so important to control and completely protect wide areas.

Olmsted recommended that the Borrego Palm Canyon, including the palm canyons and desert mountain escarpments descending into Borrego Valley and the desert area of San Felipe Valley, be associated with and preferably connected to the Santa Rosa Mountains and Salton Sea region.

The Olmsted survey, rather than encouraging preservation of the area until the state could take over its management, served to encourage speculative land investment. In addition, the publication in 1930 of Herbert E. Bolton's translation of the diaries of Anza's California expedition also focused attention on the area.

Advertisements claiming that the proposed park site would rival Palm Springs led some people to invest in the region. Speculators who bought land in nearly inaccessible places included F. Hechinger of Los Angeles, who purchased one hundred and seventy-two acres at the back of Borrego Palm Canyon in October, 1927. This land was accessible only by strenuously scrambling up the boulder strewn canyon. In June, 1930, Dana Burks, a Los Angeles and Palm Springs investor, purchased 13,500 acres in Borrego Valley and in the surrounding highlands. During the 1930s many sections of private land were sold or transferred, some of the plots being as small as two and one-half acres. Township Nine South, Range Five East, enclosing Collins Valley and Coyote Creek, best exemplified part of the problem that existed. There were more than one hundred and twenty-five individually owned parcels of land in that one area. Such investments were the cause of great concern among those who were working toward the park's creation. Tam Deering, executive secretary of the State-County Parks and Beaches Association, wrote:

> What I fear most is the danger of individuals getting a hold of strategic areas and then forcing us to buy them out at prohibitive prices, as has been done elsewhere.

Confusion concerning existing land titles presented another complication. Many persons were listed as owners of the same land. When John Forward of the Union Title Insurance Company volunteered his services in helping to clarify the titles, he discovered that what he thought would be an easy job turned out to be a real puzzle. In addition to the question of legal ownership, there was the additional problem of squatters. Part of the fault of overlapping ownership was the result of an inaccurate government survey in 1854. Section corners could not be located, making it difficult to plan park boundaries. Acquisition of the first park unit, Borrego Mesa, was delayed because the attorney general's office objected to the "indefiniteness" of the land's legal description. To help straighten out the confusion, the park commission in 1933 obtained the services of surveyor John L. Warboys to work out section corners and ownership.

Problems in selecting areas desirable for a park were compounded by the difficulties of desert travel. Rough dirt roads, automobiles prone to overheating and breakdown, lack of communication, no overnight accommodations, no service stations and little knowledge of the area all added to the delay in gathering information and acquiring land. Not until March, 1932, did the commission have sufficient information to announce an acquisition program. Listed in order of priority were five units: San Felipe or Palm Mesa, Borrego Palm Canyon, Borrego Mesa, Collins Valley and Montezuma Valley. However, private groups had already taken the initiative and were acquiring land for a state park when the commission announced its program. Private interests had obtained land on faith only, since the commission had not made arrangement for acquisition until the March meeting.

The State-County Parks and Beaches Association did more than any other private group to help create a desert park. It represented those who owned or purchased land in Borrego and were interested in selling or donating the land to the state. They spent thousands of dollars which helped carry the 1928 state park bond issue in San Diego County. They also worked to arouse public interest and support for a desert park, surveyed and negotiated for the purchase of private lands and helped secure passage of bills withdrawing government land in the Borrego Valley area.

Although it was intended that the association operate with guidance of commission representatives, the park commission at times found its work exasperating. Land owners often preferred to negotiate with the association rather than directly with the state. The association assessed land at a higher value than government surveys indicated and also made arrangements with land owners without first consulting state authorities. One such promise involved the exchange of valuable valley lands for inaccessible mountainous lands in equal amounts of acreage.

Yet it was the association that actively began the acquisition program. In 1931, Harry S. Woods and Charles and Henry Fearney, who owned land in Borrego Valley, offered to deed some of their land to the association. George W. Marston, a prominent San Diegan and the honorary president of the association who was asked to act as agent, urged the purchase of land located at the entrance of Borrego Palm Canyon. His purchase of 2,320 acres effectively secured the ultimate acquisition of the entire canyon. Later Marston purchased 5,500 acres, chiefly in the Collins Valley area, and also held these in trust for the state.

In August, 1931, Tam Deering, executive-secretary of the association, wrote to Ellen Browning Scripps, of the Scripps newspaper family and a resident of La Jolla, urging her to purchase land in the Borrego project adjacent to those purchased by Marston. Miss Scripps donated $2,500 which was eventually matched with park bond funds for the acquisition of property along the old Julian-Kane Springs Road.

In spite of these and other private donations, funding continued to be a major problem. The total amount allotted for the acquisition of all private land in the Borrego Palms Desert Park amounted to $18,000 from bond funds. That sum, matched by private donations of land and money, made $36,000 available for all land purchases. People who were out to make a profit by holding back their land for a better price made the funding problem critical. Though federal land was freely transferred to the state, filing fees still had to be paid. The effects of the Depression probably led to the November, 1930, defeat of a San Diego County bond issue to donate funds to assist the state in acquiring park lands located in the county. This added to the already sad financial plight.

Under the leadership of the State-County Parks and Beaches Association a great part of the Borrego Valley purchase was accomplished. Approximately 10,000 acres were to be deeded to the State Park by the Interior Department and 8,000 acres were to be purchased. The city of San Diego was to be the central figure in obtaining the funds to secure the acreage. Philip L. Gildred was named chairman of the fund-raising committee which also included George Marston, Julius Wangenheim, Colonel Ira C. Copley and Miss Alice Lee, all under the leadership of Deering.

The response was effective. The necessary matching funds were secured and the State Park Commission was able to close the deal then pending for Anza State Park, Palomar State Park and all of those chosen to comprise other state parks in the desert. Joseph Sefton, a San Diego banker, was the treasurer of the county committee that secured the necessary funds which included a $1,000 donation from John Forward Jr. for his family whose great interest was to obtain a site for Palomar State Park.

Unable to buy all of the proposed park land, the commission stressed procurement of key holdings, including Fearney's Well at the entrance to Borrego Palm Canyon and the Beaty Ranch at the entrance of Collins Valley. Due to limited funds, the size of the projected park was reduced to 83,840 acres from the 200,000 originally recommended by Fleming and Olmsted. The financial difficulties persisted through the following years, and finally in 1946 Borrego Valley land developer A. A. Burnand Jr. purchased many of the remaining sections of land previously held by homesteaders.

The first private lands deeded to the state, on November 17, 1932, were 2,732 acres within the Borrego Mesa unit. The land was a gift from

Louis T. and Lorraine Busch. With the procurement of this property the Borrego Palms Desert State Park became a reality. Lands within Borrego Palm Canyon were deeded on January 20, 1933. Marston lands in Collins Valley became part of the park a year later, and other private lands were obtained in following years, although commercial and investment interests continued to grow, making it even more difficult to acquire suitable land. It took another sixteen years to attain the basic boundaries of the park.

After the State Park Commission announced the general boundaries of Borrego Palms Desert State Park and organized an acquisition program, it proposed a bill calling for the transfer of government lands not used for public purposes to the state of California for park use. Representative Phil D. Swing introduced the bill in the United States Congress in February, 1933. Secretary of the Interior Ray Lyman Wilbur, the former state park commissioner, gave his full endorsement to the bill, stating that the "State of California has sensed its responsibility in preserving this unique area which cannot be duplicated elsewhere."

The only stipulation placed upon transferring federal land was the requirement that the state provide satisfactory proof that the land selected contain characteristic desert growth and scenic or other natural features which would be desirable to preserve as a part of a park system. The Swing bill was amended before passage to provide that former federal land revert back to the United States if it was not used for park purposes within a five-year period. The bill passed on March 3, 1933, making 185,034.36 acres of unappropriated federal land available to the state of California. The land was located north of the old Julian-Kane Springs Road and below the Riverside County line, extending from the Salton Sea west to Montezuma Valley and the Los Coyotes Indian Reservation.

After the passage of the Swing bill, the park commission contracted L. Deming Tilton, a landscape architect and planning expert for San Diego County, to make a study of the area and the park units in the acquisition program. His affirmative report concerning the possibility of creating a desert park of gigantic proportions excited even the most pessimistic observors.

Tilton believed the program followed by Fleming was too restricted. He called for boundaries to encompass at least 200,000 acres, a plan similar to that originally recommended by Fleming and Olmsted in 1928. He based his evaluation of the area on scenic values, not on land values, and insisted that it was necessary for the park to embrace practically all land of minimal agricultural or commercial value in order to prevent exploitation which could destroy the natural beauty of the area. His ultimate boundary lines would necessitate the procurement of private holdings. Tilton requested quick action in obtaining the land because delay had already foiled plans for an ideal park by allowing some development to occur in Borrego Valley in 1933. He reasserted the worth of the area as a park site:

> It is accessible and convenient. It is largely unspoiled, although considerable clearing and destruction of typical desert vegetation have already taken place. It has high scenic and historic value. It contains excellent groves of palms in its rocky canyons, forests of ocotillo and ironwood and masses of other interesting desert plants. It is, moreover, still in large part government or state land and is not yet afflicted with the promotional scale of land values found around Palm Springs and elsewhere.

The State Park Commission and the State-County Parks and Beaches Association endorsed Tilton's report. The association urged the commission to complete its selection and patenting of federal lands within the proposed area before any complications could arise. Included among those supporting the Tilton report and urging still further expansion of park plans were Robert Hays, secretary-manager of the El Centro Chamber of Commerce, George S. Krueger, secretary-manager of the Brawley Chamber of Commerce, and R. B. Whitelaw, conservation committee chairman of the Associated Chambers of Commerce of Imperial Valley.

The chambers of commerce had their own reasons for supporting a park. Imperial County communities had early recognized the potential benefit in being a gateway to a great state park.

FLAMING SPEARS: *Rain brings forth scarlet blossoms to grace the tips of an ocotillo, one of the thorniest plants growing in the Anza-Borrego Desert.*

BORREGO SPRINGS: *A unique town, totally surrounded by Anza-Borrego Desert State Park, it is developing in all directions beginning at Christmas Circle.*

In April, 1929, the county had urged that the Olmsted survey include the Carrizo and Vallecito valleys in the proposed park boundaries. Again, in June 1933, Imperial County renewed its request, with better results. In July, 1933, Fleming, now southern district superintendent of California State Parks, was instructed by the commission to make a preliminary study of land to be included. His report was favorable, and in 1934 the State Park Commission, through the effort of Representative George Burnham, drew up legislation calling for the transfer to California of government lands in the Carrizo and Vallecito areas.

The Burnham bills, approved on June 29, 1936, made 365,389.54 acres of federal lands available for park purposes. These bills carried the same stipulations as the Swing bill, but in addition, amended the Swing bill to provide for the exchange of federal lands for private lands in order to consolidate state park holdings and to secure strategic, privately owned areas within park boundaries.

While Congress considered these bills, the El Centro Chamber of Commerce advertised the area as a park that would ultimately embrace nearly a million acres and Fleming said it would be the largest park in the world. Collaborating with Fleming was P. T. Primm, associate landscape architect for the National Park Service, who called for all of the lands in the Burnham legislation, and in addition to all of the Salton Sea area and many acres of adjacent lands to round out the park boundaries. Both men saw the possibility of national park status:

> There are real possibilities here for developing a great National Park. Borrego Desert State Park, Cuyamaca State Park and San Jacinto State Park might all be tied together by further acquisitions of desert and forest lands to make a year round playground of this magnificent area. Over a million acres could well be included herein and portions of three counties would be required to properly complete the picture.

As park boundaries expanded, the name Borrego Palms Desert State Park seemed inadequate. Robert Hays, of the El Centro Chamber of Commerce, suggested Anza as a more fitting name. Part of Juan Bautista de Anza's route to California crossed the Imperial Valley area then being considered. On March 15, 1938, the State Park Commission approved the renaming of the area as Anza Desert State Park. The name was more fitting to the total area, and also brought to mind some of the land's rich early history. The State Park Commission divided the park into four distinct units: Borrego Desert, Vallecito Desert, Carrizo Desert and Salton Sea Desert.

On July 1, 1938, the State Park Commission made its first selection of 155,947.03 acres in the Carrizo and Vallecito units from government lands and paid the filing fees on them. But what appeared to be the last stage of an arduous acquisition program suddenly came to a tumultuous but temporary halt. Park enthusiasts had become so optimistic in their dreams of a million-acre park that would be unequalled in its grandeur and scope that they did not recognize the dangers of a growing opposition that had existed to a small degree from the beginning of the project.

One-fifth of the San Diego County electorate had opposed the park bond issue in the 1928 elections. Stronger opposition in 1930 managed to defeat a bond to help finance the creation of parks within the county. In addition, the concept of a park that would encompass the Borrego Valley area appeared menacing for the developing agricultural interests. However, the opposition did not become vocal until it found its voice in San Diego County Supervisor Walter Bellon.

The intensity of the opposition came as a shock to the State Park commission. They had believed that both San Diego and Imperial counties strongly favored the park project. Perhaps an even greater surprise was the opposition of Bellon and the San Diego County Board of Supervisors. Bellon's chief interests were metropolitan areas while Carrizo and Valecito were in the districts of two active supporters of the park project, William T. Hart and T. Leroy Richards. Hart, as a former state park commissioner and past president of the State-County Parks and Beaches Association, had supported the park extension. Richards also had declared his support for the park before Bellon began his attack. Richards told Fleming that the protests of the supervisors were only "political sop to satisfy certain disgruntled groups."

The Board of Supervisors claimed it first became disturbed after noting that the land selected in the Carrizo and Vallecito units followed the old Butterfield stage route. They suspected that the State Park Commission was being duped by interests seeking a "cannonball" highway between Imperial Valley and Los Angeles, and one which would bypass San Diego. They appealed to the California Division of State Parks and to the local federal land office, noting that the land was usable for agriculture and grazing and that the commission had failed to notice existing mining claims. They charged that the park would be a playground for Los Angeles and Imperial Valley at the expense of San Diego.

In 1938 forty-eight percent of San Diego County already was untaxable because it was national forest, Indian reservation, city and county park or military land. The county already had six state parks and it was feared that the creation of more park lands would increase the tax burden of citizens. In the eyes of the supervisors, the eastern half of the county was being changed into a state park system of aesthetic and recreational values, and the removal of taxable lands threatened the future development of San Diego County itself. Supervisor Bellon best expressed this fear:

> To place one-half of our county in a park system means the end of our future competition as a shipping port and our commercial advantage will be removed forever. The question of a great metropolitan city on the shores of our beautiful bay will be limited and our political powers . . . can no longer expand beyond its present limits. . . . We could lose all because of a park.

In May, 1939, Bellon went to Sacramento and personally pleaded his case before Governor Culbert L. Olson and members of the California Legislature. A number of organizations in the San Diego area joined the battle and protested the park's extension. A report prepared by Bellon listed forty-seven organizations, primarily agricultural and business groups, as filing protests with the State Park Commission. Though protests were filed by eight chambers of commerce within the county, the San Diego Chamber of Commerce continued to support the park extension.

This sudden and vehement opposition caused a three-year delay of the park extension while the charges were being investigated. Officials waited to see if the complaints were valid, and if any land should be excluded because of a higher value brought about by economic use. Supervisor Bellon suggested the state delay further issuance of patents for a year, pending study by a group of experts. The commission agreed and set the period of study from June 2, 1939, to June 2, 1940, to be followed by a hearing.

According to Congressional Acts of June 29, 1936, the state had five years, until June, 1941, in which to select lands for park use before the lands would again revert to federal control. Opposition and delay coming at this time were critical to the park's future. However, the commission still did not initiate a campaign to express either its objectives in desiring the Vallecito and Carrizo areas or to counter the misunderstanding and general distrust of park objectives fostered by Bellon's followers.

The Department of the Interior was the first governmental agency to counter some of the charges. The San Diego County Bureau of Mines and the Board of Supervisors had both filed protests with the General Land Office against all of the selections made in the Vallecito and Carrizo units by the State Park Commission. Reasons cited were the same as those made by the supervisors to the Division of State Parks. Fred W. Johnson, United States Land Commissioner, dismissed all of the charges:

> In the opinion of this office, if the predominant characteristic of a legal subdivision in the area described in the act of June 29, 1936, is its desert growth, scenic or other natural features, the legal subdivision is subject to selection by the State and this office cannot refuse approval of the selection solely because the tract might be made susceptible to irrigation, might be sold under the five-acre act or might be put to a so-called higher use than inclusion in a State park. . . . The State has furnished the required proof as to the character of the lands.

Unsatisfied with the opinion, Bellon's forces

DAY COMES TO CHRISTMAS CIRCLE: *Borrego Springs, town within a park, provides a man-made oasis in the midst of the dry Anza-Borrego Desert.*

IN THE VALLEY BELOW: *Water from beneath the earth's surface is pumped from wells to create an oasis in land once considered too hostile to develop.*

claimed the area did not contain characteristic desert growth and could not be selected under the provisions of the Acts of June 29, 1936. In January, 1940, at Bellon's request, the Board of Supervisors retained Dr. Philip Munz, professor of botany at Pomona College and an authority on desert flora, to make a botanical survey of lands selected in the Vallecito and Carrizo units. The results of Munz' survey were silenced by the Board of Supervisors. In his report Munz averred that his most outstanding impression of the Mason-Vallecito-Carrizo area was that "botanically it is one of the richest desert valleys I have ever seen."

The argument that the lands selected would adversely affect the tax structure of San Diego County also was found to be exaggerated. The average assessed valuation of lands in Carrizo and Vallecito valleys in 1939 and 1940 was from forty to eighty-five cents per acre. Most of the property homesteaded in the early 1900s was tax delinquent. The 1940 census listed only three families in the whole area: Robert Crawford, the county custodian of Vallecito Stage Station; Marshall South, an author and conservationist who urged the park to take over the land; and Everett Campbell, the only man in the area with land under cultivation. In a letter to the editor of *The San Diego Union,* Campbell wrote that he found no objection to the park's selection of land, nor did he see it as potential agricultural land. The park selections, he continued, "do not border on any land of agricultural value." People who owned land in the area purchased it as an investment and did not live there. Furthermore, it was impractical to bring in water as some opponents suggested. Since the lands were largely undeveloped and did not contribute significantly to the tax program, it required considerable imagination to say that the economic future of San Diego County depended on it. The county had paid little attention to this area until park enthusiasts became interested in it.

It was true that Imperial County hoped for a road into the park. As early as 1933 the Imperial Valley chambers of commerce mentioned the desire for this and even offered manpower for the construction of the necessary roads required for the proper development of the park. From the very beginning of the project, they had pictured Imperial Valley as the "gateway" to the park.

Although they persisted in their claims, members of the San Diego Board of Supervisors failed to prove that any of the lands selected by the state had agricultural or mineral value. Rich gypsum deposits in the Fish Creek Mountains were already owned by United States Gypsum Company, and according to the Act of June 29, 1936, the federal government retained mining rights in the land transfer. Hence any mining done in the park would remain under the jurisdiction of the federal government, not the State Park Commission. This has continued to the present, making Anza-Borrego the only state park in California open to prospecting.

During the period of opposition the park retained its enthusiastic supporters. There still were hopes that the tide would turn and a great desert park would evolve. The Riverside Chamber of Commerce continued to push for the extension of the San Jacinto State Park boundary southward to connect with Anza Desert State Park. The city of Riverside began in 1940 to sponsor an annual Anza celebration to draw attention to the area. Imperial Valley formed the Anza Memorial Conservation Association, the purpose of which was the protection and preservation of naturally scenic and historic areas. It also solicited money to assist the state in paying filing fees for park lands.

After the stated year of arguments, the State Park Commission held its hearing on August 16, 1940. The evidence submitted was sufficient to change the original concensus of the commission and as a result, the San Diego County Board of Supervisors employed two additional devices to cause further delays. The board hoped its opposition would put enough pressure on the commission that it would fail to file for any more land by the June 29, 1941, deadline. The first attempt to force a delay came in January, 1941, when the board, through State Senator Ed Fletcher, introduced a bill in the California Legislature providing that no government lands be given to the state for park purposes without express approval of the State Legislature. The bill was defeated in April, 1941. The board then requested hearings before the United States Land Office, which were held June 3 and 4, 1941, and represented the supervisor's last attempt to cause a delay. It resulted in a stalemate. Land Commissioner John B. Bennett, presiding at the hearings, suggested that a compromise would be the best solution since neither side was satisfied with the evidence.

The State Park Commission accepted neither the validity of the supervisor's arguments nor the idea of returning the federal lands. However, the commission had planned to pacify the opposition by returning some of the selected land even before a compromise was suggested by the land office. Prior to the hearing the commission had discussed its compromise plan, in order to assure patent of desirable federal property before the June deadline.

According to the compromise plan worked out by the commission, patent would be taken on lands on which filing fees were paid, but 46,000 acres of it considered valuable for either agriculture or mining would be used for exchange purposes. Application also would be made for an additional 130,000 acres of unappropriated land.

In September, 1941, Fleming and Park Commissioner Matthew M. Gleason met with county representatives to work out a compromise acceptable to both parties. Certain property deemed important for agriculture or mineral purposes were deleted from patent, and the protest filed with the Federal Land Office by the board was withdrawn. In addition, cattlemen were permitted to use the area for grazing under concessionary agreement.

The immediate effects of the opposition to park extension and the resulting compromise were major changes to the park boundaries and years of delay to the acquisition program. Sections of land cited as agriculturally or minerally important were excluded in park selections, creating an irregular park boundary and allowing pockets of private ownership. The most significant compromise involved the loss of Borrego Valley. Because of protests, the State Park Commission had encouraged the passage of a bill in 1939 allowing patented lands with agricultural potential located in the floor of Borrego Valley to be used for exchange purposes. The act allowed later development of Borrego Springs, an agricultural-resort community in the heart of the park. At the time of the act, Borrego Valley was almost entirely undeveloped. Plans for a million-acre park never survived the protests.

With the placation of opposing interests, the State Park Commission was able to dedicate the park and continue the acquisition program. In December, 1941, Anza Desert State Park was dedicated to the memory of Anza and to all other explorers and pioneers of the desert region. At the dedication, representatives of the California State park pledged to preserve the park in its natural state so future generations also might enjoy its intrinsic qualities. Even though the newly dedicated park was assured of selected federal properties, the state did not receive full patent to the land until May, 1948. Exchanges were made with private landholders and the basic park boundaries which exist today were established. Later years would see the addition of acreage from other private holdings, the introduction of planned management, and the long-range effects of the compromised acquisition program.

A PARK APPROACH: *An agave blossom frames a view of Borrego Springs looking northeast from Montezuma Road which descends 3,500 feet in ten miles.*

IX

The Desert: A Way of Life

After World War II, the beauty and quiet of the desert began to capture public imagination, and living and playing in the desert became even more attractive with the availability of off-road vehicles, better roads and air conditioning. As with other desert parks, the increasing use of Anza-Borrego Desert brought both management problems and threats to the desert wilderness. The problems were compounded by the presence of a town in the center of the park, the result of the compromised acquisition program. Thus, park management was challenged to provide services to visitors while protecting the desert wilderness from recreational and commercial misuse.

Although the Depression of the 1930s had kept park visitors and land developers to a minimum, Guy Fleming, southern district state park superintendent, believed the state should have a representative at the park in order to establish the fact that a state park actually did exist in the Anza-Borrego area. Consequently, one or two seasonal custodians were assigned to the park between 1933 and 1948. It was not until 1949 that the steady increase in the number of visitors merited a much larger park staff.

In 1933, Paul A. McEwen and John Fleming, the superintendent's son, were employed as the first such custodians. Their tasks included working on the Palm Canyon trail, burying abandoned car bodies, taking down wire fences and preventing visitors from removing plants growing on park land. Using a 1921 touring car and camping equipment, McEwen and Fleming began exploring the park. The custodians' salary reflected Depression wages. They received only $100 per month, to be shared equally. Because Fleming was the superintendent's son, he could receive no direct salary, but had to share McEwen's.

During the first season there were from twenty-five to thirty visitors on an average weekend. McEwen described the first tourists as "rugged people" who pitched tents in a cleared area at the mouth of Borrego Palm Canyon. The first facilities in the Palm Canyon campground also were built that year and some stoves and ramadas were constructed by the Civilian Conservation Corps.

In 1934, John Fleming again was employed as a custodian, this time assisting Richard B. Dixon. Living accommodations had improved slightly with the rental of Charles Fearney's shack, but water had to be hauled in milk cans from the Ensign Ranch in Borrego Valley. Many tourists came on weekends but few visited Borrego Palms Desert Park during weekdays.

Temporary help was still being utilized in 1935, when Donald Armstrong of Borrego Valley worked as a custodian. In 1936 a full-time civil service employee was assigned to the park, and permanent ranger's quarters were constructed with more ramadas being added to the main Palm Canyon campground by the C.C.C.

Jack Calvert, a former Azusa postmaster, served as park supervisor almost continuously from 1936 to 1952, spending summers at Lake Tahoe and winters in the desert. During his tenure as supervisor he saw the growth of the park and also the town of Borrego Springs. In the winter and spring Calvert patrolled the area, served as park guide and naturalist and attempted to define state park boundaries. While he resided at Lake Tahoe, the desert park was officially closed. The advent of electricity and refrigeration finally allowed him to live in the desert with his wife, Ella, the year around. There were few facilities for the public during those years and visitors paid no fees. A pool was added in 1941 and picnic facilities in 1942.

In 1942, the United States Army took more than 27,000 acres of Fish Creek Mountains for use as a bombing range, calling it the Carrizo Impact Area. Within a few years it was leased to the Navy which continued to use it for the same purpose. In 1959, practice bombing was discontinued and the Navy initiated a bomb-disposal program before returning the land to the state. The public was again allowed to enter the impact area, but only for a short while because in the same year a scrap dealer was killed in an explosion accidentally triggered while he was attempting to remove scrap metal. When the question of legal responsibility arose, the Navy stated such responsibility belonged to the state because they could not guarantee the safety of the park. On December 14, 1962, the State Park Commission officially closed the area to public access until such time as the Navy could guarantee the safety of it. Navy demolition crews have since been called into the area whenever a live bomb has been found by one of the patrolling rangers. However, lost to the public through these years has been some of the most scenic land in the park and a famous part of the old Southern Emigrant Trail.

Gasoline rationing as a result of World War II brought park attendance to a low ebb, and in 1944, Calvert was assigned to La Purisima State Park, near Lompoc. He returned to Anza Desert State Park in the fall of 1946 and remained in charge until 1952. During the intervening period John Fleming worked as a ranger and alternated between Palomar State Park in summer and Anza Desert State Park in winter. Despite the low number of visitors during those years, the campground facilities were overcrowded and a study of the park's recreational potential was initiated. During the fall and spring of 1946-1947 there were 10,827 visitors recorded, the largest attendance since the park's opening. The beginning of the park's use as a location for Hollywood film productions also was noted that season.

In the fall of 1947, a state park ranger, William Allison, was instructed to go to Anza Desert State Park to "see if you can find anyone." He was given a map with a circle around the general area. He had never heard of the vast park located at the bottom of the state, and when he arrived, Allison found what seemed the vestiges of the early frontier. The only law enforcement officer in the valley was San Diego County Deputy Sheriff Ed DuVall whose office was the Borrego Store and Post Office, and park Supervisor Calvert wore a pistol and carried a rifle in his car. Calvert assisted the United States Border Patrol in watching for Mexican Nationals and smugglers. During that time no more than a few fields were under cultivation. Both entertainment and contact with the "outside world" were provided by a radio that received only stations located in Australia, the Belgian Congo and Yuma, Arizona.

During his first season, Allison assisted John Fleming in a special five-month trail-building project. Because the Calverts occupied the only house in the park, Allison, Fleming and the building crew lived in campground ramadas. Many of the campers were those who had camped at the park for years. A number of persons who were considering the purchase of land—and some who had bought property, sight unseen—came to ask help in locating it. Because most visitors were interested only in the area north of Highway 78, Calvert and Allison never bothered to patrol areas south of the highway. During the winter of 1947-1948 park attendance doubled and 24,606 persons visited the campground.

The real growth of privately held land in Borrego Springs began in 1946, both encouraging park development and creating continued challenges for it. An understanding of the relationship between Borrego Springs and the park must go back to Depression days when the valley lay isolated and neglected in the triangle of major roads between San Diego, El Centro and Los Angeles. The nearest railroad shipping points were seventy miles west and fifty miles southeast. As the full effects of the Depression hit, valley population dropped. Gradually as state park acreage increased, privately held land became surrounded. Because of opposition from the

CALCITE MINE: *During World War II, this was an active and busy mine supplying optical grade calcite crystals which were used in precision bomb sights.*

San Diego Board of Supervisors and the lack of funds to purchase private lands, the state had refrained from including all of the Borrego Valley into the park plan. The consequences of that action were not to be fully realized until the end of World War II.

In 1936, when Calvert first arrived in Borrego Valley, the population already had decreased to twenty-five persons as many of the early settlers had given up their desert homes. Also in 1936, Dana Burks, a Palm Springs developer, sold his ranch to Noel Crickmer who, in spite of the Depression turned it into the Desert Lodge. With that addition, Borrego Valley could then boast a guest lodge, an elementary school and a small store.

During the war, most agricultural activities were curtailed because of gasoline shortage which prevented farmers from shipping their products to railheads. Production was generally limited to the farmer's personal subsistence. At war's end only about 300 acres were under cultivation in the valley. However, the Ensign Ranch was one exception that showed wartime growth. The Ensigns had secured a source of underground water which was used to irrigate date palms and alfalfa fields. Turkeys were raised for a number of years, and during the early 1940s the ranch was expanded to include a dairy. Dairy products were shipped to San Diego when there was a shortage in the city.

Because of its unique terrain features, the desert offered an ideal training ground for military units during World War II. In the spring of 1942, armored elements of the United States Army under the command of Major General George S. Patton conducted maneuvers in the Borrego Desert prior to being transfered to the Mojave Desert for further training in preparation for the invasion and campaigns in North Africa. Army anti-aircraft batteries stationed at Camp Callan, located on the coast in San Diego, arrived in two groups each week for exercises in the badlands near Font's Point. These activities continued until the end of the war. Also, in addition to the Carrizo Impact Area, Clark's Dry Lake was used as an aerial bombing range.

World War II brought about the mining of calcite deposits in the Borrego Badlands. Some types of calcite crystals were found to be the essential mineral required for certain gunsights because of its quality of double refraction. War meant the loss of foreign supplies of calcite, and as a consequence the mining operations in Borrego Badlands became the most important in the Western Hemisphere during the war years.

Soon after the bombing of Pearl Harbor, desert artist John Hilton had sent a sample of calcite from his claim to the Harvard University mineralogy department for analysis. Mineralogist Harry Berman believed the calcite to be of the exact quality then being sought by the government. Hilton and his partner, Ralph Willard, extracted calcite crystals as quickly as possible, but they lacked the manpower and equipment for an extensive operation and began to lose money despite their hard work.

Hilton's description of the war years in the desert is graphic:

> We lived like animals in a little cave high above our first camp and ate K-rations donated by Patton's outfit, because we were too tired to crawl off the cliff for wood to warm it up. We learned how little water a man can work on if he doesn't wash for a week at a time. We lost weight and morale in about equal proportions. Still production was spotted and low.
>
> Finally we got word that the company (a large eastern manufacturing concern who bought and consolidated most of the claims in the area) was going to send out some engineers who would mine the calcite right. We gladly sold the claims for a little more than we had invested in the project and a guarantee of jobs on the calcite mine for the duration at reasonable salaries.

Machinery arrived, a road was constructed up to some of the workings, a cook house built, tents erected and electricity connected. The Marine Corps brought in a huge water truck and storage tanks and a shower was installed. As production continued, experts developed synthetic crystal which would replace optical calcite. The operation, which by then resembled a small town, was finally sold to Jack Frost and Robert Dye who continued mining it until existing war needs were filled. After the war they mined some specimens, but their claim lapsed and a cloudburst washed the road away. Today the site of this once important operation is a scenic part of the park.

Military interest in Borrego Valley also brought about the paving of Yaqui Pass Road, which entered Borrego Valley from the south. Thus Borrego Valley was tied more directly into one of the main east-west highways. From San Diego travelers could follow the present Highway 78 through Julian and Banner and then turn north for the desert resort and agricultural areas. Once dubbed "the road to nowhere" by county officials, it was rugged, winding and twisting. However, it was the only road into the valley except for one through the Narrows and the rough Truckhaven Trail.

During the 1930s agriculturalists and land developers had recognized the potential of Borrego Valley, if the all-important water could be provided. Joseph DiGiorgio of DiGiorgio Fruit Corporation had visited the Ensign Ranch and the small scattered ranches in the valley before the war. He was particularly interested in Roy Brininger's grape vineyards, because he was looking for a warm climate in which to grow grapes that could be shipped to Eastern markets ahead of the later-maturing northern California crops. Need for water was paramount and in May, 1945, DiGiorgio persuaded the San Diego Gas and Electric Company to bring a fourteen-mile electric power line into the valley. With electric pumps to tap a water supply, grape production was assured, and in 1946 the corporation purchased 2,000 acres of land and planted vineyards. In 1948 the first crop of Thompson seedless grapes reached New York markets a month before those from other California vineyards.

With the use of hydraulic drilling equipment the DiGiorgio Corporation proved that an ample supply of underground water was present, the first step for any significant development of the valley. Others soon were attracted to the area and began to plant citrus, vegetable, cotton and flower crops. San Diego County officials became interested in the valley's potential again and asked the State Park Commission to return 25 percent of all park lands to the county tax roll to allow agricultural development. However, the park commission reported it could not abandon park lands. By 1950 Borrego Valley was a small agricultural community, and by 1955 there were 3,305 acres under cultivation.

The next person to provide a moving force in the development of Borrego Springs was A. A. Burnand Jr., who envisioned the area as a residential and resort community. In 1936, recognizing the valley's potential, Burnand purchased De Anza Ranch at the entrance of Coyote Canyon, and after the war bought most of the privately owned land in the valley. He negotiated a trade with the state to consolidate both his and state park holdings, and persuaded two Los Angeles businessmen, Lawrence Barker and Paul Grafe, to invest in the project. In September, 1946, the developers disclosed plans for turning Borrego Valley into a winter resort.

Access roads to the San Diego-El Centro-Los Angeles triangle were necessary if the valley population was to grow. Yaqui Pass Road, paved since World War II, was not adequate for the large-scale development planned. Consequently, in the same year, a new road was constructed from the valley to State Highway 78 near Borrego Mountain, and a survey of Coyote Canyon was made to find a possible route for a road to Los Angeles.

In 1947, Burnand, Barker and Grafe formed the Borrego Land and Development Company and began subdividing 1,800 acres of the 10,000 acres owned by the company into one- and two-acre lots. Plans for the residential and recreational resort community, to be named Borrego Springs, were drawn by architects and city planning experts from Palm Springs.

Burnand also introduced resort operators Frank and George Hoberg to Borrego Valley. The Hoberg brothers were looking for a winter resort location, and in August, 1946, chose the valley as the site for their project. They established the third lodge in the valley. The Crickmers had sold the original Desert Lodge to the Burnand family and had opened the Tub Canyon Guest Ranch.

Promotion literature described Borrego Springs as the gateway to the largest state park in the nation, the rival of Palm Springs desert recreational areas, and advertised many features of the park to the public. With new cars rolling off production lines and an ample gasoline supply, Southern Californians began crowding the highways on weekends, exploring Anza Desert State Park, which now offered a paved road and resort accommodations. Other promoters came into Borrego Valley, offering campaigns which prompted significant increases in park visitors between 1946 and 1948.

By 1949, a county airport had been built, bus service was established to San Diego and Jack and Ella Benson offered tours of the valley and park from Hobergs' lodge. First, actor Frank Morgan and then Leo Carrillo officially became honorary mayors. The first issues of the *Borrego Sun* discussed hopes of building a dam in Coyote Canyon, creating a permanent water supply for Borrego Springs and a lake which would be a sportsman's paradise. The first Anza Jeep Cavalcade was held that year to promote a Coyote Canyon Road. Developers also hoped to build a seventeen-mile road through Montezuma Valley to Warner Springs and San Diego and to reconstruct the Truckhaven Trail as a permanently paved highway to the Salton Sea. All of the roads crossing state park lands, except Coyote Canyon Road, have been built.

By the fall of 1948, it became apparent that the park was entering a new stage in its growth. No longer would the half-million-acre park be a one-man caretaker operation. Visitors began exploring remote areas of the park far from the Palm Canyon campground. The phenomenal development of Borrego Valley and the widespread publicity given the area and the park by developers greatly increased administrative problems, according to the State Park commission:

> The advertisements and publicity released by the local valley resorts do not, in our opinion, invite consideration of the fact that the valley is surrounded by state park land where activities are restricted for protection of the natural values. This publicity and advertising suggests hunting, digging in Indian ruins for artifacts, collection of geographical specimens, etc., etc. It has created public interest. Hunters by the dozens and in increasing numbers are invading the park lands. Desert vehicles with four-wheel drive, capable of negotiating the barest trails, radiate out over our lands.

Demands for camp, picnic and trailer facilities increased almost daily. Park attendance skyrocketed to 62,586 persons in 1949, nearly three times greater than the previous season. On one day alone some 5,000 vehicles and 15,000 persons were reported in the park as a result of widespread publicity given to the lush wildflower growth.

It became impossible to protect and manage the park area without a regular crew of trained personnel. In an attempt to meet the new demands, park administration was reorganized and facilities expanded. The staff was increased to seven in order to better manage the newly equipped Palm Canyon campground, which included thirty-seven camp sites and twenty-nine trailer spaces. A new staff residence, office and service building were constructed. Because of the additional facilities, fees were collected from visitors for the first time. A patrol of heavily visited areas, such as Coyote Canyon, Split Mountain and Font's Point was organized. Superintendent William Kenyon, who replaced Guy Fleming in 1947, asked rangers to submit written reports on all-day patrols. One report recounted the attempts of rangers to prevent persons from removing plants from park lands to reset them "at newly built houses in Borrego Springs."

In the winter of 1952-1953, Kenyon ordered regular overnight patrols. Ranger Merle Beckman took food, a map, bedroll and gasoline for a two-day patrol to Dos Cabezas and other southern areas of the park. It was an adventure for Beckman, who had never been south of Blair Valley. The patrol was successful and a permanently designated ranger position was created, and Orville Short was named to it. Short kept himself busy locating state park boundaries, watching for hunting activity and violators of park rules, assisting campers, cleaning refuse from the areas, and noting wildlife and natural features. Short traveled to one of six areas each day, recording his adventures in a daily log.

CITRUS GROVE: *Well water and modern automatic irrigation systems are now being used in the few groves which are planted near Borrego Springs.*

ALONG YAQUI PASS: *Teddy bear, cholla and hedgehog cactus grow near a well-traveled road which goes through the pass and descends to Borrego Springs.*

By 1952 it became apparent that further reorganization was needed if the park was to meet growing demands. With visitors numbering 79,288 that year, it became increasingly difficult to cover all areas of the park from the headquarters. Bids went out for construction of a new campground, residence and workshop at Tamarisk Grove. Plans were also made to divide the park into two separate parks in the following year with separate patrolmen and staff in the hopes of achieving better management of the area. From 1953 to 1957 everything north of State Highway 78, except Tamarisk Grove and Yaqui Pass, fell in Borrego State Park and everything south of it in Anza Desert State Park. The Tamarisk Grove campground became headquarters for the Anza Desert while the Palm Canyon campground remained the administration center for Borrego. In 1953, exploration of outer areas began in earnest as rangers ventured farther afield.

At that time Borrego Springs was experiencing new growth. James S. Copley, William H. Black, and the DiGiorgio Fruit Corporation bought out Burnand's partners in the Borrego Land and Development Company and soon afterward formed the Borrego Valley Golf and Improvement Company, announcing plans to construct the De Anza Desert Country Club and surrounding estates. Other developers, including George J. Kuhrts III, Burnand's stepson, and Frank Morgan, promoted other subdivisions in the valley. The *Borrego Sun* hailed these plans as the "dawn of a new era." It was predicted that by 1970 there would be a seasonal population of at least 7,000 persons. One study concluded:

> Within a few years, Borrego Springs may be a pass town on the De Anza State highway, and compete with Palm Springs for national recognition as a winter resort for the ever-growing population of the metropolitan areas of the Pacific Southwest.

In 1953, A. A. Burnand Jr. made a strong plea before the State Park Commission that it grant a right-of-way to the County of San Diego for a road through Montezuma Valley to Borrego Springs. Burnand stated that unless such a right-of-way was granted, the commission would be responsible for "bottling up" the people of Borrego Valley. He argued that the road would save between forty and forty-five minutes' driving time for a round trip between the junction of Warner Hot Springs and Borrego Springs. Burnand was optimistic about the healing of scars on the desert mountain landscape as a result of construction.

Upon investigation, the Division of Beaches and Parks concluded that the maximum driving time saved would be less than thirty-eight minutes, and the director, Newton B. Drury, felt that a scar on the west wall of Borrego Desert would never completely heal, as "the vegetation is very sparse and the present color of the mountains is caused by centuries of weathering." State Park civil engineer L. D. Ewen Sr. believed the park would not benefit by the road, aside from some possible scenic vistas, which he felt would not outweigh the negative effect on the landscape. Frederick Law Olmsted Jr. had earlier warned about the threat of man-made scars in the 1928 California State Park Survey when he wrote:

> . . . the very conditions which make a desert what it is leave every man-made scar upon its surface so completely unsoftened by natural processes as to produce a rapidly cumulative deterioration of its precious wilderness.

Despite the feelings of the Division of Beaches and Parks, the State Park Commission approved the construction of the road. Park Commissioner Leo Carrillo, a film actor, was honorary mayor of Borrego Springs at the time and possibly influenced the decision. Thus, the first battle for road access to Borrego Valley came to a close. Work on the seventeen-mile road was started in 1955 and completed in 1964.

Additional growth of Borrego Springs and its desire for more access roads took place while both parks were undergoing a period of self-discovery, from 1953 to 1957. Before that time land boundaries were vague and the park staffs had little knowledge of natural and historical features. Under the guidance of Superintendent Kenyon and supervisors Carl Whitefield and James B. Chaffee, an intensive patrol program was instituted in order to further know the parks

ANZA DESERT COUNTRY CLUB: *Golf course greens contrast sharply with the colors of the surrounding desert, and luxury homes line the fairways.*

as well as to control activities within them. Concern over the protection of desert landscape was not limited to Borrego and Anza areas. Groups such as the Desert Protective Council were formed with the purpose of safeguarding for future generations all desert areas of "unique, scenic, scientific, historical, spiritual and recreational value."

During weekdays rangers concentrated on locating section corners and park boundaries, placing signs at all access routes into the park and exploring hitherto unknown areas of both Anza and Borrego parks. Areas such as the Petrified Forest and Sandstone Canyon were discovered. Rangers also gathered valuable historical data and did research into the parks' past. Through the efforts of Patrolman Jack Welch, historical markers were placed along the Anza Trail and the Emigrant Route.

Prospecting and mining, illegal hunting, cleanup, grazing, boundary trespass and visitor safety were the most pressing problems. Tungsten and uranium were the primary minerals sought by prospectors who took little heed for the fact that their digging disturbed the natural landscape. Tungsten was actively mined in Anza Desert Park in the Granite Mountain and Sunrise Highway area until the government stopped buying the metal in 1958. As elsewhere in California, uranium prospectors were also active in the Jacumba Mountains from 1953 to 1955.

An attempt was made to obtain approximately fifty-two sections of land in Imperial County adjacent to the Borrego Badlands, an area which contains the Pumpkin Patch, Giant Sand Dunes, Four Palms Spring, Lone Palm and scenic outlook points which were originally recommended as part of the park by Frederick Law Olmsted Jr. in 1928. Multiple ownership of land combined with shortage of funds and opposition from mining interests, and the Salton City and county officials who thought the parks were large enough, resulted in the deletion of this area from ultimate boundary plans.

Dr. Horace Parker, a veterinarian who became fascinated with the parks in 1954 and began writing news articles about the area, approached Patrolman Welch and asked him to assist in the preparation of an extensive guidebook. With the approval of Superintendent Kenyon, Welch began a two-year period of accompanying Parker in exploration, mapmaking and interviews. The first edition of the guidebook was published in 1957, and Parker subsequently became a state park commissioner.

By 1957 attendance of the combined parks had increased to 389,600, a growth rate of almost 500 percent since the beginning of the patrol system in 1952. The park staffs had only grown to eleven rangers and one naturalist, an increase of 33 percent. Problems had also increased as the population enjoyed greater use of the area in a "desert movement." Rangers no longer could adequately control hunting, destruction of Indian sites, unauthorized use of motor vehicles, vandalism, removal of plant life and fossils, prospecting and mining, fires, grazing and illegal road construction over park lands.

As a result of the distressing situation, the director of the Department of Natural Resources, DeWitt Nelson, told Superintendent Kenyon either to do something about solving the problems or get rid of the parks. Kenyon worked out a control plan and in the fall of 1957 a new park organization was established, setting forth the guidelines still in use in the 1970s.

The two parks were combined again to form Anza-Borrego Desert State Park, and Clyde Strickler was selected as supervisor of the new program. The staff was increased to sixteen and eight patrol districts of about 60,000 acres each, created at Sheep Canyon, Palo Verde, Tamarisk Grove, Blair Valley, Culp Valley, Fish Creek and two districts at Bow Willow. Four new ranger outposts were built and each patrolman was assigned a radio-equipped four-wheel drive vehicle giving them twenty-four-hour contact with park headquarters. Each ranger was trained in tracking, search and rescue. Primitive campgrounds were established at Yaqui Pass, Fish Creek, Blair Valley, Dos Cabezas and Pegleg.

Programs were developed by park naturalist Dalton Merkel to acquaint the public with the park and the desert. A self-guided nature trail was installed at Palm Canyon and the first guided automobile tours to Font's Point and Fish Creek were initiated. The fragile nature of the desert and the importance of saving it for future generations were stressed in these programs. The same theme was carried out in nature walks by patrolmen. Merkel began compiling lists of park plants and animals. It also was the period of university and museum excavations to examine the park's geological and archaeological past.

Under Strickler's supervision, from 1957 to 1965, a system of protection, control and interpretation was established. Many visitors were saved from possibly serious mishaps when lost, and were assisted in other ways by the rangers, especially during summer months. A positive change also was noted in those years in the growing public respect for the parklands.

However, because of the great size of the park, the new system was not without problems. Considerable poaching occurred, off-road vehicles left track patterns over thin-crusted mud hills and desert landscapes. Commercial nurserymen gathered desert plants, and snake collectors frequented desert roads during spring and summer nights. There was significant removal of Indian artifacts, petrified wood, fossils and concretions. Prospecting, mining and grazing continued. The famed palms of Borrego Palm Canyon suffered when twenty acres of the canyon were blackened with fire in 1961. Private lands located within park boundaries also caused problems when owners developed their holdings with roads, buildings and clearings in previously undisturbed natural areas.

The never-ending battle for access roads into Borrego Valley also continued. Negotiations for a road into Coyote Canyon had begun in earnest in 1946, although no official alignment was considered by the San Diego Board of Supervisors until 1954, when state highway engineers surveyed the shortest practical route. Members of the Borrego Valley Soil Conservation District announced that such an alignment would need flood control, and recommended channelization of the Coyote Canyon wash.

In 1955, the San Diego County Planning Commission conducted public hearings on the proposed master plan for Borrego roads which included the Coyote Canyon Road, Montezuma Valley Road and the Truckhaven Trail. Approval had already been given to the Montezuma Road by the State Park Commission in 1953. At the November 21, 1958, meeting of the State Park Commission a vote was taken on the fate of Coyote Canyon. The commission voted unanimously in favor of the proposal, but the road alignment was ultimately rejected by the California Department of Parks and Recreation.

Conservationists have long fought to protect Coyote Canyon, described by Horace Parker as "perhaps the best known, best watered, most scenic, most historical, and most used area in the park." In 1957, members of the Desert Protective Council and of the State Park Commission met and decided not to oppose the construction of the Truckhaven Trail, which was completed in 1968 and renamed the Borrego-Salton Seaway. They believed that Borrego Springs residents might abandon the Coyote Canyon proposition due to this road's construction.

The next attempt to get a road through Coyote Canyon came indirectly through the efforts of the Bechtel Corporation, the California Gas Transmission Company, and the Southern California Edison Company, when in 1961 they began looking for possible gas pipeline routes across Anza-Borrego Desert State Park, and found Coyote Canyon to be the most economical route. On the recommendation of the San Diego County road department, Bechtel Corporation bought rights-of-way in private lands held in the canyon, but opposition from the Department of Parks and Recreation, the State Park Commission, and from residents of Borrego Springs forced these companies in 1962 to withdraw their application from the Public Utilities Commission. This particular battle marked the first time that a segment of Borrego Springs residents became concerned about "their" park.

With the completion of the Montezuma Road in 1964 and the Borrego-Salton Seaway in 1968, it became easier to reach some areas within the park. However, major cutbacks in the park budget caused by state fiscal policies led to the loss of three patrolmen and four ranger outposts in Sheep Canyon, Culp Valley, Palo Verde and Blair Valley. The park also lost one relief patrol-

An approximate outline of the Anza-Borrego Desert State Park is shown in this artist's relief map which includes San Diego and Imperial Counties as well as part of Riverside County and Mexico. The park, which covers nearly a half-million acres, is a region of varying landscapes and unique geologic formations. In the foreground is the City of San Diego, tightly nestled along the Pacific Ocean and surrounded by its satellite suburbs. East of the park lies the flourishing Imperial Valley, where agriculture depends upon irrigation water from the Colorado River, seen on the southern horizon as it flows into Mexico on its way to the Gulf of California. The mountains between San Diego and the park contribute to the aridity because they prevent rain from crossing over into the desert. East of the Anza-Borrego is the Salton Sea where it is 273 feet below sea level. (Map Copyright by Cooper Enterprises of La Jolla.)

ARIZONA
SONORA
MEXICO
IMPERIAL
VALLEY
SALTON
SEA
MEXICALI
BAJA
CALIFORNIA
NATIONAL CITY
CHULA VISTA
SAN
DIEGO
BAY
SALT EVAPORATION BASINS
SILVER
STRAND
BEACH
STATE
PARK
Pacific
Ocean
JACK MOFFETT
70

man and was without an officially designated naturalist for one year. In the interim Ranger Ernest Brown functioned as naturalist until 1968 when he was officially appointed.

While manpower was reduced, park attendance doubled to 600,000. The increase of off-road vehicles, motorcycles and dune buggies, and their indiscriminate use, left a toll of destruction of natural vegetation and mud hills. The task of keeping the park clean became overwhelming. During a major holiday weekend one ranger reported:

> At 1320 I spotted a rockhound club digging rocks in Palm Wash. I made them stop digging and move out, explaining that pretty rocks are our only decoration here in the desert.
>
> At 1410 hours found a group of bikes (27 in all) have a jackrabbit race on the sand flat in the vicinity of Basin Wash. They stated they felt this was OK because when the sand blew, their tracks would fill in.
>
> At 1440 hours a group of 39 bikes doing the same thing in Basin Wash; and at 1510 hours found 21 bikes having their race in Bank Wash.
>
> At 0730 counted 97 campers before I had gone 10 miles, and each camper had from two to four motorcycles attached to the camper or on trailers.
>
> At 1010 hours caught a lady washing dishes in the spring at Seventeen Palms Oasis. I asked her if she would like soap in her drinking water.
>
> A dune buggy club, 51 in all, visited Arroyo Salada restrooms this morning all at once. What a line-up! Then I cleaned them again.
>
> At 1510 hours I am in Font's Wash and it looks like Cox's Army went through here. Dune buggy and bike tracks all over the place. I visited this wash twice on Friday, once on Saturday, and one today, but they seem to know when I am coming because there's never a dune buggy or bike in sight when I am present.

Despite the setbacks, there were some improvements. Self-guided automobile tours to major areas of the park were initiated, as well as a sky tour for pilots of private planes. The Anza-Borrego committee of the Desert Protective Council was formed in 1967 and began to acquire parcels of private land within the boundaries of the park through purchases, gifts and memorial presentation. By 1972 the committee had $26,000 and purchased 1,340 acres of the 67,000 acres of private holdings. Grazing ended in 1972 when park commissioners refused to renew concessions. Also in 1972 all off-road vehicles had to be registered and were allowed only on maintained roads or designated routes. Though there were fewer park rangers, they were better trained, and through a federally funded program, an archaeologist and a naturalist were added to the staff.

Perhaps the best thing that happened to the park was an increased understanding on the part of many residents in Borrego Springs. From the beginning of the development of the town, business interests had pushed for a Palm Springs-type resort and predicted a rapid growth during the 1960s and 1970s. However, they had to be satisfied with a slow but steady growth. The Hobergs eventually sold their property and the developers of the $4,000,000 Borrego Springs Park on the Ensign Ranch placed their investment on the auction block. The slow pace of development and attitudes concerning the future were partly the result of Borrego Springs' location and the problem of roads leading through state park lands.

In the late 1950s there was a difference of opinion as to the direction Borrego Springs should take as a community. In 1959, the Borrego Valley Associates printed an article entitled "Progress" which declared:

> It is wonderful to see vineyards, grass, homes, farms, stores, and other symbols of progress where once there was only desert, but, isn't it wonderful, too, to see places where the desert will look the same to our grandchildren—as we see it now?

However, during another episode of the Coyote Canyon road battle, also in 1959, the president of the Chamber of Commerce wrote an irate letter to the editor of the *Borrego Sun*:

> I am wondering how long we as a community of roughly 2,000 people can afford the over-protective attitude of organizations such as the Desert Protective Council and the San Diego Chapter of the Sierra Club. I am sure they are all well

> meaning people but when they take the attitude that they must stop progress and growth of a community to save it for posterity, I feel for our own survival we must speak out.

Residents of Borrego Springs expressed two points of view on the future growth of the area. One group, which was the most vocal, hoped to speed development and business opportunities as expressed by the Chamber of Commerce and persistently pushed for a road through Coyote Canyon. The other group, fearing that expansion would bring an end to the peace and quiet of the desert community, opposed the Coyote Canyon Road and were instrumental in the formation of the Anza-Borrego Natural History Association in 1971. However, the association's membership reflected both points of view and took no official position on the Coyote Canyon Road question. Instead, it supported efforts to open a desert museum, sponsored field trips and lectures which helped to educate the public in preserving park values and natural features, and actively participated in annual bighorn sheep tallies.

Some business interests continued to blame the park for slow progress. Valley population fluctuated almost monthly and in 1973 permanent residents numbered about a thousand, with perhaps five hundred or more persons as seasonal residents at vacation homes. New motels had appeared, the old Desert Lodge had been converted into a quiet hotel called La Casa del Zorro, and residential structures were rising from the sand.

Rangers have worked hard to improve the park image and its relationship to the community. The staff assisted in the annual Borrego Desert Festival, was active in community affairs and presented lecture and slide programs to community groups. However, residents in Borrego Springs continued to challenge park policies, especially in regard to the building of a "recreational parkway" through Coyote Canyon. The Carrizo Impact Area remained closed because of unexploded military ordnance. The park remained open to mining and prospecting, and adverse development of private land holdings within park boundaries was a constant challenge to conservation groups. The number of people misusing the park also continued.

Such problems have not been unique to the Anza-Borrego Desert State Park. In 1970 the United States Department of the Interior conducted a study and found that the difficulties were universal to the sixteen million acres of California desert land:

> The wide open spaces of the desert beckon to millions of Americans. In this untrammeled landscape, the great urban population of Southern California, only a few miles away, can find relaxation from the pressures of city life. . . . Long considered a wasteland, the California Desert . . . is now recognized as a fragile area where the natural balance is easily upset. It is rich in a multitude of resources: minerals, unique vegetation and wildlife, historical and archaeological values, and unparalleled scenery. But the inroads of our civilization are already evident on the desert: air pollution, solid waste disposals, scars on the land surface, accidental destruction, and wanton vandalism. We can no longer afford such losses.

ELEPHANTS' KNEES: *They get their name from shapes created by irregular erosion on the strata exposed along this bluff in the Carrizo Badlands.*

The Mirages and the Myths

A story of the Anza-Borrego Desert would be incomplete without added tales of mystery—of lost ships, gold mines and strange apparitions.

Most cultures have had myths and legends. They are usually an attempt to explain the cause of something which people see or experience, and often become part of the religious and ceremonial life of a society. Modern science makes use of a "cause and effect" approach, but mythology works in reverse—it observes an effect and then creates an easily understood cause to explain it.

The Diegueño and Cahuilla myths are not unlike those of other primitive cultures. Their purpose was simple, to explain why things appeared as they did and how they got to be that way, whether it was the color of a rock or the tune a bird sings.

Everything around man was important, and one of the most important questions concerned how the earth had been formed and how people came to be placed on it. One Diegueño creation myth taught that in the beginning everything was covered by a great salt sea, under the surface of which lived two brothers. The brothers kept their eyes closed so they would not be blinded by the salt. But, finally the elder brother, Tcaipakomat, rose to the surface to look over his domain. He saw nothing but more water. His younger brother, Yokomat, also rose to the surface, but he opened his eyes and, being blinded by the water, saw nothing at all so returned to the deep darkness of the sea. Tcaipakomat, seeing the vast watery desolation, created land out of the bodies of many red ants. Then he created black, flat-billed birds, but since it was still dark, the birds became lost and could not find a place to roost. Tcaipakomat took clay, shaped it into a round plate, then threw it up into the sky where it stuck, giving off a dim light. The plate was called the moon, but it was not bright enough. Taking more clay and shaping it into another disk, Tcaipakomat threw it into the other side of the sky, where it made everything bright and was called the sun. With yet another piece of clay he created man, and from a rib of man he made woman. They and their children—called *ipai,* people—lived at a great mountain in the east, and the sounds of their singing and dancing can still be heard there, for that is where they go when they die—back to the place where everything was first created.

There are variations of creation myths, even within individual tribal groups. Although many of them have been recorded only since 1900, they have existed within the Indian oral tradition for centuries. Some elements of particular stories have overtones of European and Middle Eastern tales incorporated in them. The creation of man through the use of clay is not unusual among primitive people who made utilitarian objects from clay themselves. But the addition of man's rib being used to create woman has a Judaic-Christian element which anthropologists believe to be only a later gloss—or interpretation—inherited from Christian missionaries. However, an old Campo Indian who related this story to an anthropologist in the early years of the Twentieth Cenutry was a *bronco* (unbaptized) who called himself a Kamiyai. He apparently never was under the influence of the missions, and presumably would have had little occasion to learn stories from the Book of Genesis.

Accounts of great floods are universal in primitive myths and often include stories of the world being destroyed by water. The Old Testament story of Noah, the Babylonian flood story and tales of floods wrecking destruction in the Nile River region are perhaps the best known. The Diegueño story uses water as a source of creation, but the isolated desert Indians who continued to retell the stories of a Creator living deep in salt water which covered the earth, had little way of knowing in their own time that many square miles of their desert wasteland was once covered by just such a sea. It would have been an element passed down through the centuries—the factor of "racial memory"—and would have become a fixed part of the story.

In what today is called the Carrizo Impact Area, the Diegueños were familiar with Red Rock. To explain why it was red they chose things they knew—the rock, the coyote and death. According to the oral tradition of the Cuyamaca Mountain Diegueños, Coyote was not trusted by his brothers and sisters. They even thought he wanted to eat the body of his father. When the old man died, the animals sent Coyote far away on an unnecessary errand hoping to perform the customary funeral rites before he returned.

However, Coyote saw the billowing smoke of the funeral pyre, and on it the charred remains of his father's body. Leaping over the mourning guards he snatched the unburned heart from the pyre and raced east across valleys and mountains. Finally in the desert, Coyote stopped on a hill and there ate the heart. As he did, drops of blood fell and ruddy hues formed on the ground surrounding him. Soon the entire hillside was covered and the rock forever remained red.

Red Rock later provided the raw material from which the Diegueños extracted pigment for the crimson paint they used to barter for goods with the mountain tribes. Thus, the wiley coyote enters the myth cycle for both his treachery in stealing the heart of his father and also in his helpfulness to the desert Indians in providing them with a valuable commodity.

The personification of animals is not unusual in primitive cultures, and present day society provides a counterpart in fairy tales which give voice and human characteristics to bears, crickets and fish, although few such modern stories are as grisly as that of Coyote. The principle is the same and the accounts use a familiar vehicle through which to teach a moral lesson or explain a natural phenomenon. Animals formed an integral part of Indian life and many folk myths which the tribes created concerned those creatures with which they were all familiar. The Cahuillas had animals as central figures in legends concerning the origin of objects or occurrences. One such story was their delightful tale of the reason mockingbirds sing as they do:

> Before our tribe came from the north, only birds and other creatures inhabited the desert. For as long as anyone can remember, the birds had been happy with their desert life—until they began listening to migratory birds who regaled them with stories about other places far more lush and abundant than their home.
>
> During one unusually hot and dry year the birds, now made unhappy by the tales they had heard, assembled and decided to leave their arid surroundings in search of a better life. They flew north together—all, that is, except Mockingbird. After a while the weather in their new land turned cold, everything began to freeze and food became scarce. The errant birds once more flocked together and decided to return to the desert where they knew it would be warm. However, only a few of them survived the trip and, so they would never forget the terrible times they had been through, it was agreed that each one would compose a song to describe his experience.
>
> Daily they sang their melancholy ballads until Mockingbird became so troubled and confused by the sorrowful melodies around her she forgot her own happy tune. Ever since then, Mockingbird sings only parts of other birds' songs.

Some universal myths are also found among the tribes of the Anza-Borrego Indians. Cahuilla mothers told their children that evil spirits punished wicked boys and girls, and such techniques for controlling the behavior of children have never been unique to any particular society or era.

Few objects escaped a role in story-telling. At night the vast, cloudless heavens stretched like a sparkling canopy over the desert, and the stars became something all men shared in common. As they gazed up into the night sky they saw yet

SETTING OUT: *Noted for her authentic paintings of scenes along the historic Butterfield Mail route, Marjorie Reed (now Marjorie Reed Creese) also is well known for her bold and colorful portrayals of San Diego's back country. Commissioned by Copley Books, she has recorded on canvas the remnants of the once-booming gold town of Banner as it appeared after the exciting days of the gold rush were over. It was from Banner at the foot of the Cuyamaca Mountains that many solitary prospectors set off into the Anza-Borrego Desert in search of wealth. Most would find nothing but disappointment in the rugged and hostile landscape.*

further adventures, and both Diegueños and Cahuillas passed down to their children the dramas they saw unfold above them.

The Milky Way, they explained, was the dust kicked up by Coyote and Wildcat as they raced each other across the dark sky. The stars in Orion's belt were mountain sheep and the constellation's sword was an arrow shot at them by a hunter who was the bright star Rigel. Dancing and jumping stars seen near the horizon were especially placed there by Mukat the Creator to amuse his children, perhaps to keep them entertained and happy in an otherwise desolate land. The Diegueños even had a deep canyon they called "look at stars canyon" (*kwiluphawu* or *kwitup*), from the bottom of which they said they could see the stars during the daytime.

Much later in the day of the White man, legends became more sophisticated. Stories of rocks, coyotes and mockingbirds were replaced by tales of treasure, and as the stories were retold the treasure became greater and the circumstances surrounding it grew even more mysterious. One of the most persistent mysteries was a lost ship in the Colorado Desert. A small amount of fact and a great deal of fantasy have become so confused that it remains a chief legend of the former inland sea. Indian tales of mystery ships going up the Colorado perhaps arose from the early Spanish explorations of Hernando de Alarcón, who entered the Gulf of California in 1540 and experienced the terrifying effects of the tidal bore which pushed against the on-rushing Colorado River. Unable to sail farther north, he sent a number of small boats up the river, at least as far as Yuma and perhaps even farther upstream. He became the first White man, as far as it is known, to see the mountains of California. Along the river he was welcomed by the Yuma Indians and, being handsomely garbed, he told them he was the Son of the Sun.

Though Alarcón retired to Mexico, the legend of a lost ship in the desert persisted and a mystery vessel has been described variously as a Viking boat, a Chinese ship, a Spanish pearler and an English corsair's ship laden with treasure from the Spanish Main. Presumably the phantom ship sailed up the Gulf of California into the flooded Colorado basin and was abandoned when the water receded. Sightings of the land-locked ship have been reported geographically as far separated as the Yuha Desert, Carrizo Badlands and the Fish Creek-Split Mountain area.

In 1892 a Mexican named Santiago Socia claimed to have seen it in a narrow box canyon. He described it as a big, open vessel, half-buried in the sand and having many large, round metal objects attached to its sides. Six years later an Indian, Jesús Almanerez, supposedly sighted the ship in the Yuha Desert. He described it as a large, copper-plated canoe having a long "neck" topped with the head of a beast. Deciding the ship was a bad sign, he left the area in great haste.

Later stories which presumably described Viking ships could well be corruptions of similar tales concerning Chinese visitors. In the Sixteenth Century a Spanish narrator, Captain Pedro Monge, reported that a patrol of the expedition of Francisco Coronado, while exploring north along the mainland coast of Mexico, claimed it had found strange looking men near the mouth of the Colorado River. The men, working metal from slag brought there from some unknown region of the interior, indicated by signs that they had come across the ocean in ships having carved pelicans as figureheads.

However, other stories do point to the Norsemen whose ships crossed the Atlantic Ocean to the American continent centuries before Columbus. Even though there is no evidence of their activities in the Pacific, the Seri Indians of Tiburon Island off the west coast of Sonora in the Gulf of California had stories and songs about large, blue-eyed, fair-complexioned men who arrived at their island in a long boat powered by many oars. A version of the Seri legend also says that these strange sailors were accompanied by a woman who had her hair fixed in long braids reaching down her back. These strangers, who fit the description of Vikings, lived with the tribe for about a year before sailing away with four Indian families. They promised to bring their passengers back when they returned. However, neither the strangers nor their hapless Indian guests were ever seen again.

The story of a lost pearl ship has its origin

in a novel which combines both fact and fiction. In the early Seventeenth Century, it is said, such a ship sailed north into the Gulf of California, laden with the harvest of a successful season of pearl gathering. Its captain now sought the Straits of Anían, the legendary link between the two great oceans. Passing through a narrow and shallow channel the ship entered an inland sea and a few days later it was trapped by the lowering water level. The captain was forced to give up the ship and its treasure.

According to legend, a muleteer on an Anza expedition, one hundred and sixty years later, discovered the vessel two or three days march out of Yuma. Taking what pearls he could carry, he left the expedition and crossed the desert toward San Diego. Later, it is told he returned for more pearls but was unable to locate the ship. However, there are no official reports suggesting any such event of desertion.

A third possibility for the desert ship's identity has been assigned to the pirate vessel of Thomas Cavendish. Supposedly loaded with gold, silver, silks and perfume taken from captured Spanish galleons, she was last seen by a sister ship in November, 1587, rounding Cape San Lucas and entering the Gulf of California. It is possible that the ship's captain also was searching for the Straits of Anían and a shortcut to England.

The skeleton of the pirate ship may have been the one reported in 1923 by a solitary prospector called "Butcherknife Ike." Camping on the side of a sand dune near Split Mountain Canyon, he built a small fire to heat his dinner before turning in for the night. Although he added no more fuel to the fire the flames continued to burn brightly. During the night the prospector was awakened by rekindled flames, and, digging into the sand, found wooden beams, one of which was keeping the fire burning. In the morning he dug deeper and uncovered more beams, some encrusted with barnacles. After relating the story to Adelaide Arnold of Hemet, "Butcherknife Ike" set out again into the desert and was last seen in Borrego Valley headed toward the badlands.

However, the desert mirage is a possible explanation for the lost ship phenomenon. Both Signal Mountain and Superstition Mountain have been fashioned into the shape of a Spanish galleon by employing a combination of imagination and the distortion caused by heat waves.

Yet, there actually were two ships found in the desert, and the history of each is a matter of record. One, the steamer *Explorer,* commanded by Lieutenant Joseph C. Ives, was the first used to chart the Colorado River in 1858. Some years later it was wrecked and the hulk was not found until 1928, half-buried in the silt of the river delta.

The other vessel was a twenty-one foot skiff built in Los Angeles in 1862. It was designed for use in crossing the Colorado River on the way to the gold mines in La Paz, Arizona. Soon after being placed on wheels to be hauled across the desert, the animals pulling it became exhausted and the boat was abandoned far short of its destination. Within a few years it had become the subject of many stories, and in 1870 an expedition was organized by Charles Clusker to search for the lost ship. The expedition found it about thirty miles west of Dos Palmas near the San Bernardino and Fort Yuma Road. But, since no valuables were aboard either of those more modern vessels, the legends of old treasure-laden ships persist.

The most sought-after treasure of the Anza-Borrego Desert is not a ship, but gold—and more specifically the fabulous "Pegleg" gold mine, the most famous lost mine in the Southwest.

Thomas Long Smith was an Indian fighter, horse thief, trader, trapper, adventurer and storyteller. Born in Kentucky in 1801, he went on his first trapping and trading expedition into Kansas and Nebraska territory in 1820. In succeeding years he traveled through the west with other mountain men, including Jedediah Smith, Ewing Young, Thomas Fitzpatrick, Ceran St. Vrain, Sylvester Pratte and Milton Sublette.

In 1827, Smith's left leg was shattered by an Indian arrow. With the help of Sublette, Smith amputated his own foot, and while he was recovering, his friends made him a wooden leg and christened him "Pegleg" Smith. After a summer rendezvous at Bear Lake Valley the following year, Smith joined a group that trapped in the Virgin River area of Utah and, in early 1829

A MINE IN THE DESERT: *The entrance to an old deserted mine in Borrego Buttes frames the denuded and twisting badlands of Borrego seen in the background.*

reportedly crossed the desert to the Mexican pueblo of Los Angeles to sell the party's pelts.

Pegleg later claimed to have picked up a few black pebbles he found scattered atop one of three buttes in the Anza-Borrego area, but he said it was not until he reached Los Angeles that he found the pebbles to be gold. Apparently he was not interested in gold at that time, because he sold the pelts and used some of the money to buy whiskey. Intoxicated, he became involved in a fight and was ordered out of town by the *alcalde*. Leaving California, he acquired between three hundred and four hundred horses which he herded to Taos, New Mexico, to sell.

As the fur trade declined in the 1830s, Smith settled among friendly Ute Indians and became a trader, specializing in horses which he procured from California ranchos. For the next several years he apparently had a profitable business, and in the early 1840s established a trading post along the Oregon Trail at Bear River, Idaho. He did not leave Idaho until after the discovery of gold in California.

In 1850, Smith again returned to Los Angeles and interested a party in searching for his lost gold. They wandered about the desert unsuccessfully and Pegleg reportedly deserted them to later reappear empty-handed in Los Angeles. Again in 1853 he failed to find the three buttes and a third expedition the next year which attempted to locate the gold ledge that trapper "Dutch George" Yount supposedly found in 1826 or 1827 in the Virgin River area was also a failure.

Pegleg Smith spent his last colorful days in the San Francisco area, drinking and spinning yarns about his fabulous lost gold mine. According to Major Horace Bell, a contemporary of Smith's, Pegleg was "the most superlative liar that ever honored California with his presence." Bell believed the mine was nothing but a lie conceived by Smith to obtain free whiskey.

After he died on October 15, 1866, the legend of his gold mine continued to grow. His own death may be considered the beginning of the now-popularized story of the lost gold mine of Pegleg Smith.

The location of the fabled buttes was moved about in the Anza-Borrego Desert as the story continued to be retold and enlarged. Some students of the legend preferred the Chocolate Mountains, on the eastern edge of the Colorado Desert, but wherever the three buttes were located —if indeed they did exist—the majority of old-time prospectors claimed to have seen either the buttes or the gold, or at least to have come "very close" to finding them.

Because of the many contradictory stories surrounding the mystery of Pegleg Smith and his lost gold mine, other "Peglegs" were bound to be created in the minds of treasure hunters. One of them appears to have been John O. Smith, a guide and horse trader who in crossing the desert from Yuma to Warner's ranch attempted to find a shortcut through the Borrego Badlands. It was on that trip in 1852 that he claimed to have found the three buttes, one of which had black-coated nuggets on it. Thinking them to be copper, he took only a few and continued his journey to Los Angeles where he discovered the pieces he had were not copper, but gold. However, Smith was never successful in relocating the site from which he said they had come.

A few years later, a former soldier from Fort Yuma followed the same route as John Smith and insisted he also found the buttes and the gold. He showed samples to some friends and later led them into the desert to search for the site. Their bodies were reportedly found sometime later in the foothills of the San Ysidro Mountains.

In 1869, a miner also following a route between Yuma and Warner's ranch, climbed a hill to determine his location and discovered it was covered with particles of free gold. Emptying his saddle bags he refilled them with about $7,000 in gold, then resumed his journey to Los Angeles. After arriving he became ill and, before his death, was treated by a Dr. DeCourcy, whom he took into his confidence. For many years DeCourcy unsuccessfully conducted his own search for the gold.

According to another story, two Frenchmen discovered gold in the desert and one of them went to the mining town of Banner where he bragged about his mine and showed samples of the nuggets. He was later shot, but before he

EYE-CATCHING FLASH: *The sun's rays reflect off the mirror-like surface of a piece of pure gypsum embedded toward the top of a crusted mudhill.*

ABANDONED SHACK NEAR DOS CABEZAS: *Thorn-studded ocotillo became building material years ago and perhaps sheltered a miner or cattleman.*

died told a Negro named Jim Green the location of the mine. The other Frenchman disappeared, but from that time on Green, who worked in the Banner saloon, apparently always had a supply of gold. Green loaned money to friends and even purchased property in the Julian area.

Not all of the stories of lost gold concerned trappers and guides. Indians also supposedly had knowledge of gold in the area. In the 1870s an Indian woman, who had crossed the desert without water, staggered exhausted into a railroad construction camp and related that from the top of one of *tres picachos* she had sighted the smoke of the camp. Later she showed the crewmen black-coated nuggets which she had found on the hill and gave one to the chief engineer. Soon after she left the camp and was never seen again.

A Yaqui Indian from Sonora married a Diegueño woman from Grapevine Canyon and in the 1880s lived near what was later to be called Yaqui Well. Some time after he moved to Warner's ranch and worked in the area, making periodic trips into the desert whenever he needed money. Because he reportedly had a supply of black-coated nuggets, he was followed whenever he left for his desert forays, but no one was able to track him to the source of the gold. After the Yaqui was killed in a fight, $4,000 in gold was found in his bunk. His wife was questioned about directions to the location of the gold, but said only that her husband left at dawn, traveled east, and arrived at the gold sometime in the afternoon. The location may have been anywhere between Oriflamme Mountain and the Borrego Badlands.

The story of Thomas W. Cover, a Riverside sheriff, has led some to believe that the gold of the Yaqui Indian and that of Pegleg Smith were one and the same, and that it may be located in the Borrego Badlands. Cover met the Yaqui in the desert while he was searching for horse thieves. However, it is also possible that he may have talked to Dr. DeCourcy about the gold of the miner he had treated. Although it is not clear how many expeditions were made by Cover, one source relates he made several. On his last trip, in 1884, he was accompanied by a friend, Wilson Russell, who later reported that Cover actually had a map with directions to Pegleg's mine. He took the map with him and disappeared into the desert. Even those sources which do not indicate whether Cover had a map, do agree that he had knowledge of gold being located at the foot of the Santa Rosa Mountains in the Borrego Badlands. Cover was last seen in Borrego Valley near the mouth of Coyote Creek. Russell searched for his friend for two days, but Cover was never seen again.

Charlie McCloud, of Julian, first became interested in Pegleg's gold when he heard of Cover's search for the mine. Until his death in 1939, McCloud searched for the gold, never doubting its existence.

One thing that most prospectors are said to have in common is the blind faith and determination that they would discover the lost Pegleg mine. Always, they were on the verge of discovery, and their hope of "striking it rich" was sustained by the occasional prospector who claimed he did find gold.

As early as 1900, Henri Brandt, a French-Canadian of German ancestry, allegedly found gold in either the Superstition, Vallecito or Fish Creek mountains. For eight successive years he left his home in San Diego during the spring, and after a few months in the desert would go to Riverside where he would ship about $4,000 in gold to the San Francsico Mint. Unlike the black-coated gold nuggets of Pegleg Smith, Brandt's gold was in quartz veins.

Before his death, Brandt disclosed the location of his mine to a friend. The friend in turn allowed others to see the directions, but because they were confusing, no one was ever able to find the site. The only thing that was clear from the directions was that the gold presumably was located about three hours' walking distance to the northeast of Brandt's shack, which was east of the old Carrizo stage station. That also created problems because Brandt was crippled and walked slowly. Some people believe the mine is located within a radius of one mile from Fish Creek Mountains, part of the area within the now-closed Carrizo Impact Area.

Henry Wilson spent more than fifty years

DESERT MYSTIQUE: *The mystery of the desert, which has given rise to so many mirages and legends, is expressed in this painting of the northwest end of Borrego Valley. Hamilton G. Stalnaker Jr. is well known for his paintings of the sea as well as the desert. He is a frequent exhibitor throughout Southern California and Hawaii, and has won many first place awards in art shows in San Diego.*

Stalnaker studied art at San Diego State College under Everett G. Jackson and after World War II resumed his work with such artists as Orren Louden, Belle Baranceanu, Thelma Underhill, Ben Messick and Fred Hocks. He also studied at the former San Diego School of Arts and Crafts in La Jolla where he later taught landscape and marine painting. He maintains a studio in Spring Valley, California.

searching for the gold after thinking he saw the legendary three buttes in the early 1900s. Prospecting with Borrego homesteader John Collins somewhere between Seventeen Palms and Fish Creek, he saw three hills. Part of one was covered with black rock, but since he already was lagging behind, he made a mental note of the location and hurried to rejoin Collins. He was never able to find the hills or the black rock again.

In September of 1914 a young cowboy named Harry Yarnell and a Cahuilla Indian, Julian Cabrias, were driving cattle from Valley Center to Imperial Valley for winter feeding and made camp in Earthquake Valley. There the Indian showed Yarnell a half-dozen gold nuggets he had picked up in a gully on the way. Cabrias took Yarnell to the mouth of the gully where the cowboy constructed a rock cairn to mark the site. By the time Yarnell returned to the site, a flash flood had destroyed the cairn, and for years afterward he fruitlessly searched various gullies of the Oriflamme region for the gold.

John Mitchell, author of many tales of lost gold, also claimed to have first found, and then lost, Pegleg's gold in the mid-1920s. He collected three black nuggets at the east end of the Chuckwalla and Chocolate mountains. He found them while climbing a hill looking for a meteor crater he had been told about. Not until years later, Mitchell said, did he break off the black crust of the three nuggets and find they were gold.

Twenty years after Mitchell's report, an army sergeant assigned to an armored unit conducting maneuvers in the Mojave and Colorado deserts, claimed to have found $3,000 worth of Pegleg's black gold. While on leave from his station he prospected in the Borrego Badlands and reportedly found a low cave or crevice near the top of a hill. There, next to a human skeleton, he found saddlebags containing twenty pounds of black gold. He took it but never reported the incident. In 1945, while stationed in Italy, he told another soldier about the gold and said he thought there could be more in the area. However, he was afraid to return because he might get into difficulty for not reporting his discovery and might even have to surrender the gold to the government.

Fred Harvey also claimed to have found gold during the early 1940s. Harvey was duck hunting with a friend at the Salton Sea when a *chubasco* began blowing in from the Gulf of California. They hurriedly started back toward San Diego, but poor visibility caused them to stop somewhere west of Plaster City on the banks of Coyote Wash. The storm already had blown away about three feet of sand and even exposed the bedrock in many places. Noting some black rocks, they picked up a few and upon arriving in San Diego, discovered the rocks were gold. When they returned to the site, the desert floor again was covered with a thick blanket of sand. Later, they returned equipped with metal detectors but found only a few widely-scattered nuggets.

While some prospectors set off into the desert in quest of Pegleg Smith's legendary lost gold and hope of instant riches, some men did find their fortunes in the surrounding mountains.

Although about $7,000,000 in gold was taken from the San Diego County mines beginning in 1870, there was only one reported gold mine producing in the present park area. Originally two separate claims—Lincoln Ledge and Warpath—the mine was named Oriflamme when patented in 1882 by E. W. Morse. Located on the west side of Oriflamme Creek Canyon, its peak production was probably between 1870 and 1885, although sporadic work continued until 1905. It is estimated that less than $25,000 came from the Oriflamme Mine, and an attempt to get it into operation in the mid-1920s proved unsuccessful.

West of the desert, rich strikes also were made in 1870, several at the mountain community of Julian and others near Banner, on the desert road from Julian. The Washington and Stonewall Jackson were important Julian mines and in the Banner area there were the Ready Relief, Golden Chariot, Redman and Ranchita.

Gold was also found in the rugged Cargo Muchacho Mountains east of the desert, with perhaps as much as $13,000,000 being taken from the earth.

During the early 1940s the Roberts Mine,

just inside the park in the San Diego County, was actively producing celestite, a major source of strontium material, used in the manufacture of explosives and in certain steel-hardening processes. Although the mine was closed in 1946, small amounts of celestite were brought out as late as 1957. Prospecting on park land has greatly diminished over the years, but there is still some being done.

Many people have searched for gold or "sighted" lost ships in the formerly uncharted wastelands, while others have seen apparitions which both fascinated and terrified them.

In 1892, prospector Charles Knowles told of seeing lights that resembled fireballs exploding in mid-air on the western edge of the Valley. One plausible theory used to explain this particular phenomenon has been that Knowles saw signal fires built by people smuggling Chinese emigrants into the United States from Mexico.

In legends concerning the different gold mines, ghosts also wandered the desert. Skeletons were reported guarding mines, one being described as having flickering light in its chest that shone out through its ribs.

An "apparition" that can be seen by park visitors is located on a mountain northeast of Borrego Valley. With a little imagination a strange-looking natural scar can be fashioned into an angel. As with the ancient Indian myths, a story was created to account for the angel's presence. Supposedly the second Anza expedition, one which included women and children, became lost in the Borrego Valley while journeying north to build a settlement at San Francisco. An angel appeared to them and pointed the way to Coyote Canyon which led to Mission San Gabriel, thus saving the expedition and ensuring its safety and success. Official records make no mention of such a phenomenon and it is notable that Anza placed more faith in Indian guides than in imaginary angels.

Park visitors can also see the "tracks" of ancient dinosaurs at Split Mountain. For many years stories circulated that indeed they were tracks from the days when giant reptiles once roamed the earth. However, the tracks have subsequently been proven to be the result of a peculiar erosion in the sandstone.

Whether or not lost ships, gold mines or apparitions truly exist in the park is not really important, for the real treasure is the enjoyment the legends create. They are only one aspect of a many-faceted desert gem. The Anza-Borrego Desert has been, and will continue to be, many things to many people. In addition to its beauty, romance and mystery, it is a home, an outdoor laboratory and school, a playground and refuge, a source of wealth, a place of quiet enchantment and a battleground for developers and environmentalists.

But more importantly, it is a trust for future generations of people who will find their own special relationship with our historic desert.

Author's Acknowledgments

This book is based on a thesis submitted for a Master's degree which is on file at San Diego State University. The purpose of the study was twofold: first, to provide a much-needed overall picture of such a large and significant park to researchers and those interested in park interpretation, management and conservation; and second, to compile the main sources relating to geology, archaeology, biology and history of man within the park area.

For chapters of geology, biology and the Indians, sources were primarily technical papers, government bulletins and university publications. The chapter on Indians was the most difficult to put together because dating and interpreting of artifacts is highly controversial. Sources for chapters on Spaniards, Mexicans and early Americans in the park were primarily published diaries, journals and newspaper accounts.

Recreating the story of the park's formation presented some difficulty since many sources have been discarded by the California Department of Parks and Recreation. Thus, material was drawn primarily from various personal collections, unpublished manuscripts, interviews, newspaper articles and other existing published material. Information on park management was obtained through questionnaires sent to all previous park supervisors.

To the many persons who have offered assistance and read the manuscript I wish to offer thanks. From California State University, San Diego, were Gordon Gastil, former chairman of the Geology Department; Richard Phillips, professor of geology; Paul Ezell, professor of anthropology; Abraham Nasatir, professor of history; and members of my thesis committee, Douglas Strong, Ned Greenwood, and my chairman, David Weber.

I am also indebted to the following: Theodore Downs, chief curator of Earth Sciences Division of the Los Angeles County Natural History Museum; Lowell Bean, professor of anthropology at California State University, Hayward; Kenneth E. Hedges, curator of the San Diego Museum of Man; John Sloan, curator of herpetology, and Helen Witham, assistant curator of botany, both at the San Diego County Natural History Museum; Mitchel Beauchamp, authority on San Diego County botany; Ernest Brown, park naturalist, William Seidel, park archaeologist, and Maurice Getty, manager, all of the Anza-Borrego Desert State Park Headquarters; Robert Begole and Morlin Childers, avocational archaeologists; Roscoe Poland, conservation chairman of the San Diego Chapter of the Sierra Club and librarians of the California Room at San Diego Public Library, Junipero Serra Museum in San Diego, and Bancroft Library in Berkeley.

For information on Borrego Springs and the park's early history I thank Virginia DeMarais of Borrego Springs; Betty Remlein of the Borrego Springs Chamber of Commerce; editor Richard Davis who kindly sent me many back issues of the *Borrego Sun;* Lois von Voigtlander, news editor of the *Borrego Sun;* Mrs. Guy Fleming of La Jolla; Mrs. Jack Calvert; Eugene Velzy; Harvey Moore; Maurice Morgan; Jack Welch; Leo Crawford, William Allison; John Fleming; Richard B. Dixon; Paul McEwen; Frank Fairchild; Merle Beckman; Douglas Bryce; William Reinhardt; Wesley Cater; Clyde Strickler; and

Jack Hesemeyer.

Many individuals within the Department of Parks and Recreation in Sacramento were helpful: John H. Michael, supervisor of Interpretive Services; Frederick A. Meyer, supervisor of Environmental Resources Section; James P. Tryner, chief of the Division of Resource Management and Protection; Newton B. Drury, former chief of the Division of Beaches and Parks; and Earl P. Hanson, former deputy chief of the division.

COPLEY BOOKS ACKNOWLEDGMENTS

Copley Books appreciates the professional assistance of those who read the final manuscript of this book, and whose suggestions have been incorporated in the text: Dr. David Weber, professor of history, Dr. H. Lee Wedberg, professor of botany and associate dean of the College of Sciences, and Dr. Richard L. Threet, professor of geology, all at California's San Diego State University; Ken Hedges, associate curator of the San Diego Museum of Man; Clark R. Mahrdt, herpetologist at San Diego Museum of Natural History; and Mr. Philip L. Gildred of San Diego.

ART CREDITS

General desert photographs by Ed Neil, Thane McIntosh and Rex Salmon, Union-Tribune Publishing Co. Photographs of desert snow by Mauricc Getty, Anza-Borrego State Park Manager, and of desert bighorn sheep by Jack Turner, Research Biologist in Palm Desert. Sketch of ram's head by Eric Poulson and maps of trails by Bob Fasset, Union-Tribune Publishing Co. Indian pictographs are courtesy of Ken Hedges, San Diego Museum of Man.

Bibliography

ARCHAEOLOGY, GEOLOGY AND TOPOGRAPHY

Apostolides, Alex. *Field Report: Archaeological Survey of the Anza-Borrego State Park,* 1969. Copy at Anza-Borrego State Park Headquarters.

Bartholomew, M. J. *San Jacinto Fault Zone in the Northern Imperial Valley, California.* In: *Geological Society of America Bulletin,* LXXX, October, 1970.

Blackwelder, Eliot. *Geomorphic Processes in the Desert.* In: *Geology of Southern California,* Bulletin No. 170, California Division of Mines, San Francisco, 1954.

Bowers, Stephen. *Reconnaissance of the Colorado Desert Mining District.* Sacramento: California State Mining Bureau, 1901.

Dibblee, T. W. Jr. *Geology of the Imperial Valley Region, California.* In: *Geology of Southern California,* Bulletin No. 170, California Division of Mines, San Francisco, 1954.

Downs, Theodore. *Airlift for Fossils.* In: *Museum Alliance Quarterly,* VI, Summer, Los Angeles Count Museum of Natural History, 1967.

.... *Fossil Vertebrates of Southern California.* Berkeley: University of California Press, 1968.

..............., and White, John A. *A Vertebrate Faunal Succession in Superposed Sediments from Late Pliocene to Middle Pleistocene in California.* In: *Report of the 23rd International Geological Congress.* Prague, Czechoslovakia, 1968.

..............., and White, John A. *Anza-Borrego Desert Faunal List.* Downs Files, Los Angeles County Museum.

Durham, J. Wyatt. *The Marine Cenozoic of Southern California.* In: *Geology of Southern California,* Bulletin No. 170, California Division of Mines, San Francisco, 1954.

Gastil, R. G.; Phillips, R. P.; and Allison, E. C. *Reconnaissance Geology of the State of Baja California.* Part IV, Geological Society Memoirs, in press.

Getze, George. *State Park Contains Giant Fossil Preserve.* In: *Los Angeles Times,* July 18, 1966.

Gunn, Douglas. *San Diego: Climate, Productions, Resources, Topography,* Etc. San Diego: Union Steam Book and Job Printing Office, 1886.

Hillinger, Charles. *Skeleton of Human 21,500 Years Old Found in Desert.* In: *Los Angeles Times,* October 8, 1972.

Hilton, John. *Mining for Gunsights.* In: *Desert Magazine,* XIII, October, 1950.

Hinds, Norman E. A. *Evolution of the California Landscape.* Bulletin No. 158, California Division of Mines, San Francisco, 1952.

Howard, Hildegarde. *Fossil Birds from the Anza-Borrego Desert.* In: *Contributions in Science,* No. 73, Los Angeles County Museum, 1963.

.... *The Incredible Teratorn Again.* In: *The Condor,* LXXIV, Autumn, 1972.

Jahns, Richard H. *Investigations and Problems of Southern California Geology.* In: *Geology of Southern California,* Bulletin No. 170, California Division of Mines, San Francisco, 1954.

Jones, Barry. *Paleontology, Anza-Borrego Desert State Park, Fossil List.* Anza-Borrego Desert State Park Headquarters, 1972.

Meighan, Clement W. *Archaeological Resources of Borrego Desert State Park.* Report for Interpretive Services, California Division of Beaches and Parks, Sacramento, 1958-1959.

Miller, William J. *California Through the Ages: The Geologic Story of a Great State.* Los Angeles: Westernlore Press, 1957.

Moriarty, James Robert III. *The San Dieguito Complex: Suggested Environmental and Cultural Relationships.* In: *Anthropological Journal of Canada,* VII, No. 3, 1969.

Moyle, J. R. *Water Wells and Springs in Borrego, Carrizo and San Felipe Valley Areas, and San Diego and Imperial Counties, California.* Bulletin No. 91-15, U.S. Department of Water Resources, 1968.

Newman, William L. *Geologic Time: The Age of*

the Earth. U.S. Department of the Interior, Geological Survey. Washington, D.C.: Govt. Printing Office, 1970.

Oakeshatt, Gordon B. *California's Changing Landscape: A Guide to the Geology of the State.* New York: McGraw Hill, Inc., 1971.

Peterson, G. L.; Gastil, R. G.; and Allison, E. C. *Geology of the Peninsular Ranges.* In: *Mineral and Water Resources of California,* Bulletin No. 191, California Division of Mines, San Francisco, 1966.

Pourade, Richard F., ed. *Ancient Hunters of the Far West.* San Diego: Union-Tribune Publishing Co., 1966.

Putnam, William C. *Geology.* New York: Oxford University Press, 1964.

Sauer, Carl. *Land Forms in the Peninsular Range of California as Developed about Warner's Hot Springs and Mesa Grande.* Publications in Geography, Vol. III. Berkeley: University of California Press, 1929.

Schroeder, Albert H. *A Brief Survey of the Colorado River from Davis Dam to the International Boundary.* Boulder City: Bureau of Reclamation, 1952.

Sharp, Robert V. *San Jacinto Fault Zone in the Peninsular Ranges of Southern California. In: Geological Soc. of America Bulletin,* LXXVIII, June, 1967.

.... *Geology: Field Guide to Southern California.* Dubuque, Iowa: Wm. C. Brown Co. Publishers, 1972.

Stewart, Richard M. *Geology and Mineral Resources of Anza-Borrego State Park.* Report to California Division of Mines, San Francisco, October, 1956.

Taylor & Taylor, Consulting Engineers. *Borrego Valley Water Report.* Los Angeles: Taylor & Taylor, 1946.

U.S. Department of the Interior, Geological Survey. *The Borrego Mountain Earthquake of April 9, 1968.* Professional Paper 787. Washington, D.C.: Govt. Printing Office, 1972.

Wallace, William J. *Archaeological Explorations in the Southern Section of Anza-Borrego Desert State Park, California.* Report, Interpretive Services, California Division of Beaches and Parks, Sacramento, No. 5, 1962.

Wallace, William J., and Taylor, Edith S. *Preliminary Excavations at the Indian Hill Rock Shelter, Anza-Borrego Desert State Park.* Report, Interpretive Services, California Division of Beaches and Parks, Sacramento, 1959.

.... *The Surface Archaeology of Indian Hill, Anza-Borrego Desert State Park, California.* In: *The Masterkey,* XXXIV, January-March, 1960.

.... *The Indian Hill Rockshelter, Preliminary Excavations.* In: *The Masterkey,* XXXIV, April-June, 1960.

Wallace, William J.; Taylor, Edith S.; and Kritzman, George. *Additional Excavations at the Indian Hill Rockshelter, Anza-Borrego Desert State Park.* Interpretive Services, California Department of Parks and Recreation, Sacramento, June, 1961.

Weber F. Harold, Jr. *Geology and Mineral Resources of San Diego County, California.* County Report No. 3, California Division of Mines, San Francisco, 1963.

White. John A. *A New Porcupine from the Middle Pleistocene of the Anza- Borrego Desert of California.* In: *Contributions in Science,* No. 136, Los Angeles County Museum, February, 1968.

.... *Late Cenozoic Bats from the Anza-Borrego Desert of California.* In: *Miscellaneous Publications,* No. 51, University of Kansas Museum of Natural History, n.d.

.............., and Downs, Theodore. *A New Geomys from the Vallecito Creek Pleistocene of California.* In: *Contributions in Science,* No. 42, Los Angeles County Museum, 1961.

Willey, Gordon R. *North and Middle America.* Vol. I of *An Introduction to American Archaeology.* Englewood Cliffs, N.J.: Prentice-Hall, Inc., 1966.

THE LIFE AND CLIMATE OF THE DESERT

Banks, Richard C. *The Rodents of Anza-Borrego Desert State Park, San Diego, California.* Report No. 4-022-032, Interpretive Services, California Division of Beaches and Parks, Sacramento, September 30, 1964.

Beattie, George William, and Beattie, Helen Pruitt. *Heritage of the Valley, San Bernardino's First Century.* Oakland: Biobooks, 1951.

Brown, Ernest H. *The Desert Bighorn of Anza-Borrego.* In: *News and Views,* XXV, September, 1968.

.... *Anza-Borrego Desert State Park Mammals, Reptiles and Amphibians.* California Department of Parks and Recreation, Resources Agency, 1969.

.... *Revised and Annotated List of Birds Noted in and around Anza-Borrego Desert State Park.* California Department of Parks and Recreation, Resources Agency, 1969.

Burdick, Arthur J. *The Mystic Mid-Region, the Deserts of the Southwest.* New York: G. P. Putnam's Sons, 1904.

California Department of Parks and Recreation, Resources Agency. *Borrego Palm Canyon Na-*

ture Trail Guide. February, 1962.

Chase, J. Smeaton. *California Desert Trails.* New York: Houghton Mifflin Co., 1919.

Cowan, Ernie. *Anza's Living Fence.* In: *Desert Magazine,* XXXI, March, 1968.

.... *Pupfish Find Haven in State Park Pond.* In: *Borrego Sun,* October 24, 1970.

Edwards, E. I. *Lost Oases along the Carrizo.* Los Angeles: The Westernlore Press, 1961.

Felton, Ernest L. *California's Many Climates.* Palo Alto: Pacific books, 1965.

Henderson, Randall. *Palm Oasis in Mortero Canyon.* In: *Desert Magazine,* IV, November, 1940.

.... *Wild Palms of the San Ysidros.* In: *Desert Magazine,* VIII, July, 1945.

.... *Vanishing Oasis of Palm Wash.* In: *Desert Magazine,* VIII, August, 1945.

.... *On Desert Trails Today and Yesterday.* Los Angeles: Westernlore Press, 1961.

Higgings, Ethel Bailey. *Annotated Distrbutional List of the Ferns and Flowering Plants of San Diego County, California.* In: *Occasional Papers,* No. 8, San Diego Society of Natural History, November, 1949.

Jackson, Howard E. *Elephant Trees.* In: *Pacific Pathways Magazine,* II, August, 1948.

Jaeger, Edmund C. *Denizens of the Desert: A Book of Southwestern Mammals, Birds, and Reptiles.* New York: Houghton Mifflin Company, 1922.

.... *Desert Wild Flowers.* Stanford: Stanford University Press, 1941.

.... *The California Deserts.* Stanford: Stanford University Press, 3rd ed., 1955.

James, George Wharton. *The Wonders of the Colorado Desert.* 2 vols. Boston: Little, Brown, and Co., 1906.

Leadabrand, Russ. *Let's Explore a Byway—Into the Anza-Borrego Desert State Park.* In: *Westways,* LIV, November, 1962.

Leetch, George. *Find no Fish at Fish Creek?* In: *Borrego Sun,* March 16, 1968.

Leopold, A. Starker. *The Desert.* New York: Time Incorporated, 1961.

Merkel, Dalton E. *Flowers, Trees and Ferns of Anza-Borrego Desert State Park.* California Department of Parks and Recreation, May, 1965.

Munz, Philip A. *California Desert Wildflowers.* Berkeley: University of California Press, 1969.

Preston, Dudley A. *Checklist of Some of the Ferns, Cone-bearing and Flowering Plants of Anza-Borrego Desert State Park.* California Department of Parks and Recreation, District VI Headquarters, San Diego, 1964.

San Diego Museum of Natural History. *Some Common Desert Birds and Mammals of San Diego County.* Mimeographed information sheet, 1971.

.... *Desert Vegetation.* Mimeographed information sheet, n.d.

Seymour, George. *Coyote.* California Department of Fish and Game, Resources Agency, n.d.

.... *Ringtail.* California Department of Fish and Game, Resources Agency, n.d.

Shreve, Forrest, and Wiggins, Ira L. *Vegetation and Flora of the Sonoran Desert.* 2 vols. Stanford: Stanford University Press, 1964.

Sloan, Allan J. *Springtime and Snakes.* San Diego Museum of Natural History, n.d.

Sutton, Ann, and Sutton, Myron. *The Life of the Desert.* New York: McGraw-Hill Book Company, 1966.

Van Dyke, John C. *The Desert.* New York: Charles Scribner's Sons, 1901.

Witham, Helen. *The Trees of the Desert Are Different.* In: *California Garden,* LX, December-January, 1969-1970.

.... *Colorado Desert Ferns.* Unpublished MS in Witham files, Borrego Springs, 1971.

INDIAN OCCUPATION OF ARID LANDS

Barrows, David Prescott. *The Ethno-botany of the Coahuilla Indians of Southern California.* Banning, Calif.: Malki Museum Press, 1967.

Bean, Lowell John. *Mukat's People: The Cahuilla Indians of Southern California.* Berkeley: University of California Press, 1972.

............, and Lawton, Harry. *The Cahuilla Indians of Southern California: Their History and Culture.* Banning, Calif.: Malki Museum Press, 1965.

............, and Saubell, Katherine Siva. *Temalpakh: Cahuilla Indian Knowledge and Usage of Plants.* Banning, Calif.: Malki Museum Press, 1972.

Burnett, E. K. *Inlaid Stone and Bone Artifacts from Southern California.* In: *Contributions,* American Indian Heye Foundation, XIII, 1944.

Cook, S. F. *The Conflict between the California Indians and White Civilization.* In: *Ibero-Americana,* XXI, January, 1943; XXII, February, 1943; XXIII, April, 1943.

Cowan, Ernie. *Survey of Indian Sites Urged for Desert Park.* In: *San Diego Evening Tribune,* June 19, 1972.

Curtis, Edward S. *The North American Indians.* 20 vols. Norwood, Mass.: The Plimpton Press, 1926.

Drucker, Philip. *Cultural Element Distribution:* Southern California. Anthropological Records. Vol. I. Berkeley: University of California Press, 1939.

DuBois, Constance Goddard. *The Religion of the*

Luiseño Indians of Southern California. In: *Publications in American Archaeology and Ethnology,* Vol. VIII, University of California Press, Berkeley, 1908.

Englehardt, Father Zephyrin. *The Mission and Missionaries of California.* 4 vols. Santa Barbara: Mission Santa Barbara, 1929.

Farb, Peter. *Man's Rise to Civilization as Shown by the Indians of North America from Primeval Times to the Coming of the Industrial State.* New York: E. P. Dutton & Co., Inc., 1968.

Forbes, Jack D. *Warriors on the Colorado: The Yumas of the Quechan Nation and Their Neighbors.* Norman: University of Oklahoma Press, 1965.

.... *Native Americans of California and Nevada.* Healdsburgy, California: Naturegraph Publishers, 1968.

Gifford, Edward Winslow. *Clans and Moieties in Southern California.* In: *Publications in American Archaeology and Ethnology,* Vol. XIV, University of California Press, Berkeley, 1918.

.... *The Kamia of Imperial Valley.* U.S. Bureau of American Ethnology, Bulletin No. 97. Washington, D.C.: Govt. Printing Office, 1931.

Hayden, Julian D. *Of Hohokam Origins and Other Matters.* In: *American Antiquity,* XXXV, No. 1, 1970.

Hedges, Kenneth Everett. *An Analysis of Diegueño Pictographs.* Master's thesis, San Diego State College, 1970.

Heizer, R. F., and Whipple, M. A. *The California Indians, A Source Book.* Los Angeles: University of California Press, 1951.

Hicks, Frederic Noble. *Ecological Aspect of Aboriginal Culture in the Western Yuman Area.* Ph.D. dissertation, University of California Press, Los Angeles, 1963.

Hooper, Lucile. *The Cahuilla Indians.* In: *Publications in American Archaeology and Ethnology,* Vol. XVI, University of California Press, Berkeley, 1920.

Jackson, Helen Hunt. *A Century of Dishonor: A Sketch of the United States Government's Dealings with Some of the Indian Tribes.* Boston: Roberts Brothers, 1886.

Kroeber, A. L. *Handbook of the Indians of California.* Berkeley: California Book Company, Ltd., 1953.

Loomis, Noel M. *The Garra Uprising of 1851.* In: *The Westerners Brand Book, San Diego Corral,* 1971.

Moriarty, James Robert III. *The San Dieguito Complex: Suggested Environmental and Cultural Relationships.* In: *Anthropological Journal of Canada,* VII, No. 3, 1969.

Pourade, Richard F. *Time of the Bells.* San Diego: Union-Tribune Publishing Co., 1961.

Ruby, Jay William. *Cultural Contact between Aboriginal Southern California and the Southwest.* Ph.D. dissertation, University of California, Los Angeles, 1970.

Spicer, Edward H. *Cycles of Conquest: The Impact of Spain, Mexico, and the United States on the Indians of the Southwest, 1533-1960.* Tucson: The University of Arizona Press, 1962.

Spier, Leslie, *Southern Diegueño Customs.* In: *Publications in American Archaeology and Ethnology,* Vol. XX, University of California, Berkeley, 1923.

Strong, William Duncan. *Aboriginal Society in Southern California.* In: *Publications in American Archaeology and Ethnology,* Vol. XXVI, University of California, Berkeley, 1929.

Swanton, John R. *The Indian Tribes of North America.* Smithsonian Institution, Bureau of American Ethnology, Bulletin 145. Washington, D.C.: Government Printing Office, 1952.

Thurman, Frank. *The Cahuillas and White Men of San Carlos and Coyote Canyon.* In: *San Bernardino County Museum Association Quarterly,* XVII, Spring, 1970.

Treganza, Adan E. *Possibilities of an Aboriginal Practice of Agriculture among the Southern Diegueño.* In: *American Antiquity,* Vol. XII, January, 1947.

Wallace, William J. *Archaeological Explorations in the Southern Section of Anza-Borrego Desert State Park, California.* Report, Interpretive Services, California Division of Beaches and Parks, Sacramento, No. 5, 1962.

Wallace, William J., and Taylor, Edith S. *Preliminary Excavations at the Indian Hill Rock Shelter, Anza-Borrego Desert State Park.* Report, Interpretive Services, California Division of Beaches and Parks, Sacramento, 1959.

.... *The Surface Archaeology of Indian Hill, Anza-Borrego Desert State Park, California.* In: *The Masterkey,* XXXIV, January-March, 1960.

.... *The Indian Hill Rockshelter, Preliminary Excavations.* In: *The Masterkey,* XXXIV, April-June, 1960.

Wallace, William J.; Taylor, Edith S.; and Kritzman, George. *Additional Excavations at the Indian Hill Rockshelter, Anza-Borrego Desert State Park.* Interpretive Services, California Department of Parks and Recreation, Sacramento, June, 1961.

Weber, F. Harold, Jr. *Geology and Mineral Resources of San Diego County, California.* County Report No. 3, California Division of Mines, San Francisco, 1963.

MIGRATIONS OF THE SPANIARDS AND MEXICANS

Bean, Lowell John, and Mason, William Marvin, eds. *Diaries & Accounts of the Romero Expeditions in Arizona and California, 1823-1826.* Los Angeles: Ward Ritchie Press, 1962.

Beattie, George William. *Reopening the Anza Road.* In: *The Pacific Historical Review,* II, March, 1933.

Bolton, Herbert Eugene, ed. *Anza's California Expeditions.* 5 vols. Berkeley: University of California Press, 1930.

.... *In the South San Joaquin ahead of Garcés.* In: *California Historical Society Quarterly,* Vol. X, September, 1931.

Bowman, J. N., and Heizer, Robert F. *Anza and the Northwest Frontier.* Southland Press, June, 1967.

Dixon, Ben F. *The Saga of San Felipe.* n.d. Bibliographic material on San Felipe Valley at Junípero Serra Museum, San Diego.

Elias, Don José. *Jornadas.* In: *Noticias estadisticas del estado de Sonora.* Mexico: José Francisco Velasco, 1850.

Fages, Pedro. *The Colorado River Campaign, 1781-1782.* Edited by Herbert Ingram Priestly. In: *Publications,* III, Academy of Pacific Coast History, May, 1913.

Guinn, J. M. *The Sonoran Migrations.* In: *Publications,* VIII, Historical Society of Southern California., 1909-1910.

Hutchinson, C. Alan. *Frontier Settlement in Mexican California: The Híjar-Padrés Colony and its Origins, 1769-1835.* New Haven: Yale University Press, 1969.

Pourade, Richard F. *The Explorers.* San Diego, Calif.: Union-Tribune Publishing Co., 1960.

.... *Anza Conquers the Desert.* San Diego, Calif.: Union-Tribune Publishing Co., 1971.

Rensch, Hero Eugene. *Fages' Crossing of the Cuyamacas.* In: *California Historical Society Quarterly,* Vol. XXXIV, March, 1955.

.... *Fages Through Borrego and Coyote Ahead of Anza and Garcés in 1772.* MS in files of Interpretive Services, California Department of Parks and Recreation, Sacramento, 1956.

AMERICAN PIONEERS AND MILITARY MARCHES

Bancroft, Hubert Howe. *History of California.* 7 vols. San Francisco: The History Company, Publishers, 1886.

Bartlett, John R. *Personal Narrative of Explorations and Incidents in Texas, New Mexico, California, Sonora, and Chihuahua, Connected with the U.S. and Mexican Boundary Commission during the years 1850-1853.* 2 vols. New York: D. Appleton & Co., 1854.

Bean, Lowell, and Mason, William Marvin, eds. *Diaries & Accounts of the Romero Expeditions in Arizona and California, 1823-1826.* Los Angeles: Ward Ritchie Press, 1962.

Beattie, George William, and Beattie, Helen Pruitt. *Heritage of the Valley, San Bernardino's First Century.* Oakland: Biobooks, 1951.

Chamberlin, William H. *From Lewisburg to California in 1849.* In: *New Mexico Historical Review,* Vol. XX, July, 1945..

Conkling, Roscoe P., and Conkling, Margaret B. *The Butterfield Overland Mail 1857-1869.* 3 vols. Glendale: The Arthur H. Clark Company, 1947.

Cooke, Philip St. George. *The Conquest of New Mexico and California: An Historical and Personal Narrative.* New York: G. P. Putnam's Sons, 1878.

Couts, Cave J. *From San Diego to the Colorado in 1849, Journal and Maps.* Los Angeles: Arthur M. Ellis, 1932.

.... *Hepah, California! The Journal of Cave Johnson Couts from Monterrey, Nuevo Leon, Mexico, to Los Angeles, California, during the Years 1848-1849.* Tucson: Arizona Pioneers' Historical Society, 1961.

Dixon, Ben F. *The Saga of San Felipe.* n.d. Bibliographic material on San Felipe Valley at Junipero Serra Museum, San Diego.

Emory, W. H. *Notes of a Military Reconnaissance from Fort Leavenworth, in Missouri, to San Diego, in California, Including Parts of the Arkansas, del Norte, and Gila Rivers.* New York: H. Long & Brothers, 1848.

Foreman, Grant. *The Adventures of James Collier, First Collector of the Port of San Francisco.* Chicago: Blackcat Press, 1937.

Hafen, Leroy R., ed. *The Mountain Men and the Fur Trade of the Far West: Biographical Sketches of the Participants by Scholars of the Subject.* 8 vols. Glendale: The Arthur H. Clark Company, 1966.

Hall, J. Austin. *San Diego.* In: *The Californian Illustrated Magazine,* III, Feb., 1893.

Hayes, Benjamin. *Pioneer Notes from the Diaries of Judge Benjamin Hayes, 1849-1875.* Los Angeles: Marjorie Tisdale Wolcott, 1929.

Hill, Joseph J. *The History of Warner's Ranch and Its Environs.* Los Angeles: privately printed, 1927.

Johnston, Captain Abraham Robinson. *Journal.* Washington, D.C.: Government Printing Office,

1848.
Jones, Newell. *Tracks of Old Stage Line Guarded Carefully by S. D. Kin of Driver.* In: *San Diego Evening Tribune,* April 9, 1937.
Krythe, Maymie. *Port Admiral, Phineas Banning, 1830-1885.* San Francisco: California Historical Society, 1957.
Lang, Walter B., ed. *The First Overland Mail, Butterfield Trail, St. Louis to San Francisco, 1858-1861.* Washington, D.C.: Walter B. Lang, 1940.
Lindsay, Diana. *Henry A. Crabb, Filibuster, and the San Diego Herald.* In: *Journal of San Diego History,* XIX, Winter, 1973.
Loomis, Noel M. *The Garra Uprising of 1851.* In: *The Westerners Brand Book, San Diego Corral,* 1971.
Mitchell, Virgil L. *California and the Transformation of Mountain Men.* In: *Journal of the West,* Vol. IX, July, 1970.
Ormsby, Waterman L. *The Butterfield Overland Mail.* San Marino, Calif.: Huntington Library, 1942.
Orton, Richard H., ed. *Records of California Men in the War of Rebellion, 1861 to 1867.* Sacramento: State Office, 1890.
Pattie, James O. *The Personal Narrative of James O. Pattie of Kentucky.* Vol. XVIII of the *Early Western Travels 1748-1846.* Edited by Reuben Gold Thwaites. Cleveland, Ohio: The Arthur H. Clark Company, 1905.
Phillips, George H. *Indian Resistance and Cooperation in Southern California: The Garra Uprising and its Aftermath.* Ph.d. dissertation, University of California, Los Angeles, 1973.
Pourade, Richard F. *Time of the Bells.* San Diego: Union-Tribune Publishing Co., 1961.
.... *The Silver Dons.* San Diego: Union-Tribune Publishing Co., 1963.
.... *The Glory Years.* San Diego: Union-Tribune Publishing Co., 1964.
Reed, Lester. *Old Time Cattlemen and Other Pioneers of the Anza-Borrego Area.* Palm Desert: Desert Printers, Inc., 1963.
.... *Old-Timers of Southeastern California.* Redlands: Lester Reed, 1967.
Rensch, Hero Eugene. *Woods' Shorter Mountain Trail to San Diego.* In: *California Historical Society Quarterly,* XXXVI, June, 1957.
Rolle, Andrew F. *California: A History.* New York: Thomas Y. Crowell Company, 1963.
San Diego Herald. 1851-1857.
Stott, Kenhelm W. *Stage Coach Operation in San Diego and Imperial Counties 1857-1874.* Unpublished monograph, San Diego State College, 1950 (copy at Serra Museum, San Diego).
Stout, Joe A. *Henry A. Crabb, Filibuster or Colonizer.* In: *The American West,* VIII, May, 1971.
Sweeny, Thomas W. *Journal of Lt. Thomas W. Sweeny, 1849-1853* Los Angeles: Westernlore Press, 1956.
Tyler, Sgt. Daniel. *A Concise History of the Mormon Battalion in the Mexican War, 1846-1847.* Chicago: The Rio Grande Press, Inc., 1964.
U.S. Congress, House. *War of the Rebellion: A Compilation of Official Records of Union and Confederate Armies.* Series I, Vols. I to LV, 55th Cong., 1st Sess., H.R. 59. Washington: Govt. Office, 1897.
U.S. Department of War. *Reports of Exploration and Survey, to Ascertain the Most Practicable and Economical Route for a Railroad from the the Mississippi River to the Pacific Ocean Made under the Direction of the Secretary of War, in 1853-1854.* Acts of Congress, 12 vols. Washington: Beverly Tucker, 1856.
Van Dyke. T. S. *San Diego County, California.* San Diego: Gould, Hutton & Co., 1890.
Warner, J. J. *Reminiscences of Early California from 1831 to 1846.* In: *Publications,* Vol. VII, Historical Society of Southern California, 1906-1908.
Weber, David J. *The Taos Trappers: The Fur Trade in the Far Southwest, 1540-1846.* Norman: University of Oklahoma Press, 1971.
Welch, Jack P. *The Butterfield Overland Mail.* In: *News and Views,* Vol. XX, June, 1963.
Whipple, Amiel W. *The Whipple Report, Journal of an Expedition from San Diego, California, to the Rio Colorado, from Sept. 11 to Dec. 11, 1849.* Los Angeles: Westernlore Press, 1961.
Woodward, Arthur. *Lances at San Pasqual.* California Historical Society, 1948.
.... *Feud on the Colorado.* Los Angeles: Westernlore Press, 1955.

RANCHERS AND SETTLERS IN THE DESERT

Avitt, Pearl M. *Desert Kaleidoscope.* In: *Union Title Trust Topics,* XV, December, 1961.
Bellon, Walter. *Report Compiled from Public and Private Records for the Citizens of San Diego County Concerning Borrego, Vallecito and Carrizo Units.* April, 1940. Mimeographed copy in Serra Museum, San Diego.
Borrego Land and Development Company. *Facts about Borrego Springs, Your Place in the Sun.* n.d. Mimeographed information sheet, author's files.
Borrego Springs. Collections of interviews of early residents of Borrego Valley and miscellaneous material on the history of the valley at; Borrego

Springs Chamber of Commerce; California Room, San Diego County Library; and Serra Museum, San Diego.
Borrego Sun, 1949-1973.
Botts, Myrtle. *History of Julian.* Julian: Julian Historical Society, 1964.
Bryson, Jamie. *Author Built House on Mountain in Desert, Lived there 16 Years.* In: *The San Diego Union,* March 30, 1969.
Colbert, Frederick J. *Mary's Store at Agua Caliente Oasis.* In: *Desert Magazine,* XIV, March, 1951.
Curti, G. Philip. *Borrego Valley: The Birth of a Desert Community.* Master's thesis, University of California, Los Angeles, 1955.
DeMarais, Virginia. *A Brief History of the Borrego Springs Unified School District.* Typescript, n.d., DeMarais files, Borrego Springs.
.... Collection of miscellaneous MSS, correspondence and articles relating to the history of Borrego Springs. Borrego Springs, Calif.
Davis, Edward H. *Forgotten Tragedy of Carrizo Creek.* In: *Desert Magazine,* III, July, 1940.
Fleming, Shannon. *A. A. 'Doc' Beaty, Borrego Pioneer,* n.d. MS in files of the Borrego Springs Chamber of Commerce.
.... Notes on Borrego Springs Chamber of Commerce. n.d. Files of the agency.
Heath, J. H. *Borrego Valley is Developing as Farm Area.* In: *The San Diego Union,* May 6, 1928.
Hellyer, David. *He Planned to Change the Desert Climate.* In: *Desert Magazine,* XII, June, 1949.
Hood, Amorita. *As Far as I Know.* n.d. Typewritten statement in files of Borrego Springs Chamber of Commerce.
Jasper, James A. *Trail-breakers and History makers of Julian, Ballena, Mesa Grande, Oak Grove, Warner Ranch, Banner, and Cuyamaca in San Diego County, Calif.* n.d. Unpublished MS in two volumes at Serra Museum, San Diego.
Kelly, J. L. *Camping on the Colorado Desert.* Unpublished MS, July 1918. Copy available at Serra Museum, San Diego.
Lamb, Taze, and Lamb, Jessie. *Dream of a Desert Paradise.* In: *Desert Magazine,* II, June, 1939.
Lindsay, Diana. Collection of correspondence, ranger patrol reports, miscellaneous material and interviews. Author's files.
Mason, James. Files, Serra Museum, San Diego.
McCain, John. Files, Serra Museum, San Diego.
Mathes, Albert L. *To the Valley of the Sun.* March, 1929. MS in DeMarais files, Borrego Springs.
Nolan, Patrick. *Ensign Ranch Story.* MS in files of Borrego Springs Chamber of Commerce.
Oliver, Harry. *Harry Oliver's Desert Rat Scrap Book.* Thousand Palms, Calif.: privately printed, n.d. Issues available at Bancroft Library.
Reed, Lester. *Old Time Cattlemen and Other Pioneers of the Anza-Borrego Area.* Palm Desert: Desert Printers, Inc., 1963.
.... *Old-timers of Southeastern California.* Redlands: Lester Reed, 1967.
Roche, H. W., and Kepner, Roy, Jr. *The Date Palm Industry in Borrego Valley.* Report to the San Diego Dept. of Agriculture, 1944.
.... *How about a Few Dates, Mates?* In: *San Diego County Employee,* April, 1946.
Roy Wenzlick & Co. *Market Potential, Borrego Springs, California.* Report to La Casa del Zorro, January, 1963. Files, DeMarais, Borrego Springs.
San Diego Directory Co. *San Diego City and County Directory.* 1930.
Sentenac, Paul. Files, Junipero Serra Museum, San Diego.
South, Marshall. *Campbells of Vallecito Valley.* In: *Desert Magazine,* III, December, 1939.
Wilson, Henry E. W. *Before the Law Came to Borrego.* In: *Desert Magazine,* XIX, February, 1956.

DEVELOPMENT OF ANZA-BORREGO STATE PARK

Anza-Borrego Desert State Park. Collections of correspondence and miscellaneous material at: park headquarters; California Department of Parks and Recreation, District VI Headquarters, San Diego; California Department of Parks and Recreation, Interpretive Services, Sacramento; Junipero Serra Museum, San Diego; and San Diego Chapter of the Sierra Club.
Bellon, Walter. *Report Compiled from Public and Private Records for the Citizens of San Diego County Concerning Borrego, Vallecito and Carrizo Units.* April, 1940. Copy in Serra Museum, San Diego.
Borrego Sun. 1953-1973.
Calexico Chronicle. 1941.
California Department of Natural Resources, Division of Beaches and Park. *Proposed Imperial County Additions to Borrego and Anza Desert State Parks.* Interpretive Services, Sacramento, 1955.
.... *Re-establishment of Ultimate Boundary Lines, Anza Deseret & Borrego State Park, San Diego County.* Interpretive Services, Sacramento, 1955.
.... *Chronology of State Park Movement in California in Relation to Save-the-Redwoods League.* Digest of Minutes of Save-the-Redwoods League. Drury Collection, Bancroft Library, Berkeley.

.... *Anza-Borrego Desert State Park Acquisition Map.* Sacramento, 1965. Copy at ABDSP headquarters.

California Department of Parks and Recreation, Resources Agency. *Anza-Borrego Desert State Park.* Sacramento, n.d.

.... *Statistical Report for Fiscal Years 1963-1971.* Files, Anza-Borrego State Park.

.... *California State Park System.* Sacramento, 1967.

California Department of Parks and Recreation, State Park Commission. *Annual Report of the California State Park Commission to Hon. Earl Warren. Gov., for the Fiscal Year 1948-1949.* Interpretive Services, Sacramento, 1950.

Calvert, J. W. *Anza Desert State Park.* In: *News and Views,* VII, April, 1949.

Colby, William E. *Borrego Desert Park.* In: *Sierra Club Bulletin,* XVIII, April, 1933.

Cowan, Ernie. *Anza-Borrego's Forbidden Canyons.* In: *Desert Magazine,* XXXIV, April, 1971.

Drury, Newton B. Collection of correspondence and miscellaneous material on the creation of the California State Park System. Bancroft Library, University of California, Berkeley.

.... *California State Park System Record of Land Acquisitions.* Report to the California Department of Natural Resources, Division of Beaches and Parks, August, 1940.

El Centro Chamber of Commerce. *Entering the New California State Desert Park Via El Centro Gateway.* n.d. Pamphlet in Fleming files, University of California, San Diego.

Fairchild, Frank, and Beckman, Merle E. *Unit History, Anza-Borrego Desert State Park.* ABDSP headquarters.

Fleming, Guy L. *Borrego Palms Desert Park Project Map, 1928.* Fleming files, University of California, San Diego.

.... *Borrego Palms Desert Park, Revised Minimum Taking Plan and Ownership Map, 1932.* Fleming files, University of California, San Diego.

.... *Borrego Desert Project.* Typewritten summary of lands in the project, Sept. 1, 1933. Fleming files, University of California, San Diego.

.... Collection of correspondence and miscellaneous material on the creation of the California State Park System. University of California, San Diego, and Serra Museum, San Diego.

Hanson, Earl P. Files, California Department of Parks and Recreation, Interpretive Services, Sacramento.

.... *Anza Desert and Borrego State Parks Take on Added Significance.* In: *News and Views,* XII, April, 1955.

.... *The Better Ranger: Operation '58.* In: *News and Views,* XVI, Feb., 1959.

Henderson, Randall. *Where Anza Blazed the First Trail.* In: *Desert Magazine,* II, April, 1939.

Jennings, Bill. *Desert Folks Get Results Quietly.* In: *Riverside Daily Enterprise,* May 5, 1972.

Kenyon, William L. *Report on Trip to Anza Desert State Park, May 4 to 6, 1949.* Hanson files, Interpretive Services, Sacramento.

.... *Anza Desert State Park, Discovery of Sandstone Canyon.* In: *News and Views,* III, January, 1956.

Kepner, Roy M., Jr. Files, San Diego County Department of Agriculture.

Lindsay, Diana. Collection of correspondence, ranger patrol reports, miscellaneous material, and interviews. Author's files.

Marston, George. Files, Junipero Serra Museum, San Diego.

Marston, Mary Gilman. *George White Marston, A Family Chronicle.* Los Angeles: The Ward Ritchie Press, 1956.

Munz, Philip. *Report on Botany of Proposed Anza Desert State Park.* Copy in Fleming files, University of California, San Diego.

Olmsted, Frederick Law Jr. *Report of State Park Survey of California.* Sacramento: California State Printing Office, 1929.

Parker, Horace. *Anza-Borrego Desert Guide Book.* Balboa Island: Paisano Press, Inc., 1957.

.... *Key Inholdings within the Anza-Borrego Desert State Park.* Report prepared for the California State Park Commission, 1967. Available at the San Diego Chapter of the Sierra Club and in Parker Collection, Corona del Mar.

.... Collection of papers, correspondence, etc., while state park commissioner, Sherman Foundation Library, Corona del Mar.

Primm, P. T., and Fleming, Guy L. *Report on National Park and/or State Park Possibilities of Lands Included in H.R. 1994 and H.R. 1995,* Together with Adjacent Areas. February, 1935. Fleming files, University of California, San Diego.

Ramona Sentinel. 1932.

Reeder, Hazel I. *List of Taxpayers with Legal Descriptions and Number of Delinquent Acres in Township 9 South - Range 5 East.* 1933. Fleming files, University of California, San Diego.

San Diego Evening Tribune. 1937-1973.

Stanley, Kenneth T. *Borrego State Park, Nov. 9.* In: *News and Views,* VIII, Dec., 1950.

The San Diego Union. 1936-1973.

The Tribune-Sun. 1940-1941.

Tilton, L. Deming. *A Report upon Problems of Acquisition and Development of the Borrego Desert Park.* Prepared for the California State Park Commission, July 31, 1933. Copy in Fleming files, University of California, San Diego.

U.S. Congress, House. *A Bill to Provide for the Selection of Certain Lands in the State of California for the Use of the California State Park System. H.R.* 14534, 72nd Cong., 2d Sess., 1933.

.... *A Bill to Amend Public Law Numbered 425, 72nd Cong., Providing for the Selection of Certain Lands in the State of California for the Use of the California State Park System, Approved March 3, 1933.* H.R. 1997, 74th Cong., 2nd Sess., 1936.

.... *An Act to Provide for the Selection of Certain Lands in the State of California for the Use of the California State Park System.* Pub. 838, 74th Cong., 2d Sess., 1936, H.R. 1597.

.... *An Act to Provide for the Selection of Certain Lands in the State of California for the Use of the California State Park System.* Pub. 839, 74th Cong., 2d Sess., 1936, H.R. 1597.

U.S. Department of the Interior, Bureau of Land Management. *The California Desert: A Critical Environmental Challenge.* Proposal by the California State Office, Jan., 1970.

Wade, Kathleen Camilla. *Anza Desert State Park.* W.P.A. Project 465/03/133, State of California Dept. of Natural Resources, 1937. Typescript at Junipero Serra Museum, San Diego.

Welch, Jack P. Ranger patrol reports. Author's files.

LEGENDS, MYTHS, MIRAGES AND TREASURE

Bailey, Philip A. *Golden Mirages.* New York: The MacMillan Co., 1949.

Bell, Horace. *On the Old West Coast: Being further Reminiscences of a Ranger.* New York: William Morrow & Co., 1930.

Caine, Ralph L. *Legendary and Geological History of Lost Desert Gold.* Los Angeles: Gedco Publishing Co., 1951.

Coolidge, Dane and Coolidge, Mary Roberts. *The Last of the Seris.* New York: E. P. Dutton & Co., 1939.

Desert Magazine: Issues containing articles on myths, treasure, lost gold and Pegleg Smith: April, 1936; Jan. and Sept., 1939; Nov. and Dec., 1944; June, 1945; Nov., 1946; Dec., 1947; March, June, Oct. and Dec., 1948; Feb. and April, 1949; Feb., 1951; March, 1953; May and Nov., 1954; Jan., 1956; July, Oct. and Dec., 1964; March, May, June, July, Aug.-Sept., and Dec., 1965; June and Aug.-Sept., 1966; Oct., 1967; Feb., April, May and July, 1968; and Jan. and May, 1969.

Drago, Harry Sinclair. *Lost Bonanzas: Tales of the Legendary Lost Mines of the American West.* New York: Dodd, Mead & Co., 1966.

DuBois, Constance Goddard. *The Mythology of the Diegueños, Mission Indians of San Diego County California, as Proving their Status to be Higher than is Generally Believed.* In: *Proceedings of the 13th International Congress of Americanists.* New York, 1902.

.... *The Story of the Chaup: A Myth of the Diegueños.* In: *Journal of American Folk-lore.* XVII, Oct.-Dec., 1904.

Hooper, Lucile. *The Cahuilla Indians.* In: *Publications in American Archaeology and Ethnology,* XVI, University of California, 1920.

Humphreys, Alfred Glen. *Thomas L. (Peg-leg) Smith.* In: *The Mountain Men and the Fur Trade of the Far West* (edited by LeRoy R. Hagen). Vol. IV. Glendale: The Arthur H. Clark Company, 1966.

Johnson, Mary Elizabeth. *Indian Legends of the Cuyamaca Mountains.* Privately printed, 1914.

Niehuis, Charles C. *Lost Ship of the Desert.* In: *Desert Magazine,* II, Jan., 1939.

Oliver, Harry. *Desert Rough Cuts, a Haywire History of the Borego Desert.* Los Angeles: The Ward Ritchie Press, 1938.

Patencio, Francisco. *Stories and Legends of the Palm Springs Indians.* Palm Springs: Caroline S. Snyder, 1943.

Spier, Leslie. *Southern Diegueño Customs.* In: *Publications in American Archaeology and Ethnology.* University California, XX, 1923.

Strong, William Duncan. *Aboriginal Society in Southern California.* In: *Publications in American Archaeology and Ethnology,* Univ. of Calif., XXVI, 1929.

Templeton, Sardis W. *The Lame Captain, the Life and Adventures of Pegleg Smith.* Los Angeles: Westernlore Press, 1965.

Waterman, T. T. *The Religious Practices of the Diegueño Indians.* In: *Publications in American Archaeology and Ethnology,* Univ. of Calif., VIII, March, 1910.

Weight, Harold O. *Lost Ship of the Desert: A Legend of the Southwest.* Twentynine Palms: The Calico Press, 1959.

Wilhelm, Paul. *A Ghost of the Vikings?* In: *Indio Date Palm,* Oct., 1951.

Williams, Brad, and Pepper, Choral. *The Mysterious West.* Cleveland: The World Publishing Co., 1967.

.... *Lost Legends of the West.* New York: Holt, Rinehart, and Winston, 1970.

Yount, George C. *Chronicle of George C. Yount.* In: *California Historical Society Quarterly,* II, April, 1923.

PERSONAL INTERVIEWS CONDUCTED BY THE AUTHOR

William Allison, Mitchel Beauchamp, Ernest Brown, Perry Burnand, Ella Calvert, Leo Crawford, Noel Crickmer, Virginia DeMarais, Richard B. Dixon, Dr. Theodore Downs, John Fleming, R. G. Gastil, Maurice Getty, Kenneth E. Hedges, Paul McEwen, John Michael, Harvey Moore, Maurice Morgan, Horace Parker, Richard Phillips, Betty Remlein, John Sloan, Mabel G. Small, Clyde Strickler, Banning Taylor, Richard L. Threet, Eugene Velzy, Jack Welch, and Helen Witham.

Index

Abbott, Clinton G., museum director, 86
Admiral, Don, naturalist, 16
Agave plant, 14, 31
Agriculture, 78, 80, 93, 94, 96, 97, 100, 102, 103, 105, 110
Agua Caliente, 8, 34
Alarcón, Hernando de, Spanish explorer, 118
Allison, William, ranger, 100
Alluvial fans, 2
Amador, Rafael, Mex. courier, 55
Angel, Vance, Buck and Jack, cattlemen, 76
Animal life, 1, 12, 17, 22-23, 32; coloration of, 24; distribution of, 24; number of, 17; protected species, 25; water sources of, 17, 24
Antonio, Juan, Cahuilla Indian chief, 62
Anza-Borrego Natural History Association, 113
Anza celebration, Riverside, 96
Anza, Juan Bautista de, route of first expedition, 8, 41-46, 54; colonizing expedition, 46-48; use of trail, 51, 54, 55, 59
Anza Memorial Conservation Association, 96
Apache Indians, 42, 46
Appreciation of desert, 61, 65, 78, 109, 112, 113
Archaeological investigations, 4, 7, 27-31, 109
Argüello, Luís Antonio, Calif. gov. (Mex.), 53
Argüello, Lt. Santiago, trail of, 54
Armstrong, Donald, park custodian, 99
Arrillaga, José, Calif. lt. gov. (Spanish), 51
Arroyo Salado, 2, 4
Arroyo Seco Diablo, 2
Arroyo Tapaido, 2

Badlands topography, 1-2
Bailey, Howard, prospector and hunter, 76, 78
Banks, Richard C., zoologist, 24, 25
Banning, Phineas, wagon contractor during Civil War, 70
Barker, Lawrence, resort developer, 103
Bartlett, Russell, boundary commissioner, 63
Basin Wash, 82
Battle of San Pasqual, 56
Bean, Lowell, anthropologist, 31, 39
Beaty, Alfred Armstrong, homesteader, 78, 79, 80, 83
Bechtel Corporation, 109
Beckman, Merle, ranger, 104
Bell, Major Horace, 121
Bellon, Walter, county supervisor, 93, 94, 96
Bemis, Harold W., homesteader, 80
Bennett, John B., U.S. land commissioner, 97
Benson Dry Lake, 2, 4
Benson, Jack and Ella, 104
Benton, Ralph, cattleman, 76
Berman, Harry, mineralogist, 102
Bighorn sheep, 1, 12, 24, 32, tallies of, 25, 113
Birch, James, bids on overland mail route, 66
Bird fossils, 7
Bird life, 17, 20-21, 24
Blair Valley, 8, 34, 108, 109
Blake, William Phipps, geologist of railroad survey, 65, 66
Bombing range, 100, 102
Borica, Diego de, Calif. gov. (Spanish), 51
Borrego Badlands, 2, 4, 48, 102
Borrego Fruitlands Association, 79
Borrego Land and Development Company, 103, 106
Borrego Mountains, 11
Borrego Palm Canyon, 14, 25, 30, 49, 73, 87, 88, 89, 109
Borrego-Salton Seaway, 109
Borrego Springs, 79, 92, 95, 98; development of, 97; growth of, 100, 103, 106, 112: name of, 71; population, 112, 113; resort development, 103, 104, 106, 112; settlers, 74; temperature, 13; township formed, 83
Borrego Valley, 8, 75, 80, 127
Borrego Valley Associates, 112
Borrego Valley Chamber of Commerce, incorporated, 80
Borrego Valley Golf and Improvement Company, 106
Borrego Valley Land Company, 79
Borrego Valley Post Office, 83
Borrego Valley School District, formed, 80, 83
Borrego Valley Soil Conservation District, 109
Bowers, Stephen, geologist, 76
Bow Willow Canyon, 30
Box Canyon, 57, 58, 68
Brandt, Henri, prospector, 123
Brice, Ruth, first valley teacher, 80
Brininger, Roy, grape grower, 103
Brittle bush, 14
Brown, Aaron, U.S. Postmaster General, 66
Brown, Ernest, park naturalist, 25, 112
Bucksnort Mountain, 8
Burdick, Arthur, desert writer, 78
Burks, Dana, land developer, 88, 102
Burnand, A. A., Jr., resort developer, 89, 103, 106
Burnett, Peter H., Calif. gov., 62
Burnham Bills, to transfer govt. land, 93
Burnham, George, U.S. rep., 93
Busch, Louis T. and Lorraine, first donation of private land, 90
Butterfield Stage, 66, 68, 70, 74

Caballero, Father Felix, Dominican priest, 53, 54
Cabrias, Julian, cattledriver, 126
Cacti, 14, 16, 31, 105
Cactus Oil Company, 76
Cactus Wren, 24
Cahuilla Indians, 25, 31, 34, 37-38, 46, 62
Calcite mining, 102-103
California Gas Transmission Company, 109
Calvert, Jack, park supervisor, 99, 100, 102
Campbell, Everett W., rancher, 79
Campbell, Richard, trader, 54, 56
Campgrounds, 99, 100, 104, 106, 108, 109
Camp Independence, at Yuma, 62
Canyon Sin Nombre, 2, 81, 84
Capron, John G., road builder, 71
Carleton, Col. James H., during Civil War, 71
Carrillo, Leo, honorary mayor, 106
Carrizo bandlands, 4, 114, 118
Carrizo Canyon, 34, 57, 61
Carrizo Creek, 16, 45, 56, 57, 59, 66

Carrizo Creek Oil Company, 76
Carrizo Gorge, 8, 61
Carrizo Impact Area, 99, 113
Carrizo Mountains, 11, 16
Carrizo Stage Station site, 67
Carrizo Valley, 8
Carson, Kit, guide and mountainman, 54, 55
Carstesen, Charlie, propsector, 76
Casa del Zorro, 113
Cattle, drives, 61, 62; grazing, 73-75, 78, 97, 112
Chaffee, James B., park supervisor, 106
Chamberlin, William H., immigrant, 59
Chapuli, Los Coyotes chief, 62, 63
Chase, J. Smeaton, homesteader, 79
Childers, W. Morlin, amateur archaeologist, 27
Chillwell, Archie, cattleman, 76
Chuckwalla, 17, 25
Civil War, 70-71
Clark, Fred and Frank, cattlemen, 75
Clark Valley, 8
Clark's Dry Lake, 2, 30, 75, 102
Climate, ix, x, 7, 13
Clusker, Charles, search for lost ship, 119
Collins Valley, 8, 30, 37, 75, 79, 88,
Cocomaricopa Indians, 54
Cocomaricopa trail, 53, 54
Collier, Col. James, first port collector in San Francisco, 61
Collins, John and Ella, homesteaders, 74-75, 126
Collins, Valley, 8, 30, 37, 75, 79, 88, 90
Colonists, Anza expedition, 46, 48-49, 51
Colorado Desert, 8, 13, 16
Colorado River, 7, 8, 30, 41, 42, 53, 54, 55, 76, 110
Combs Peak, 8
Confederate forces, 70-71
Cooke, Lt. Col. Philip St. George, commander of Mormon Battalion, 56, 57
Copley, Ira C., fund raiser, 89
Copley, James S., resort developer, 106
Coronado, Francisco, Spanish explorer, 118
Coulter, Thomas, Eng. scientist, 55
Country Club, 106, 107
Couts, Lt. Cave Jr., escort of International Boundary Commission, 59, 61
Cover, Thomas W., prospector and sheriff, 123
Coyote Canyon, 34, 42, 44, 45, 46, 51, 74-75, 78, 80, 103, 104, 109, 112-113
Coyote Creek, 25, 30, 37, 40, 41, 46, 78
Coyote Mountain, 8, 84
Crabb, Henry A., filibusterer, 65
Craig, Col. L. S., action in Indian uprising, 63
Crawford, Robert, stage station custodian, 96
Creosote bush, 14
Crickmer, Noel, lodgeowner, 102, 103
Cross, Harry, homesteader, 79
Culp Valley, 8, 30, 108, 109
Cupeño Indians, 38, 62
Cuyamaca Mountains, 54, 57

Date Industry, 80
Davis, Edward H., naming of elephant trees, 16
Davis, Jefferson, Secy. of War, 65
De Anza Desert Country Club, 106, 107
De Anza Ranch, 78, 103
Deering, Tam, of State-County Parks and Beaches Association, 88, 89
Deguynos Canyon, 2
Desert Land Act, 79
Desert Lodge, 102
Desert pavement, 2
Desert Protective Council, 109, 112
Desert tortoise, 24
Diáz, Father Juan, on Anza expeditions, 42, 46, 51
Diegueño Indians, 31, 34, 37-38, 45, 63
DiGiorgio, Joseph, fruit grower, 103
DiGiorgio Fruit Corporation, 103, 106
Dixon, Richard B., park custodian, 99
Dos Cabezas, 7, 34, 79, 108
Downs, Theodore, archaeologist, 4, 7
Drucker, Philip, anthropologist, 31
Drury, Newton B., on roads, 106
Du Vall, E., landowner and deputy sheriff, 79, 100
Dye, Robert, calcite miner, 102

Earthquake Valley, 8, 24, 54, 56
Ebens, Theodore, homesteader, 76
Echeandía, José María de, Calif. gov. (Mex.), 54
Eixarch, Father Thomás, Spanish missionary, 46
El Centro Chamber of Commerce, promotion of park, 93
Electric power supply, 99, 103
Elephant trees, 1, 14, 15, 16-17
Ella Wash, 2
Elsinore fault zone, 8
Emory, Lt. W. H., report of, 55, 56
Ensign, O. H., fruit grower, 79-80
Ensign Ranch, 80, 102, 112
Erosion, 1, 2, 5, 8, 114
Etsudillo, Lt. José María, on Romero expedition, 53, 54
Evans, Charles Edward, survivor of filibuster expedition, 65
Ewen, L. D., state park engineer, 106
Fages, Lt. Pedro, routes of, 44, 45, 46, 51, 54, 57
Fain, William B., cattleman and homesteader, 38, 74
Farb, Peter, anthropologist, 39
Farwell, J. M., news correspondent, 70
Fault systems, 7, 8, 11
Fauntleroy, Col. Thomas T., Confederate Army, 70
Fearney, Charles and Henry, homesteaders, 89
Ferguson, Charles, homesteader and prospector, 76, 80
Fig Tree Spring, 51
Figueroa, José, Calif. gov. (Mex.), 55
Filibusterers, 65
Fish Creek, 4, 6, 16, 79, 108
Fish Creek Mountains, 8, 76, 118
Fish Creek Wash, 2, 4
Fitzgerald, Major E. F., in Indian uprising, 62
Fitzpatrick, Thomas, mountainman, 119
Fleming, Guy L., park superintendent, 86, 90, 93, 97, 99, 104
Fleming, John, ranger, 99, 100
Fletcher, Ed, state senator, 96
Font, Father Pedro, diarist on Anza expedition, 24, 46, 48, 51
Font's Point, 2, 10, 48, 50, 104, 108
Forbes, Jack D., historian, 38
Fort Yuma, 71
Forward, John, Jr., donations of funds, 89
Forward, John, title clearance of land, 88
Fossil sites, x, 1, 4-5, 7
Fox, Frank and Will, horse thieves, 75
Frémont, John Charles, in California conquest, 55
Frost, Jack, calcite miner, 102

Gadsden, James, purchase of Mex. land, 65
Gálvez, José de, Spanish Inspector General, 41
Garbani, Harley J., rancher, 4
Garcés, Father Francisco Hermengildo, on Anza expeditions, 41, 42, 45, 46, 47, 51
García-Conde, Pedro, Mex. boundary team, 61, 63
Garra, Antonio, Indian revolt, 62-63
Geologic ages, 4, 7, 13, 27
Ghost Mountain, 83
Gifford, E. W., anthropologist, 31
Gildred, Philip L., fund-raising committee, 89
Glanton, John, desperado, 62
Gleason, Matthew M., park commissioner, 97
Gold rush of 1849, 59, 61, 62; mining at Julian, 71, 126; prospectors, 76 78, 117, 119-123, 126-127
Grafe, Paul, resort developer, 103
Granite Mountain, 76
Grape cultivation, 103
Grapevine Canyon, 8, 30, 34
Grapevine Mountain, 8
Gray, Andrew B., boundary commission engineer, 61
Green, Jim, prospector, 76, 123

Grijalva, Sgt. Juan Pablo, on Anza expedition, 46, 48

Hall, Warren F., establishes stage route, 68
Hapaha Flat, 8, 34
Haraszthy, Agoston, S.D. sheriff, 62
Hardy, Dad, prospector, 76
Harper, Julius D. and Amby H., cattlemen, 76
Hart, John and Jane, Vallecito store managers, 71
Hart, William T., park commissioner, 93
Harvey, E. M., U.S. Dept. of Agriculture, 16
Harvey, Fred, prospector, 126
Hawk Canyon, 30
Hayes, Benjamin, immigrant, 61
Hays, Robert, El Centro Chamber of Commerce, 90, 93
Hechinger, F., land investor, 88
Hedges, Kenneth, curator, S.D. Mus. of Man, 32
Heintzelman, Maj. Samuel P., in Garra revolt, 62, 63
Hellhole Canyon, 30, 60
Helm, Chatham, homesteader, 38
Henderson Canyon, 30, 50
Highway S-2, 8
Highway 78, 30
Hilton, John, calcite miner, 102
Holland, Charles F., homesteader, 74
Homesteading, 73, 75, 78-80

Imperial County, 108
Imperial Valley, 11, 75, 76
Indian Canyon, 30
Indian Hill, 28, 30, 34
Indians: artifacts, 27; ceremonies, 34, 37; culture, 27-28, 34-39; desert tradition, 28; dialects, 31; food, 27, 31-32, 66; industries, 32-34; lineages, 37-38; myths, 37, 115-116, 118; population, 28, 30, 38-39, 55; quarry site, 27; reservations, 38-39, 63; rock painting, 33-35; taxation, 62; tools, 27, 28; uprisings, 51, 62-63; village sites, 30-31, 34, 37-38, 51; weapons, 27
International Boundary Commission, 61, 63
Invertebrates, 17
Irrigation, 73, 75-76, 78, 80, 102, 103, 110
Iturbide, Augustín, Mex. emperor, 53
Iturbide, Felipe de J., Mex. Boundary Comm. interpreter, 61
Ives, Lt. Joseph C., commander, steamer used to chart Colorado River, 119

Jackass Mail, 68, 69
Jackson, David E., mountainman, 54
Jackson, Helen Hunt, writer, 38
Jacumba, Indian village site, 34
Jacumba Pass, 61, 65
Jacumba Valley, 7, 8
James, George Wharton, desert writer, 78
James, William J., prospector, 76
Jasper, James A., county supervisor, 38, 78
Jasper, Ralph, cattleman, 73
Johnson, Fred W., U.S. Land Commissioner, 94
Johnston, Capt. Abraham, with Kearny's army, 56
Johnston, Gen. Albert Sidney, Confederate Army, 70
June Wash, 2

Kane Springs, 46
Kane Springs Road, 27, 90; completed 78, 83
Kangaroo rat, 17
Kearny, Gen. Stephen Watts, U.S. Army 55, 57
Kelly, J. L., cattleman, 74
Kelsey, Joseph A., justice of the peace, 80, 83
Kenyon, William, park superintendent, 104, 106, 108
Kino, Father Eusebio Francisco, Jesuit missionary, 41; trails, 42
Kit fox, 25
Knowles, Charles M., prospector, 76, 127
Kroeber, A. L., anthropologist, 31, 39
Krueger, George S., Brawley C. of C., 90
Kuhrts, George J. III, developer, 106

Ladder Wash, 5
Lake Cahuilla, 7-8, 30, 65, 70
La Laguna, Indian village site, 34
Land acquisition, 88-89, 90, 93-97, 108, 109, 112
Landforms, 1-4, 8-11, 65-66
Lanz, Fred and Henry, homesteaders, 80
La Posta, Indian village site, 34
Lassitor, James, homesteader and Vallecito Stn. Mgr., 68, 71
LeDuc, Maurice, trapper, 55
Lincoln, Abraham, U.S. President, 85
Lizards, 25, 32
Luiseño Indians, 34

McCain, George and Bob, cattlemen, 76
McCain, John, cattleman, 74
McCloud, Charles, prospector, 76, 123
McEwen, Paul A., park custodian, 99
McVickers, Charlie, prospector, 76
Magruder, Maj. J. B., action in Garra uprising, 63
Mail service, 66, 68, 69
Mammal fossils, 7
Marshall, Bill, renegade, 62
Marshall, James, discovers gold, 59
Marston, George W., donates land and funds, 89, 90
Mason, James E., homesteader and stage driver, 68, 73, 74, 75
Mason Valley, 8, 16, 34, 54, 56, 57
Mathes, Albert L., homesteader, 80
Meighan, Clement W., archaeologist, 30
Merkel, Dalton E., naturalist, 17, 108, 109
Merriam, John C., Pres., Save-the-Redwoods League, 85
Mesquite, 14, 16, 32
Mesquite Oil Co., 76
Mexican-American War, 55, 56, 57
Military training groups, 100, 102
Mining, 94, 108, 113; calcite, 102-103; celestite, 126-127; gold, 76, 78; gypsum, 96; prospectors, 121, 123, 126-127
Minter (John) Ranch, 70
Miracle Hotel, 83
Missions; San Gabriel, 42, 46, 51, 53; San Miguel, Baja California, 53; Santa Catalina, Baja California, 53, 54; Yuma missions, 51
Mitchell, John, writer, 126
Mojave Desert, 53, 54
Montezuma Valley Road, 98, 109
Moore, Bert, cattleman, 76
Moore, Charles S., cattleman, 74
Moraga, Lt. José Joaquín, officer on Anza expedition, 46, 48
Morgan, Frank, honorary mayor, 104, 106
Moriarty, James III, archaeologist, 27
Mormon Battalion, 56-57, 58
Mortero Canyon, 14
Mountain building, 7, 8
Mountainmen, 53, 54, 55, 56, 119
Mountain Palm Springs, 8, 14, 30
Mountain Springs Road, 71
Munz, Philip, botanist, 96
Myths: Indian, 37, 115-116, 118; ghosts, 127; lost ships, 118-119; Pegleg's gold, 119-121, 123-126

Name of park, 86, 93, 97, 108
Nance Canyon, 75
Narbona, Antonio, gov. of Sonora, 53
National Science Foundation, 4
Nature programs, 106, 108-109
Nelson, DeWitt, dir., Dept. of Natural Resources, 108

Ocotillo plants, 14, 91
Ocotillo Wells, 27
Oil wells, 76
Oliver, Harry, writer and homesteader, 79
Olmsted, Frederick Law, Jr., architect, report on desert, 86, 106, 108
Olson, Culbert L., Calif. gov., 94
Oriflamme Canyon, 54, 57
Ormsby, Waterman L., newspaper correspondent, 68, 70

Pacheco, Lt. Romualdo, army engineer, 54
Pacific Railroad, proposed routes, 65
Palm trees, 2, 14, 15, 31, 32, 64, 66, 70, 72, 73, 90

Palm Spring, 4, 15, 51, 57, 66, 68, 70
Palm Spring Oil Co., 76
Palomar State Park, 89
Palo Verde Wash, 2, 108
Parke, Lt. J. G. railroad survey party, 65
Parker, Horace, desert writer, 108, 109
Patrol districts, 99, 100, 104, 106-107, 108
Pattie, James Ohio, trapper, 53, 54
Patton, Maj. Gen. George S., wartime exercises, 102
Peninsular Range, 13, 41
Pesqueira, Ygnacia, gov. of Sonora, 65
Petrified Forest, 108
Phainopepla, 24
Pico, Andreas, Mexican lancer, 56
Pinto Basin Culture, 28
Pinyon Mountain, 8, 34
Pinyon pine tree, 32
Plant life, 1, 13-17, 18-19, 32, 90, 96; distribution, 16-17; drought resisters, 14; seed germination, 16, 67
Plum Canyon, 74
Pluvial periods, 7
Polk, James Knox, U. S. President, 55
Population, Borrego Springs, 83; California, 59; Indians, 28, 30, 38-39; park area, 96, 113
Porter, Milo C., Borrego Springs constable, 83
Portolá, Gaspar de, Spanish expedition, 41, 42
Pratte, Sylvester, mountainman, 119
Preston, Dudley A., botanist, 13
Primm, P. T., landscape architect, 93
Pumpkin Patch, 2, 64
Pupfish, 25

Rainfall, ix, 7, 13, 28
Rangers, 99, 100, 104, 108, 112
Raousset-Boulbon, Gaston Raoul de, filibusterer, 65
Rattlesnakes, 17, 24, 25
Redbud plant, 16
Red Rock Canyon, 5, 26
Reed, Joel, homesteader, 74, 75
Reed, Lester, cattleman, 74, 75, 78
Reptiles, 17, 24, 25
Richards, T. Leroy, state park commissioner, 93
Rider, W. B., chief, California Forestry Service, 86
Rivera, Fernando y Moncado, death of, 51
Road Construction, 71, 78, 83, 96, 100, 103, 104, 106, proposed, 104, 109, 112-113
Roadrunner, 24
Rock, Gilbert, homesteader, 80
Rockhouse Canyon, 30, 37, 76
Rodents, 24, 25
Rogers, Malcolm J., archaeologist, 27, 28
Romero, Captain José, Mexican expedition, 53, 54
Routes: American, 54-59, 61, 70; Indian, 53-54; Mexican, 53-54; Spanish, 41-42. *See:* Anza, Fages, Romero.
Running, Charles F., newspaper correspondent, 68
Russell, Wilson, prospector, 123

St. Vrain, Ceran, mountainman, 119
Salton Sea, 8, 11, 76, 110
Salton Trough, 11
San Andreas Fault, 8
San Carlos Pass, 46
San Diego, 57, 61, 69, 110
San Diego Chamber of Commerce, support of park, 94
San Diego County Board of Supervisors, opposition to park, 93-97
San Diego County Planning Commission, 109
San Dieguito Culture, 27-28
Sand dunes, 4
Sandstone Canyon, 2, 108
Sandstone concretions, 2
San Felipe Creek, 8, 30, 45, 66
San Felipe Fault, 8
San Felipe Valley, 8, 54, 56
San Felipe Wash, 48
San Gorgonio Pass, 11, 53, 65, 66
San Pasqual, battle, 56
San Sebastian, 45, 48, 51
Santa Anna, Antonio Lopez de, Mex. president, 55
Santa Catarina Springs, 46, 47, 51
Santa Rosa Mts., 8, 25, 44
San Ysidro Mts., 8, 44, 87
Save-The-Redwoods League, 85, 86
Sawday, George, cattleman, 73
Scissor's Crossing, Indian village site, 34, 73
Scripps, Ellen Browning, donation of funds, 89
Seidel, William, park archaeologist, 31
Sentenac Canyon, 24, 73
Sentenac Canyon Road, 65, 83
Sentenac, Paul, homesteader, 38, 73
Seri Indians, 118
Sera, Father Junípero, Spanish missionary, 41
Seventeen Palms Oasis, 77, 79
Sheep Canyon, 25, 108, 109
Shinn, Lt. John B., Civil War, 71
Ships, in desert, 118-119
Short, Orville, ranger, 104
Shoshonean Indians, 28, 30, 31
Showalter, Don, Confederate volunteer, 70
Sibley, Maj. Henry H., Confederate Army, 70
Sierra Club, 85
Signal Mountain, 42, 119
Simmons, Bert, prospector, 76
Size of Park, 1, 86, 89-90, 97, 110
Sloan, John, herpetologist, 25
Small, Mabel G., homesteader, 80
Smith, Jedediah Strong, trapper and mountainman, 54, 119
Smith, John O., horse trader, 121
Smith, Thomas Long "Pegleg," trapper, 55, 119; myth of lost gold, 121, 123, 126
Socia, Santiago, reports mystery ship, 118
Society for the Conservation of Big Horn Sheep, 25
Solá, Pablo Vicente de, Calif. gov. (Mex.), 53
Sonora Road, 54, 55, 56, 57, 59
Southern Calif. Edison Co., 109
Southern Emigrant Trail, 54, 57, 59, 65, 68, 69, 71, 75, 100
Southern Pacific Railway, survey party, 65-66, 71
South, Marshall and Tanya, experiment in primitive living, 83, 96
Spadefoot toad, 24
Stage lines, 66-70
Split Mountain, 6, 8, 9, 15, 16, 127
Staff, of park, 104, 108, 109, 112
State-County Parks and Beaches Assoc., 88-89, 90
Stockton, Commodore Robert F., U. S. Navy, 55
Stockton, Dr. T. S., mineralogist, 73
Stone, Arthur, cattleman, 76
Strickler, Clyde, park supervisor, 108, 109
Strong, Wm. Duncan, archaeologist, 37
Sublette, Milton, mountainman, 119
Sunrise Highway, 16
Superstition Mountain, 11, 119
Swartz, Nicolas, prospector, 76
Sweeney Pass, 84
Sweeney, Lt. Thomas W., at Yuma, 62, 63, 65
Swing Bill, to transfer govt. land to Calif., 90, 93
Swingle, Walter T., date grower, 80, 86
Swing, Phil D., congressman, 90
Swycaffer, Joseph, established military mail service, 66

Tarabal, Sebastián, Indian guide for Anza expedition, 42, 45
Temperature, ix, 13, 17, 56
Tilton, L. Deming, landscape architect, 90
Treaty of Guadalupe-Hidalgo, 57, 59, 61
Trees, i, 14, 16, 32, 64, 67, 105
Tripp, Chester and Ozro, prospectors, 76
Tripp, William and Shasta, cattlemen, 75
Truckhaven quarry site, 27
Truckhaven Trail, 82 ,83, 103; paved, 104; completed, 109
Tub Canyon Guest Ranch, 103

U. S. Gypsum Co., 96

Vail, Walter, cattleman, 75
Valdes, Juan Bautista, soldier on Anza exp., 42

Vallecito, 7, 8, 16, 24, 54, 56, 79; county park, 74, homesteaded, 73, 74; immigrant camp, 59-61; Indians, 63; military depot, 66; stage station, 68, 70, 71, 74
Vallecito Badlands, 4
Vallecito Mountain, 8
Vallecito Oil Co., 76
Vandalism, 30, 108, 109, 112
Van Dyke, John C., desert writer, 78
Vicente, Augustín Fernandez de, explorer, 53
Visitors, number of, 99, 100, 104, 106, 108, 112
Vista del Malpais, 2
Voles, 24
Vulture, fossil, 7

Wallace, William J., archaeologist, 28
Wangenheim, Julius, fund-raising committee, 89
Warboys, John L., park surveyor, 88
Warner, Jonathan Trumbull, trapper and rancher, 55
Warner's Ranch and Hot Spring, 41, 54, 57, 62, 68, 75
Warnock, Sam, establishes military mail service, 66
Weaver, Pauline, mountainman, 56, 57
Webb, Dr. Thomas H., 63
Welch, Jack, ranger, 108
Wells, 79, 80
West, Lt. Col. Joseph R., in Civil War, 70
Whipple, Amiel Weeks, command of Int. Boundary Comm., 61
Whitefield, Carl, supervisor, 106
Whitelaw, R. B., conservation committee, 90
Wilber, Dr. Ray Lyman, park commissioner, 86, 90
Willard, Ralph, calcite miner, 102
Williamson, Lt. Robert S., railroad surveyor, 65
Wilson, Henry E. W., prospector, 76, 123
Wilson, John C., stage driver and station manager, 71
Witham, Helen, botanist, 17
Wolfskill, William, mountainman, 54
Woillard, Eugene P. "Doc," early healer, 83
Woods, Harry S., landowner and promoter of park, 80, 89
Woods, Isaiah Churchill, agent for Birch Stage contract, 68
Wozencraft, Oliver Meridith, early irrigation plan, 73
Wueste, Col. R. C., hunter from San Diego, 74
Wyllie, Henry I., road surveyor, 71
Wynn, E. A., store owner, 79

Yaqui Pass, 105, 108
Yaqui Pass Road, built, 83, paved, 103
Yaqui Well, 34, 42, 44, 73, 74
Yarnell, Harry, cowboy, 126
Yosemite Valley National Park, formed, 85
Young, Clement C., Calif. gov., 86
Young, Ewing, mountainman and trapper, 54, 55, 119
Yount, "Dutch George," trapper and prospector, 121
Yuba Oil Co., 76
Yucca plant, 14, 32
Yuma, Fort, 70, 71
Yuma Indians, 42, 54, 55, 62
Yuman culture, 28, 30, 31

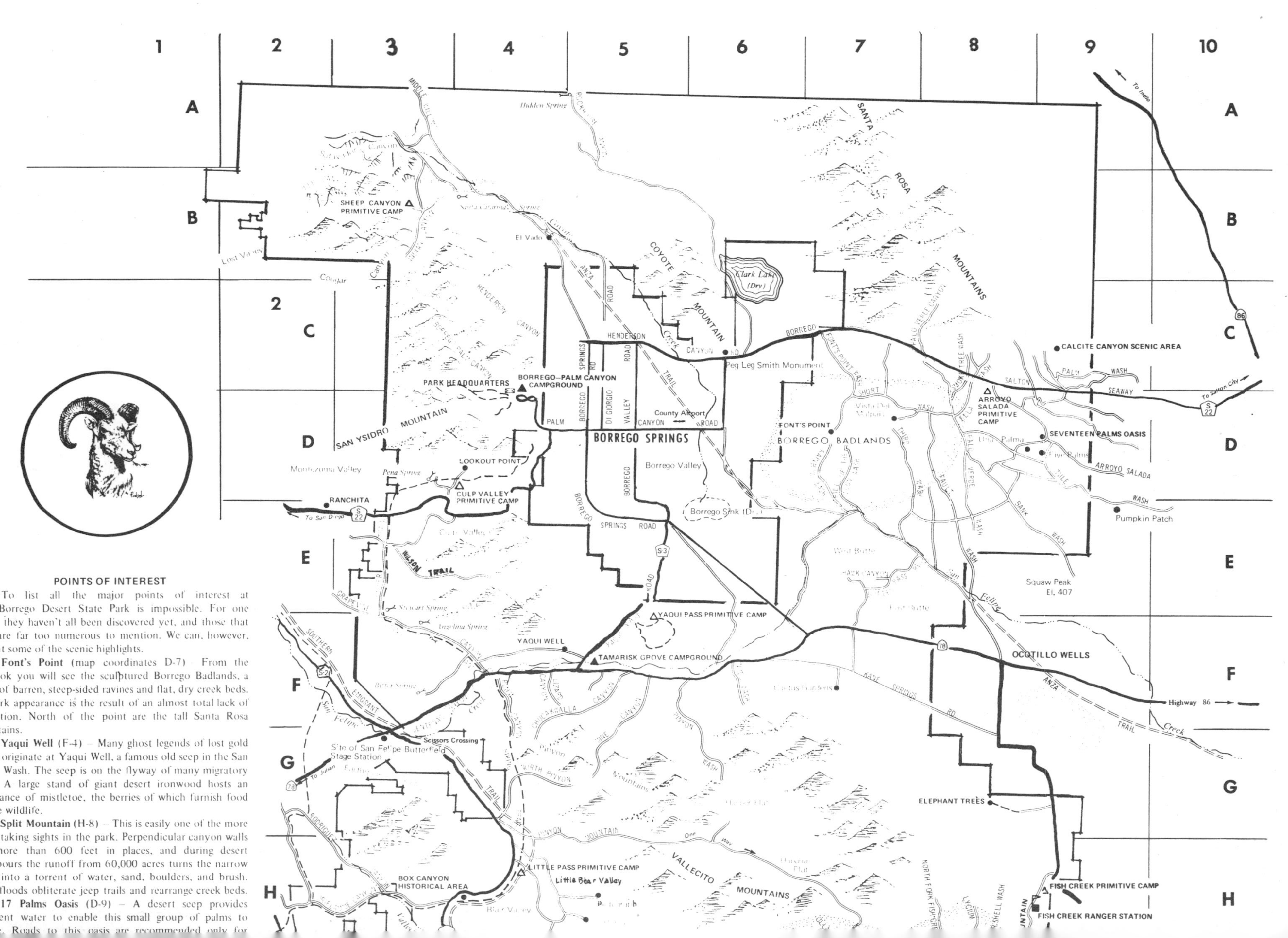

POINTS OF INTEREST

To list all the major points of interest at Anza-Borrego Desert State Park is impossible. For one thing, they haven't all been discovered yet, and those that have are far too numerous to mention. We can, however, present some of the scenic highlights.

Font's Point (map coordinates D-7) – From the overlook you will see the sculptured Borrego Badlands, a maze of barren, steep-sided ravines and flat, dry creek beds. Its stark appearance is the result of an almost total lack of vegetation. North of the point are the tall Santa Rosa Mountains.

Yaqui Well (F-4) – Many ghost legends of lost gold mines originate at Yaqui Well, a famous old seep in the San Felipe Wash. The seep is on the flyway of many migratory birds. A large stand of giant desert ironwood hosts an abundance of mistletoe, the berries of which furnish food for the wildlife.

Split Mountain (H-8) – This is easily one of the more breathtaking sights in the park. Perpendicular canyon walls rise more than 600 feet in places, and during desert downpours the runoff from 60,000 acres turns the narrow gorge into a torrent of water, sand, boulders, and brush. Flash floods obliterate jeep trails and rearrange creek beds.

17 Palms Oasis (D-9) – A desert seep provides sufficient water to enable this small group of palms to survive. Roads to this oasis are recommended only for